I raise my eyes to say Yes

Ruth Sienkiewicz-Mercer
and Steven B. Kaplan

Whole Health Books
West Hartford, Connecticut

Whole Health Books
41 Crossroads Plaza #300, West Hartford, CT 06117
(860) 233-3000

Cover Design Sorano/Barrow Design, Inc.

Library of Congress Cataloging in Publication Data:
Sienkiewicz-Mercer, Ruth.
I raise my eyes to say yes / Ruth Sienkiewicz-Mercer
and Steven B. Kaplan p. cm
1. Sienkiewicz-Mercer, Ruth—Health. 2. Cerebral palsied—
Massachusetts — Biography. 3. Physically handicapped—
Massachusetts — Biography.I. Kaplan, Steven B. II. Title.
RC388.s45 1996
362.1'96836'0092—dc20
[B]   96-8200
CIP

Whole Health Books Revised edition May 1996.
Printed in the U.S.A.
10 9 8 7 6 5 4 3 2 1

To Marian Sienkiewicz and Ruth Case

Introduction

Ruth Sienkiewicz-Mercer was born in 1950.

She has never spoken a word, never written or typed a sentence. She has had little formal education, and reads, at best, at a first-grade level, recognizing only simple words placed before her in a familiar context.

Ruth has been confined to a wheelchair or a bed for every waking hour of her life. She has never walked, never fed herself, never combed her own hair, never dressed herself.

She is a quadriplegic, a victim of cerebral palsy. Aside from her eyes, ears, nose, digestive system, and vocal cords (which can produce about ten distinct sounds), Ruth's body is functionally useless. Her hands do not point or gesture, her feet and legs cannot kick or support the weight of her seventy-five-pound body.

Ruth has lived in virtually every situation possible for a severely handicapped person. She spent her early years at home with her deeply caring parents and two younger sisters and brother, first in Amherst, then in Springfield, Massachusetts. She enjoyed three and a half years at a wonderful private facility, the Crotched Mountain Rehabilitation Center in Greenfield,

New Hampshire. Then, in 1962, she was committed to a state institution, the Belchertown (Massachusetts) State School.

Two years after her arrival at Belchertown, a legislative commission concluded that "the institution had not yet emerged from the Dark Ages in its treatment of the residents." Nine years later, another commission called the conditions at Belchertown "shocking and outrageous." As a result of a lawsuit initiated by friends and relatives of the residents, the federal district court assumed direct operation of the institution in late 1973 and implemented drastic reforms.

Ruth remained at the State School until June 1978, when, along with four handicapped friends and fellow residents, she left to live in her own private apartment in Springfield. Currently she resides in Northampton, Massachusetts, with her husband.

This book tells the life story of Ruth Sienkiewicz-Mercer, as recounted by her. It is her autobiography, written with my assistance. She began work on this project in 1976, while still a resident of the Belchertown State School. Her narrative, and this book, were completed in 1988.

I was introduced to Ruth in January 1979, when I was hired as a teacher for a program called FREE — Fundamental Right to Equal Education. This program provided individualized educational and socialization training to Ruth and the four other severely handicapped people who were Ruth's fellow Belchertown refugees. Although it usually convened at the University of Massachusetts campus in Amherst, FREE was not affiliated with the university. It was, and still is, run by Shelton's, Inc., a nonprofit corporation that provides support services for handicapped individuals.

In 1979 I had just received a master's degree in English from U. Mass. and was planning to attend law school in the fall. One of my primary activities with the FREE program was to help Ruth write her autobiography. Although she had begun working on it nearly three years earlier, only a brief outline and several pages of roughly drawn anecdotes had been completed. From January through August, we worked on Ruth's book several times a week. In interview sessions that usually lasted about two hours, Ruth told me anecdotes from various times in her life and filled in details in response to my many questions. Ruth indicates "yes," "no," and "maybe" with facial expressions. A curled-lipped frown means no, and usually is accompanied by a slight raising of her forearms. The more pronounced the curl of her lip, the more emphatic the negative. Raised eyes indicate yes, often punctuated by a smile. Ruth frequently growls, coos, sighs, chirps, yelps, chortles, or even chatters her teeth to add tone to her pronouncements. She indicates maybe with a relatively bland hybrid of her basic yes and no modes.

By utilizing this limited physical repertoire, Ruth can produce verbal communication on her word boards. These are laminated pieces of white cardboard, approximately sixteen by twenty inches, on which words, phrases, and numbers are arranged in rows and columns. The entries are grouped logically on each board in sections, delineated by borders of various colors. Different sections include pronouns, the names of prominent people in Ruth's life, verbs, adverbs, adjectives, prepositions, interrogatives, common expressions, familiar places, things to eat, colors, articles of clothing, and several expletives. There is also a section for the alphabet and the numbers 1 through 10.

Over the past ten years, Ruth has used two or three such boards, with entries on both sides of each. When we first met in 1979, her boards consisted of about 400 entries. Several months later, Ruth, Laura Lee Jones (the first director of the FREE program), and I developed new boards that contained about 800 entries. Her current boards include over 1800 entries.

Ruth can neither hold the boards nor point to her chosen words or phrases. The listener must position the boards in front of her; using her facial expressions, Ruth then selects the appropriate board. She guides her listener to the desired section of that board either by looking at it or by answering yes-or-no questions as to location with her face. She pinpoints the exact word or phrase in the same fashion.

Here is a typical conversation with Ruth via her word boards: I hold the boards in front of her, and Ruth selects Board 1 by giving a raised-eye yes when I ask, "This board?" She looks at the top part of the board to lead me to the section containing people's names. I then run my finger slowly across that section; she stops me at the correct column by raising her eyes. I run my finger down the column and she raises her eyes again to stop me at the name Shari. I know that one of Ruth's sisters is named Shari, and also that she once had an attendant by that name, so I ask, "Do you mean your sister Shari?" Her positive eye response identifies the subject of discussion.

If we are simply chatting, I might ask, "Did Shari call you recently?" or "Did you see her?" When we were working on this book, I might have asked, "Do you want to tell me a story about Shari?" Depending on her response, I would either ask several more establishing questions or solicit further information on her boards.

An anecdote involving Shari appears in an early part of Ruth's narrative. During one of our first working sessions on the book, Ruth indicated the word "Shari" on her board. I asked her several yes-or-no questions and established that she wanted to tell me a story that occurred when she was ten years old and living at home with her family. (For obvious reasons, the more one knows about Ruth's activities, personal history, friends, and family, the easier it is to facilitate her communication.)

Ruth then directed me to her spelling chart on another board. She did this by looking at the upper corner of the board in use and curling her lip negatively—her signal to change boards. (Ruth's boards now are marked in the upper corner as Board 1, Board 2, and so forth, so she can change boards quickly.)

Whenever we land at the spelling chart in our travels across the word boards, I take a deep breath and mutter to myself, "Here we go again—adventures in spelling." Owing to her limited education, as well as her nonexistent writing capacity and her inability to sound out words, Ruth's spelling skills are very rudimentary.

In this particular instance, however, she did quite well. First she spelled out .D.O.L., meaning "doll." Several follow-up questions identified the doll as Ruth's. She then spelled out .G.R.E.T.L.

Her doll's name was Gretel.

The next, and final, clue in this sequence was "soap."

By generating .SHARI.DOL.GRETL.SOAP. and by answering a few dozen yes-or-no questions, coloring her responses with various facial expressions and sounds, Ruth told me the story of how she asked her kid sister Shari to wash the hair of her doll, Gretel, in the middle of the night. My follow-up questions pertained to Shari's response, what came of the incident, and its emotional and personal significance.

This conversation lasted about an hour. It would have taken a speaking person less than five minutes to tell the story in her own words.

At some point after that conversation, I referred to my notes and wrote a narrative of the event from Ruth's point of view. Then I reviewed the draft with Ruth and carefully explored her reaction to the written version, taking care that she felt comfortable with the descriptive language and commentary. The Shari/Gretel story was relatively easy to write because the subjective elements of the event came out during our initial discussion. Yet even in this case, as with all of the other anecdotes in this book, I returned to Ruth with additional questions.

Throughout the narrative, I have attempted to present events from my source's perspective. In every instance, Ruth and I painstakingly reviewed the written account, sometimes through four or five drafts. Each time, Ruth approved, or edited, or altered, or added to her original account and my rendering of it.

Although Ruth's words and phrases are set forth wherever feasible, either as headings to specific anecdotes (for example, .SHARI.DOL.GRETL.SOAP.) or within the text itself, her story is by no means her own word-for-word account. She has described to me the notable events, people, places, and things of her life, and I have put her account into words. Most of the words were not generated by Ruth; she neither spoke them nor transmitted them directly from her creative mind to the written page. But the thoughts and emotions, the impressions and observations expressed by these words, are Ruth's alone.

How to write for Ruth . . .

The idioms and vocabulary, the tone, the nuances of language she would use if she could express herself on paper—all of this is a mystery that will never be resolved. Ruth talks through her eyes, facial expressions, grunts and sighs and other sounds, and selects two- or three-word messages/fragments/clues from her word boards to germinate a conversation.

But how does the voice in her mind speak? What words does it choose? I have posed these questions to Ruth. Her response has been that yes, she thinks like everyone else, that her inner voice talks in words and phrases, sentences, even paragraphs.

But does she think in words and phrases alone? Are her mental utterances like the speech she hears others speak, or are they more akin to the shorthand speech she produces on her word boards? Do visual images figure more prominently than words in her internal dialogues? And what does her inner voice sound like? Since she has never spoken, does she perceive that inner voice as an extension of her own spirit? Or does she perceive it as some disembodied intelligence that drops by for frequent chats?

Does that voice, Ruth's inner voice, speak in a flowing dialect of words, phrases, and sentences? Or is it assisted by internal sounds and evocative nonverbal images?

This is a woman who has never walked or run, never jumped in the air, never clapped her hands or even scratched her face, a woman whose most prodigious self-propelled physical movement was rolling around on the living-room carpet in childhood. Her most acute independently generated movement since then has been to stand semi-upright in her wheelchair for a few seconds. For this woman, thinking is the most active of verbs.

I don't know how anyone else thinks, but I wonder whether Ruth thinks like everyone else. How could she? How couldn't she?

For anyone who knows Ruth well, soliciting her thoughts poses no problems that time and patience won't solve. She usually expresses herself quite clearly and directly. She has no choice but to choose her words more carefully than anyone I have ever known. The limitations placed on her communicative faculties by her physical handicap have forced her to utilize an economy of language that eliminates most, if not all, of the trivial verbiage found in casual conversation. Communication is too precious a commodity for her to waste the attention of her audience on meaningless or misleading statements. She is clever and innovative in expression, yet always blunt. She uses conversation to reveal, not to mask, her thoughts.

Ruth's communication is, in the most fundamental sense, pure poetry. By necessity, she speaks symbolically. Her every verbal utterance engages language at its most compressed, essential, yet suggestive level.

It took me only a few conversations with Ruth to appreciate that handicapped or not, she is thoughtful, sensitive, and exceptionally bright. This isn't just some cute, energetic little cripple who signals yes and no like a trained seal.

Ruth spent the first twenty years of her life talking with her eyes and face, supplemented only with various sounds. Since then she has used her word boards to express herself in an ever-expanding verbal shorthand. Yet her eyes remain her true "voice," and her face never lies.

Ruth's magical, hot-chocolate eyes have cried the pain of a lithe spirit trapped within a useless body, imprisoned for so many years in a warehouse for the blameless repugnancies of our society. Yet those same eyes, having witnessed such misery, characteristically smile and sparkle with mischievous delight at the simplest and subtlest of pleasures.

Early on, I was unsure about the breadth of her genius. I suspected that Ruth was at best clever, that she settled too quickly for the easy answer in our conversations. It seemed that if she liked my interpretation of her clues and cues, she eagerly appropriated my suggestions as her original thoughts:

"So you feel depressed. Why? Okay, this board? This one? Yes? This section—are you looking up here? This column? Mother? Father? Sister—sister, which one, Shari? Yes? Does Shari have something to do with your being depressed? Yes? You were depressed because of Shari when you left home that time? Had she been mean to you? No—just the opposite? She'd been good, so good? Yes, that's it? She'd been so good—and after you left, you missed her? Because you'd been so close, and then you were gone for so long and lost contact with her, and she grew up and you grew up and you were apart from each other, and then you weren't even like sisters anymore? Is that it? Exactly? Anything more on this point? Okay, let me write that down."

Quite a mouthful, considering that Ruth had provided .DEPRESSED. and .SISTER. as clues. But the snowballing *umph* of her responses kept telling me I was on the right track.

During our first two months of working together, I wasn't sure whether I was improving as a guesser or Ruth was simply tired and thus willing to accept my earnestly offered semitruths. After all, that would have been a lot easier than splitting hairs, confusing the message, and getting nowhere as a result of insisting on my precise comprehension of her thoughts.

But her eyes said otherwise — repeatedly.

Ruth's eyes always told me if I was getting it just right, and if not, how far off I was. And it wasn't my intuition alone that managed to embrace the broader context of what she was trying to tell me. Whatever talents I brought to the party, ultimately I was a receptive subject. Ruth's eyes and mind utilized me — my mind, my eyes, my voice, my endless questions, and my writing faculties — as her word processor.

Every time I attempted to provide words for Ruth's thoughts, I questioned whether the written product accurately represented her commentary or unwittingly embodied too many of my own projections. Although this remained a primary concern, my skepticism diminished as I got to know her better. In particular, there were several times in those first few months when we floundered over an obscure detail in a story and Ruth insisted that we get it just right. This made me realize that once she begins to tell someone something on her word boards, she never willingly permits that person to misconstrue the message. I had discovered the one absolute rule of Ruth's approach to conversation: once she begins to express a thought, she is as obstinate as the proverbial dog with a bone. Her correspondent either perceives her message accurately or tears his or her hair out trying.

I share that doggedness. As a result, Ruth and I endured some exasperating sessions trying to give voice to a thought that proved particularly resistant. More often, however, there was an exhilarating payoff when Ruth's message finally emerged. Usually I experienced a mental flash as her clues clicked into place, their imaginative concomitance revealed.

At other times (mercifully few and far between), a conversation ended with my frank expression of my immediate thoughts:

"That's it? We spent the last half-hour on that? But you told me that two months ago, you swiss-cheese brain."

On very rare occasions, the riddle eluded both my powers of comprehension and Ruth's abilities of expression. In those instances we shrugged our shoulders and forged ahead.

There was no single revelatory conversation that convinced me of Ruth's credibility as a storyteller. The effect was cumulative. But I did stop doubting her once I had tested her stories a few times. After we began to put our initial material into writing, I discovered that she didn't remember telling me every anecdote, especially as the months passed and my notebook began to swell. I would read material to her that she had recounted months earlier, and suddenly she would light up or start chirping softly with surprised delight over something she had forgotten telling me.

It was at this time that I began to feed her sporadic suggestions that I believed were a bit off the mark. I wanted to see if she would accept a plausible, immediate, and partially inaccurate summary. But Ruth wouldn't compromise. Although she became frustrated by my failure to offer quick and accurate interpretations of her messages, this only prompted her to search for more precise clues.

Even more revealing was her response when I questioned her again about something she had already told me. When she didn't remember the earlier discussion and didn't remind me that we had already reviewed that subject, she usually repeated her original description, sometimes in identical fashion.

I didn't waste much time on these tests, primarily because Ruth responded so convincingly. Meanwhile, she never suspected my duplicity. Her eyes were too busy straining to talk to me for her to ponder why I seemed so much slower-witted on some days than on others.

Ruth never latched on to my thoughts for her story. If I got it wrong, she clamped on that teeth-baring, lip-curling "no" face that's the closest thing she owns to a mean look. This was her story all the way, and she made sure that I got it right. I could choose the words to express her thoughts and feelings best — that Ruth left mostly to my judgment. But that's why I was there; if she had been able to fashion the words herself, she could have dictated her story to a typist.

If I wanted to help her focus her stories, or highlight an emotion or observation that seemed critical, that was great — as long as it was authentic. If I rounded out the written version of her viewpoint accurately, if it felt right to her, she accepted it. Otherwise, it was corrected or deleted.

The first time Ruth heard me read back some of her narrative, she knew she had found a speaking voice. True, it wasn't really her own voice, not the one we would hear were her mouth able to speak, or read were her hand able to write. But it was an accurate evocation of her experiences, a reconstruction of her viewpoint. It was the subjective element, not the word selection, that counted, and we were getting the emotional responses right. Ruth's story was finally being told.

It was late in March 1979 that I read to Ruth the first thirty or so pages I had written up. It took some trial and error to find a suitable persona for her narrative. Although we continually refined that narrative voice thereafter, the core emerged very early in the process.

Our success became apparent when, after I had read about ten pages of her early childhood reminiscences, she gave me this message on her word boards: .I.FEEL.TALKING. She was excited. Not giggly or jittery, as she is when someone surprises her or she has to do something she has been dreading, but inwardly excited, even ecstatic. She was reveling in the present success and intuitively relishing the future possibilities.

I paused for a moment and realized that I was thrilled too. Ruth had just told me that for the first time in her life, she felt as if she were talking.

We both knew that it wasn't precisely her voice, but it was close enough. Although I don't think she realized it at the time, she had just cleared a major obstacle: she had discovered a voice that could talk and make people listen to her. I don't mean that I was that voice, not like some walking public address system hooked into her mind. Ruth had broken through to another realm of language, one that went well beyond the level of "I'll have a hamburger for lunch" or "Please take me to the bathroom." And she had done it by the sheer force of her determination.

Perhaps the best way to describe what happened during the early stages of our work together is to say that Ruth was tasting language, real talking-about-things-going-on language, for the first time in her life. She had always known that process within her own head, through her inner voice, but she had never been able to express the words, *her* words, nimbly enough, never heard her ideas spoken in detail for others to hear, never been able to focus her perceptive powers on her just-expressed thoughts in order to evaluate how they sounded.

Philosophy is usually generated within the seclusion of one's mental processes. But observations and concepts must be expressed in order to be tested. Ideas must reverberate in the air and trigger a response; their essence takes shape interactively. Consider the following representative discussion Ruth and I had in May 1979 about one aspect of her life at the Belchertown State School.

.COAT.
  "The girls were wearing coats? On the ward?"
  Yes.
  "Why, were they cold?"
  No.
  "Was there something special about their coats?"
  Yes.
  "What was it?"
  .NOT.HURT.THEY.

"Their coats didn't hurt them?"
No.
"Who wasn't hurting someone? The girls or the attendants?"
(Ruth smiled at me patiently.)
"Okay, let's take it one at a time. Had the girls been hurting someone?"
Yes.
"Who were they hurting? You?"
No.
"Other people on the ward?"
No.
.THEY.
"The girls had been hurting they — them? Themselves, they'd been hurting themselves?"
Yes. (with a laughing groan for emphasis)
"And the coats, they wore the coats so they wouldn't hurt themselves. Coats, coats . . . of course, they wore straitjackets, the attendants put them in straitjackets, right?"
Yes. Yes! (big smile and chuckling sound to indicate a direct hit)
"They put those girls in straitjackets? Really?"
Yes. Yes.

Ruth started giggling, then burst into the high-pitched chirping sound she makes to tell you that you're right on and also "Isn't that the craziest/funniest/dumbest thing you've ever heard?"
We both laughed. Then she returned to work.

"Are we still talking about those girls in the straitjackets?"
Other.
"There were other girls in straitjackets?"
No.
.BATHROOM.BABY.
"These other girls used a baby bathroom?"

No.

.LIKE.BABY.

"They went to the bathroom like a baby?"

Yes.

.WEAR.

"Wearing what, wearing diapers? They were wearing diapers?"

Yes. Yes.

"Just to be sure, who are we talking about now? Just these other girls, or the girls in the straitjackets?"

No.

"No, just the other girls, they were wearing diapers, correct?"

Yes.

"Where, on Ward Four?"

Yes.

"And these other girls, were they older than you?"

No.

"Okay, younger, how much younger—a couple of years? About three years?"

Yes.

"How many other girls? More than five?"

No.

"Less, like one or two? Two?"

Yes.

Ruth made a droning, monotonic sound that meant she had more to say about this and wanted to get back to her word boards. I held the two boards together in a little stack and showed Board 1 to her, about three feet from her face. "This board?"

No.

(I placed the first board underneath the other one and showed Board 3 to Ruth.) "This one?"

No.

(I turned that board over and showed her the flip side, Board 4.) "This board?"

Yes.

"Top part? This column?" (I pointed with my finger.)

.BABY.

"Right, you still mean diapers, those other girls wore diapers. But you told me that nearly everyone on Ward Four wore diapers."

(Ruth looked down at her watch.)

"Something about the time? Are you looking at your watch? It's not time for lunch yet."

(She grimaced sourly to say no and raised her hands a few inches toward her face for emphasis, which isn't unusual. But she continued to look at her hands as she did it, which is unusual.)

"Your hands, something about your hands. Is the clue the word 'hand'?"

Yes.

"The girls in the straitjackets. They hit themselves with their own hands, is that what you mean?"

No. Other.

"Something the other girls did with their hands, the girls with the diapers?"

Yes.

"Oh, I know, they reached into their diapers and rubbed shit all over the place, like the others you told me about a few weeks ago."

Ruth literally squealed with delight, then began laughing so hard that her teeth were chattering. Then she made her board sound, and I held the word boards in front of her again.

.PUT.ON.

"Put on those girls, on the shit-rubbers? Straitjackets, did they wear straitjackets too?"

No.

(Ruth looked back down at her hands again.)

"Something was put on their hands, right? To keep them from going into their diapers?"

Yes.

.HIT.THEM.

"Who hit whom? The shit-rubbers hit people too? Or did the attendants hit them? Which one?"

No.

.HIT.THEM.

"We're talking about the shit-rubbers? And you said 'Hit,' but now you say 'No hit.' I'm confused. Tell me some more, okay?"

.HIT.

"Were people hitting other people?"

No.

"Does the hitting have to do with what they put on the shit-rubbers' hands?"

Yes.

.BOX.

I looked into Ruth's eyes and thought for a moment. She looked back with the trace of a smile starting to form, first in her eyes and then at the corners of her mouth. Then the picture popped into my mind and we both started laughing.

"Of course, I get it now. That's a riot."

We looked at each other again and laughed some more. She knew that I knew, and I knew that she knew that I knew, but I had to say it out loud to make it real: "Boxing gloves. They put boxing gloves on their hands to keep them from groping around in their diapers. How creative!"

Ruth giggled for several seconds, until she ran out of breath and sputtered. Then she paused, took a deep breath, and collected herself. She was starting to get tired from all the laughter and the intense concentration of leading me around her word boards with her eyes. But she hadn't finished telling the story yet; she made the board sound again.

.HEAD.HIT.

"They hit their heads too? Who did, the shit-rubbers?"

Yes.

.HEAD.

"Something happened to their heads? Did they get hurt?"

.STOP.HIT.

"They stopped hitting. Something stopped them from hitting their heads? Was it something or someone who stopped them?"

.ON.HEAD.

"Something on their heads? The attendants put something on their heads?"

Yes.

"Because they hit their heads. What, against the walls?"

Yes.

"Some kind of helmet? No, they made them wear helmets so they wouldn't hurt their heads? To go along with their boxing gloves — what were they, football helmets?"

Yes. No.

"You're not sure. But it was some kind of a helmet. Was it smaller, more like a hockey helmet?"

Yes.

"Okay, hockey helmets. Tell me, did they make you wear a scuba mask because you talked too much?"

(Ruth laughed heartily. She loves wisecracks, even corny ones.)

"How long did they wear the boxing gloves and hockey helmets?"

.3.

"Years? Three years? For sure or about? Pretty sure? And what about the other ones, the ones in the straitjackets? Did it bother you to see them all wrapped up like that?"

No.

"Why not, because they hurt people? Did they ever hurt you?"

No.

"Only scared you?"

Yes.

"Is that it? End of story? All right, I've got to write this stuff down."

I stopped seeing Ruth on a daily basis in August 1979, when I moved to West Hartford, Connecticut, to attend the University of Connecticut School of Law. By that time we had written up about half of her story in a readable draft, and compiled most of the information for the remainder.

During the next twelve months, I met with Ruth at her apartment once every few weeks and worked on the book in my spare time. We continued to make progress. Unfortunately, my spare time vanished in the face of law school, my subsequent legal career, the birth of my three children, and intensifying family obligations. From late 1983 through 1986, Ruth and I kept in touch but could do little to complete the book together.

Even during those years when Ruth's book was sitting on the shelf, neither she nor I doubted that someday we would finish telling her story. In the fall of 1986, she attended a writer's workshop conducted by our editor, Dick Todd. With characteristic chutzpah and some assistance from an attendant, Ruth wheeled up to Dick, introduced herself, plopped the unfinished manuscript into his hands, and asked him to read the first half of her life story. The result of that encounter was a publishing contract, a re-energizing of our efforts, and this book.

After I reviewed the existing manuscript, my copious notes, and various other material we had compiled, Ruth and I picked up where we had left off. We received invaluable assistance from Ruth's friend and attendant Linda Binney, who patiently read and reread to Ruth the various drafts of material that I sent in the mail. Linda sensitively and intelligently recorded Ruth's responses, comments, and corrections. This enabled me to get the most out of my bimonthly meetings with Ruth, when we reviewed her editorial remarks on the work in progress and consolidated information for the remaining sections. Throughout 1979 and 1980, Ruth and I had spoken with her parents a number of times, interviewed her friends, attendants, teachers, and speech therapists from the Belchertown days, and obtained copies of her records from the State School. The information gleaned from these sources provided background details and verified some names and dates of which Ruth was uncertain.

Having spent about two thousand hours with Ruth—talking with her, being talked to by her, watching her talk to and interact with others—I can only concur with the opinion shared by everyone who truly knows her. She is a genius, blessed with a rare, sparkling, feisty, unaffected, and vulnerable resilience which inhabits those remarkable eyes and that limp, waifish body.

Most people who encounter Ruth look past, simplistically dismissing her as a tragedy on wheels. They relegate her to a subhuman twilight zone, sufficiently out of mind if not out of sight. But this label, this attitude, is grossly inaccurate.

In classic tragedy, the good guy loses. The hero struggles valiantly, then succumbs to overwhelming forces. Sometimes those forces are beyond his control; sometimes the victorious enemy comes from within the hero himself. This story, Ruth's life, is in the classic sense a comedy—the good guy wins!

Ruth's very existence embodies the predominant symbol of our century: the concentration camp. With Auschwitz, Dachau, and comparable abominations darkly defining the existential parameters of our epoch, there is something transcendent about this tiny woman. Arbitrarily imprisoned within a useless body, deprived of speech and motion, she nevertheless has overcome her irrevocable, natural concentration camp, as well as all the obstacles that society has thrown in her path, to tell her story for posterity. Such triumph over both the infirmities of the flesh and the nightmares made by man raises heroic comedy to mythic proportions.

Ruth Sienkiewicz-Mercer has accomplished this extraordinary double victory with personal tools most people would consider subhuman. But her life is no myth, and powerful lessons are to be learned from it.

STEVEN B. KAPLAN

*I Raise My Eyes
to Say Yes*

1

My story begins at the Cooley Dickinson Hospital in Northampton, Massachusetts. I was born there on September 23, 1950: Ruth Christine Sienkiewicz, a healthy baby girl weighing six pounds, three ounces, the first child of Marian and Charles Sienkiewicz. Since there were no complications at birth, my parents took me home to nearby Amherst.

At the age of five weeks, I suddenly became very ill. I developed an extremely high fever, grew severely dehydrated, and went into convulsions. My parents returned me to the hospital immediately. I spent the next three weeks being treated for a viral infection that the doctors thought was some form of encephalitis. After three weeks, I seemed to have recovered completely. Once again my parents took me home, to begin what everyone assumed would be a happy and healthy childhood.

According to my parents, I was a bright, alert, and engaging infant, and there were no more problems to speak of during my first year of life. But Mother and Father began to be quite concerned when they realized that by the age of thirteen months, I was not making much progress toward sitting up or talking. Our doctor in Amherst, Dr. Holden, referred us to the Boston Floating Hospital for a week of comprehensive physical testing to determine what was holding me back.

The Boston doctors reported that I was suffering from cerebral palsy, with marked spasticity in my arm and leg muscles. They agreed that my earlier illness almost certainly had been encephalitis, and they theorized that the high fever I had experienced had severely damaged my central nervous system. The doctors predicted that my limbs would remain weak and inflexible, and that my progress in speaking and walking would be severely impaired. But they also believed that with proper physical and speech therapy, and with dedication and hard work by my parents and myself, I should be able to walk and talk normally — someday.

My parents were dismayed. They knew nothing about cerebral palsy except what the doctors told them. Understandably, they relied on their religion to try to make sense of this tragedy. Father was a Roman Catholic, Mother a Protestant. Both believed that the hand of God had singled them out in some way. Father felt that my disability was a kind of punishment for his sins. Mother thought that it was God's way of testing them — that God had chosen our family because he knew we would be able to overcome the special problems that it would present. My parents agreed, however, that my situation was not hopeless, and they vowed to do everything they could to help me overcome my infirmity.

First they took me to see Dr. Gary De Hough in Springfield, who was amazed by, and openly skeptical about, the sunny prognosis given by the Boston doctors. He warned my parents that there could be no guarantees with a disease like cerebral palsy.

Then we began a daily routine of physical therapy at home, prescribed for us by the Clinic for Crippled Children in Springfield and updated every three months according to my progress. These exercises were intended to increase the flexibility and strength of my neck and limbs. Mother saw that I kept to the program, and we spent countless hours working at it. With Mother's help, I would raise my arms and move them in a swimming motion over my head, bend and rotate them, extend my forearms and flex my wrists, bend my hands and fingers, and go through a series of leg exercises lying on my back.

By 1955 we also were working on a complete program of speech therapy, although Mother had been using her own informal method with me since I was an infant. A speech therapist instructed her to concentrate on several areas, using exercises for my lips, tongue, and jaw. Every day Mother shaped sounds on my lips with her fingers, and closed my lips and hummed to encourage me to make an "m" sound. For my tongue, we worked on sounds like "la," "da," and "ba," and I practiced breath control by blowing bubbles in water or blowing on a feather so that I could see the strength of my exhalation.

My progress was painfully slow, but Mother never despaired — at least, not in front of me. I took my cues from her, so I didn't despair either. Although I retained the physical needs of an infant throughout my childhood — I could not walk, talk, or feed myself — I was mentally sharp. Since Mother and Father always managed to meet my needs without treating me like a cripple, I never looked on myself as one.

I don't remember too many incidents from my early years. Father had a number of different jobs: driving a bus at the university, managing a lumberyard, and selling ice cream. Until I was three, he ran a gas station in Amherst, and Mother used to take me down there in the afternoon with our dog, Prince.

Prince was unusually sensitive to my physical limitations. If he wanted to show his affection for me, he licked my hand rather than jumping all over me. Strangers had to be careful of approaching me when Prince was around, and he slept in my room for a good many years.

In November 1953 we moved to Springfield. Four months later, in March, my sister Marie was born. The doctors had told my parents that I had developed cerebral palsy as a result of encephalitis, so Mother and Father never thought that anything similar would happen to Marie. Fortunately, they were right. She was delivered safe and sound, and we soon were vying with each other to be the center of attention.

I loved having Marie for a playmate, although I experienced the usual sibling jealousy about having a newcomer around. But since I received constant attention during feeding, physical therapy, and other activities, I did not feel slighted by my sister's arrival.

Marie presented a different kind of problem for Mother. Part of the reason we moved to Springfield was that Father had taken a sales job that required him to travel frequently. Since we could not afford to hire help, the burden of caring for the family was left to Mother. My Nana Sienkiewicz and Aunt Jane both helped take care of me while Mother was pregnant and immediately after Marie was born, but after that Mother really had her hands full. Not only did she look after Marie and me while continuing with my therapy, but she also worked out of our home by doing telephone canvassing, which she continued for many years. The full workload took its toll on her back, which she had injured years before I was born.

My mother received some relief from her mother, Gramma Ruth Case, after whom I was named. Gramma Ruth lived in Springfield and visited our house regularly when Marie and I were kids. A widow, she was a small, quiet, sweet lady who was always making dresses for me. She also used to read me stories, fairy tales about princesses and far-off places to which we would journey together in our imaginations. Ever since those sessions with Gramma Ruth, one of my favorite activities has been to have a book read to me.

My father's parents, Charles and Christine Sienkiewicz, were also familiar figures throughout my childhood. They lived in Northampton, about twenty miles north of Springfield, and we used to drive up for visits on Sunday afternoons. Gramps and Nana were very cheerful, spirited people. Gramps was a short man — he had eight sons and four daughters, and they were all taller than he was. I recall that he loved to grow vegetables in his back yard, and he kidded me a lot.

Nana Christine, the source of my middle name, was also quite a bit taller than Gramps. She was a real character. She was one of the few people other than my mother who fed me. (Gramma Ruth didn't, for some reason.) Nana Christine loved to sit me on her knee and tell me wild stories that she made up as she went along. She also told me secrets about the family, which I promised never to repeat to anyone — a safe promise, since I couldn't talk.

My Aunt Jane was married to one of my father's brothers. She looked a lot like my mother, and acted a lot like her too. Aunt Jane was the only person other than Mother who had that perfect touch in caring for me. She could tell if something was wrong even before I attempted to point it out with a sound or a facial expression. Aunt Jane was boisterous and fun-loving, and like Nana Christine, she taught me at an early age that life was full of humor.

Physically, I was like an infant when Marie was born, although I was three and a half years old. One crucial goal that I continually struggled to achieve was to hold my head firmly upright. Unfortunately, my body would not cooperate. Cerebral palsy, like the development of the body's motor capacities, starts at the top of the nervous system and works its way down. As a result, I couldn't develop my head and neck muscles sufficiently to sit up, and I couldn't develop my arm and leg muscles enough to crawl or walk. My feet were relatively stronger than my legs, my legs were relatively stronger than my arms, and so on. It was harder to hold my head upright than to wiggle my toes. I never did conquer that first important step in learning how to walk — keeping my head aloft.

I could move around some, however, by turning myself over or doing a sort of roll on the floor. One of my favorite tricks when

I was little was to slide quietly out of bed and roll onto the floor. Sometimes I did this when I wanted to go to the bathroom, which was right next to my bedroom. But before I was able to maneuver myself out of my room, Mother or Father always came in and discovered me on the floor, giggling about the surprise I'd provided.

My parents hoped that I might develop more rapidly after Marie was born, by mimicking her normal development from infant to toddler. But Marie soon outstripped me, and I remained unable to sit up or talk while she mastered these functions. As a child of four, capable of laughing, cooing, sighing, and screaming nearly as well as the next kid, I was frustrated beyond belief by my limitations. Not being able to hold my head up and sit upright, I could not look at everything I wanted to see. I also was pretty much stuck in one place, while Marie could crawl, then walk, and then run all around. Even worse, I couldn't talk back when other kids teased me. I couldn't even tell Mother when Marie did something mean to me.

Although I was unable to express my thoughts in words, I did work out a basic system of communication: smiling for yes and frowning for no, providing emphasis with a number of different vocal sounds and facial expressions. I would make a noise to attract someone's attention and then respond to an endless series of yes-or-no questions about what was on my mind. Eventually, I changed my yes signal from a smile to raising my eyes; it was easier for me to do and easier for others to understand.

This system took care of my basic communication needs as a child, and it is one that I still use today. But it did not provide me with much of a chance to develop my skills of self-expression. As a result, I had to learn to talk with my eyes. To begin to understand what this was like, try permitting yourself to communicate with other people only by saying yes or no. Do not use any other words. You will soon discover that going through life playing a perpetual game of twenty questions is extremely frustrating.

To make matters worse, I was small for my age, and people constantly spoke to me in baby-talk. They even talked about me in my presence as if I couldn't understand what they were saying. This kind of attitude, whether based on good intentions or sheer ignorance, has always been insulting at best. Many times it has done me serious damage.

.LEAVE.HOME.SCARED.

When I turned five, in September 1955, Mother was in the hospital with a slipped disk. Apparently, carrying both Marie and me on her hip had worsened her bad back. For the next three months she walked around in a body cast. Since she no longer could carry me, she pulled me around the house on a blanket. Meanwhile, her doctor was telling her that she had to ease up or undergo back surgery.

At this same time my parents decided that I was not making enough progress at home, despite the fact that we were keeping up with the physical and speech therapy rigorously. My doctors in Springfield suggested that I go someplace where I could receive professional help on a full-time basis, and my folks agreed that this would be the best thing for me.

The State School in Lakeville, Massachusetts, had a good reputation for its work with physically handicapped children. Its program consisted of intensive physical therapy for six months to a year; afterward, the school outlined a total program that the client could follow in the future. After a visit and a successful application, I went to Lakeville, in January 1956.

I was very apprehensive about leaving home for the first time and being with new people in a strange place. But I understood the reason for going to Lakeville, and I was excited about the prospect of working as hard as I could to reach my fullest potential.

After I arrived at the school, I was given a while to acclimate myself to the environment before the real program began—a program aimed at getting me to creep, crawl, and eventually stand and walk on my own. During this transitional period I was subjected to a series of neurological tests. The result was very tragic, and totally avoidable. The state sent a newly graduated psychologist to Lakeville to test a group of children, including me, for intelligence. This young man determined that I was an imbecile, with a mental age of four months.

I do not remember exactly what kind of tests he used to arrive at this conclusion, nor do I recall whether he attempted to compensate for my physical handicaps, but I can assure you that I was no imbecile! Since I couldn't talk or walk, I hadn't interacted with my peers as some of the other children had. But I hadn't exactly been locked in a closet either, and I was perfectly normal in terms of passive intelligence. That is, I understood and appreciated everything that was going on around me, from simple conversations to the nuances of relationships, and I freely commented on things as much as my eyes, facial expressions, sounds, and yes-and-no system allowed. But this particular psychologist either didn't know how to evaluate someone like me or didn't care enough to try.

Despite the good reports Mother was receiving from the hands-on staff, my stay at Lakeville was abruptly terminated in March, only two months after my arrival. My parents were called to take me home.

I didn't understand why I had to leave so suddenly. Nobody told me then that the Lakeville psychologist thought I was an imbecile. But Mother and Father realized immediately that a horrible mistake had been made. None of the staff members had gotten to know me well in that short time, so they simply accepted the determination of the psychologist, who recommended that I be placed in an institution for mentally retarded children. Even if someone had sensed that I hadn't been judged fairly, I doubt there was much they could have done about changing the official evaluation. Any hopes I had nurtured about improving myself at Lakeville were shattered. As the situation became clearer to my parents and to me, we were all overcome by sadness at the cruel trick fate had once again played on me.

2

.CROTCHED MOUNTAIN.

Anger soon prevailed over sadness. We were still eager for me to go somewhere that could deliver on what Lakeville had promised, and my parents continued the search. Our pediatrician also wanted us to try again. Through the United Cerebral Palsy Foundation of Springfield, in which my parents were quite active, we heard about the Crotched Mountain Rehabilitation Center in Greenfield, New Hampshire. Crotched Mountain was a private facility, but the state of New Hampshire sent many children there to receive intensive therapy for polio and other crippling diseases.

Since we were not residents of New Hampshire and couldn't afford to pay for the services at Crotched Mountain, we thought I wouldn't be able to go there. But almost by magic, our luck changed as soon as we began to consider this facility seriously. Father was employed at the time by the Pittsburgh Plate Glass Company. We discovered that the company had some kind of financial connection with Crotched Mountain, and that the expenses of my enrollment would be minimal for my father as an employee.

My parents and I visited the grounds at Crotched Mountain in the summer of 1956, and soon afterward, my application for admission was submitted and accepted. I arrived at the center in October of that year; I stayed until March 1960.

I spent some of the happiest moments of my life at Crotched Mountain. It was a wonderful place. The facilities were excellent, and the grounds and surrounding wooded mountains were quite beautiful. The center offered a variety of programs to its residents, among whom were people of all ages with various types of physical handicaps. There were about 120 residents, half male and half female.

Some of the older people there had private or semiprivate rooms, but most lived in a ward-type arrangement. I lived in an area with about thirty other females, ranging in age from four to forty. Even though it was a ward, the atmosphere was pleasant. I never felt like I was "institutionalized" at Crotched Mountain. The fact that there were picture windows everywhere to bring the countryside in had a lot to do with this, but more important was the staff ratio: about one for every five residents, not counting the specialized personnel. Most important, however, was the staff's attitude. Every resident was treated with respect for his or her individual needs, from feeding and dressing to physical therapy and basic social interaction.

Soon after my arrival I was fitted with braces for my back and legs, so I could attempt to learn how to walk. In my daily physical therapy sessions, I struggled to stand up on my own while staff members hovered on either side of me. Initially this was a frightening experience, because I had never been up on my legs before. But fright soon gave way to pure pain and frustration as my efforts met with repeated failure. Although I continued these sessions up to the day I left Crotched Mountain, I never did manage to stand during my three and a half years there.

Another aspect of physical therapy involved learning how to feed myself. Since my hands and arms were fairly flexible at that age, the staff thought that I might learn by using specially adapted silverware. As part of my afternoon exercises I would attempt to feed myself a dessert with a wooden spoon that had an especially thick handle. I could grasp the handle all right with my hand and had no problem directing it toward my mouth, but I wasn't able to complete the simple task. My arms were too stiff and weak to raise the spoon high enough to eat from it. This was particularly exasperating, for even though an attendant fed me the applesauce or pudding after the therapy session, my failure turned the whole torturous experience into a kind of ordeal. The difference between success and failure was only a few inches, the distance that I could not lower my head or raise my hands. After three months of trying, we gave up. I was very upset when I realized that I would never be able to feed myself, but it was one more fact of life that I just learned to accept.

Despite my unavoidable dependency on others for physical assistance, I am a very independent person in thought and spirit. I have always striven to be as self-reliant as possible. For this reason, I had hoped to master feeding myself, at least partially. But disheartened as I was by my failures at this and at standing, there was one other area in which I retained high hopes at Crotched Mountain, something that was infinitely more important to me than anything else — talking. Every afternoon after my physical therapy, I received speech therapy. The speech program followed the same basic approach Mother and I had used at home, but with the center's staff and facilities, the sessions were more demanding and exhaustive.

I would love to be able to say that at such and such a time, I made the breakthrough and uttered my first word. Sadly, this never happened. Before I left Crotched Mountain, the staff concluded that the high arch of my palate, combined with my lack of control over the weak muscles of my larynx, tongue, lips, and mouth, made it impossible for me to speak.

I was crushed. Without a doubt, my inability to speak has been the single most devastating aspect of my handicap. If I were granted one wish and one wish only, I would not hesitate for an instant to request that I be able to talk, if only for one day, or even one hour.

At Crotched Mountain I began to face these dismal facts as the realities of my life. Although many of my efforts met with failure, the attempts certainly were worth it. After all, it was inevitable, and necessary, for me to discover the extent of my capabilities.

Regardless of my failures, I had a wonderful time at Crotched Mountain. One of my favorite activities was to splash around in the indoor pool with the other kids. We were held securely afloat by attendants, but we still managed to raise a ruckus in the water. One time I was cavorting in the pool near a girl who was about my age and who suffered from polio. She came by us with her attendant, floating on her stomach; I was being held with my back in the water. Suddenly the girl's leg hooked into mine. Since neither of us had much control over our legs, we became locked together, and I experienced my first accidental dunking. It was scary, though it only lasted for a second and no real harm was done to either of us. We shared a good laugh about it later.

The best place at Crotched Mountain was the library. I loved to sit there, surrounded by all the books, listening to an attendant read a story in the quiet atmosphere. I let my imagination roam as I gazed out the window at the trees and distant mountains. Like most other little girls, I enjoyed fairy tales; "Sleeping Beauty" and "Goldilocks" were my favorites.

I attended school every morning in a class of about fifteen kids my age. We learned the same things other youngsters learn: the alphabet, spelling, primary reading skills, numbers, simple arithmetic, and various kinds of general knowledge. We didn't always work, however, and we played the usual array of schoolchildren's games, albeit with some special twists. For example, we played musical chairs, including both that half of our class in wheelchairs and the half who walked with crutches. Instead of jockeying for a vacant chair when the music stopped, we aimed for an empty spot in the circle, and whoever was left without a spot was out of the game. As with our activities in the swimming pool, our group needed some help from the attendants to enjoy musical chairs, but once this help was provided, we had great fun.

.JIMY.

I made many friends at Crotched Mountain, but there were two who remain very special to me. One was a boy named Jimmy Saywich, who was my boyfriend during my last two years at the center. It wasn't exactly love at first sight, but we did like each other for quite some time before we confessed it to each other.

Jimmy was in a wheelchair because of polio, but he talked normally and was able to wheel himself around under his own power. He was very handsome, with sandy blond hair, and he usually ignored me because he was too shy to talk to me. I began to suspect that Jimmy really liked me, but he played hard to get, asking his friends to give me messages ("Hey, Sinky, Jimmy wants to know how you're doing today!").

Eventually we broke the ice, and we became steady companions. Jimmy loved racing cars and had a bright red 9 painted on the back of his wheelchair. He liked to pretend he was drag racing, making the noises of the cars as he zoomed down the corridor. Sometimes he would push my chair with his foot while he turned his wheels with his hands, which was the equivalent of taking a walk together. We couldn't go outside for any long treks, but by being able to move across the lounge under our own power to get some privacy, we asserted our independence. Jimmy and I usually sat together at the movies on Saturday nights, and all of the other kids knew we were "going out."

After I left the center, I never saw Jimmy again. I still think of him from time to time and wonder what has happened in his life.

.SUE.FEEL.HOT.WATER.HELPED.

My very best friend at the center was a girl I met the day I arrived. Her name was Sue, and she had short brown hair and fair skin and was the normal size for a girl of six. She had a disease that made her limbs very weak and numb, so she needed braces on her legs and had to use crutches to walk. Although she could speak normally and was ambulatory, we hit it off right away. I managed to tell Sue almost everything by using my eyes, expressions, and sounds.

We all were kept very busy during the day, but Sue and I managed to play together in the evenings and on weekends. We each had dolls, which we treated as if they were babies. Like most little girls, we dressed our dolls up, fed them, and made a general fuss over their imaginary needs. They were not handicapped, of course, so they did not have to worry about things like wheelchairs and metal leg braces. We also used to play the children's game giant step. I was the giant, and Sue asked permission to do the stepping. (If we had swapped roles, the game wouldn't have gotten very far. . . .) Almost every night we got mad at the attendants because they interrupted our fun and put us to bed earlier than we wanted. Television was not a big concern during the week, but on Saturday mornings we watched cartoons in the lounge with the other kids.

Sue and I were like sisters at Crotched Mountain. Someone who doesn't know me might think that because I was stuck in a wheelchair and had limited communication abilities, my relationship with her was one-sided. That was not the case, however, as one incident that occurred during my second year at the center illustrates.

Sue was being given a bath, and I was sitting in my chair nearby, keeping her company. The water running into the tub was very hot, so hot that I noticed steam collecting in the air. The attendant must have been talking to somebody with her back turned to Sue, because she didn't see the steam. Since Sue had no feeling in her limbs, she wasn't aware that the water was too hot and was already beginning to burn her skin. But I was sure of this from looking at that steam, so I started to scream as loudly as I could—which was, and still is, quite loudly—thus managing to draw the attendant's attention. She looked at me, I looked frantically over at Sue, and catastrophe was narrowly averted.

Granted, I didn't engage in such heroics very often, but I didn't feel that I needed to, either, in order to keep up my end of the friendship with Sue. Since I couldn't tell jokes, I laughed at hers; since I couldn't speak in words, I expressed my thoughts with my face and sounds; since I couldn't talk, I listened; and since I could respond to my friend in my own fashion, I did.

.CHRISTMAS.WHITE.DRESS.

Life at Crotched Mountain was structured around a regular routine, but several special events did occur while I was there. At Christmas parents and relatives visited the center, and in many cases took their kids home for the holidays. While all of our visitors were there, we presented an annual Christmas pageant. I always seemed to be cast as an angel, costumed in white from head to toe, replete with a shiny halo. Maybe it was because the part came naturally to me. Whatever the case, everyone gave me rave reviews, and my parents loved it. The pageant set the holidays off on the right note for us.

Starting with my years at Crotched Mountain, we established a regular family tradition at Christmas. As soon as I came home, Father took the children out to look for a tree. I always made the final selection. After the subsequent tree trimming, we all went out together for last-minute Christmas shopping. During all the years that I came home for Christmas, we kept to that tradition, which remained very special to me.

I experienced an altogether different kind of thrill when I was eight years old. One afternoon my parents picked me up at the center and took me to Boston for the day. We visited the statehouse, where I had my picture taken with the governor of Massachusetts, Foster Furcolo. Evidently Crotched Mountain was launching an advertising campaign in Massachusetts. Since I was a resident of the commonwealth and wasn't an unseemly-looking little girl, they selected me as their representative. My picture with Governor Furcolo appeared in the *Boston Record-American*, and the trip provided us with an exciting afternoon.

.MOVIE.

A year later, Crotched Mountain was in turmoil for several weeks over another promotional activity, a film about the center. A professional company invaded and rearranged everything to make their filming easier, shuffling the tables and beds around to make room for their equipment. Using the staff and residents as actors in real-life situations, they filmed almost everyone doing something or other. We were surrounded by lights and cameras. My big scene showed me being taken outside in my chair for a stroll around the grounds. I was dressed for the part in a ruffled pink party dress. The costume consultants topped the Shirley Temple look with pink barrettes, some very cute pink ankle socks, and a matching necklace and bracelet.

All of the kids were thrilled about the project, and we had great fun watching the filming. We saw the finished product several times, but the first time was the best. Helen Hayes narrated, and the whole thing was very professionally done. It was thrilling to see ourselves and our friends on the screen.

As a promotional device, the movie was meant to show all the good things that were being accomplished at Crotched Mountain. Even so, when I saw myself in it, I wasn't very pleased. I looked tiny, almost lost, in my wheelchair, and much younger than I really was, partly because of the cutesy outfit I was wearing. My dress was almost grotesquely humorous in contrast to the thick metal braces on my legs and my cumbersome corrective shoes. This was the first time I'd ever seen myself wearing the braces, and it scared me. Besides, the back brace that I was wearing underneath my dress made me look fat.

Thinking about that film now, I'm annoyed that we all were scrubbed up and dressed in costumes for it. The crew filmed me eating, but did not include that segment in the final version; it was probably too messy and unsettling for the idealistic effect they were trying to achieve. Perhaps the realistic element was better left unshown, but the film was sentimental in other ways. Rather than just showing a boy struggling heroically to walk with an artificial leg, or the kids whooping it up in the pool, they might have informed the public about some of the more frustrating aspects of handicapped people's lives.

The center was achieving some remarkable things and there was no need to romanticize it. But I suppose that the general public's attitudes toward the handicapped in 1959 had a great deal to do with determining the tone of the film.

3

.BAD.SAD.NERVOUS.HAPPY.

During my years at Crotched Mountain, I went home for a week every Christmas and for two weeks every summer. Father used to coordinate his vacation from work with mine from school so that the whole family could be together at a cottage at Shaker Pines Lake in Connecticut. About the only things I remember about those summer vacations are fooling around with Prince in the water and the fact that I enjoyed them immensely. Nonetheless, I was always happy to return to the center and resume my rehabilitation program.

In March 1960 I went home for what was supposed to be a two-month vacation. Although this came at an unusual time of year and seemed a bit long, I didn't think much about it. There was added incentive for me to stay at home for a while: my brother, Howard, was only six months old, and the only time I had seen him had been at Christmas. I hardly knew my sister Shari, who had been born during my first year at Crotched Mountain. I was also looking forward to spending time with my parents, Marie, and Prince.

Although I expected to return, I had a teary farewell when I left the center. This was going to be an extended absence, and I wasn't sure if all of my friends would be there when I came back. But I promised to write, especially to Jimmy, and he promised to write too.

In the past when I'd visited home, things had been pretty hectic, what with the holidays and many of our relatives and friends dropping by. This time I had to adjust to being home as one of the regular inhabitants on an everyday basis. Almost immediately I established a routine, but it was much more relaxed than my schedule at Crotched Mountain.

I shared a room upstairs with Marie, who was six years old at the time. (I was nine and a half.) Every morning Mother came in to wake us up with a perfectly dreadful rendition of "Oh What a Beautiful Morning." As she entered the room, singing away, she headed straight for the windows and threw open the blinds, inviting the bright sun to come shining in on us. The combination of glaring sunlight and Mother's off-key warbling drove Marie out of bed like a shot and straight into the bathroom. Unfortunately, I had to surrender unconditionally to both the blinding and the ear-breaking as Mother helped me out of bed and into my clothes.

She then carried me downstairs and put me in my wheelchair (because of the layout of the house, we never brought my wheelchair upstairs), and I was fed breakfast along with Marie and Shari. Then Marie headed off to school and I played with Shari while Mother tended to Howard. After that, Mother strapped the metal braces on my legs, laid me down on two big towels spread out on the living room floor, and put me through my physical therapy session. Then there was more play with Shari while Mother did some telephone work, lunch a little later on, and another physical therapy session after lunch.

In the afternoon Mother set me up in the living room in front of the television and locked my braces to keep my legs straight while I watched my favorite shows—the soap operas. I usually napped for an hour or so until Marie came home from school, sometimes bringing a friend with her. Then I would go back into my wheelchair and we all would play together until dinner. This gave Mother a chance to finish her day's work on the telephone. We weren't allowed to stay up too long after dinner, so evening consisted of baths and bedtime.

After two months of this routine, I was eager to return to Crotched Mountain. Being home was fun, but I missed my friends and the super programs and great facilities at the center. My parents and I were beginning to wonder if something was wrong, because every time we called to ask about scheduling my return, the people at the center told us to call back in a week.

Soon it became apparent that I wouldn't be returning. The people at Crotched Mountain had concluded that I was "unable to take full advantage" of their program. Mother and Father questioned this explanation. My father had left the Pittsburgh Plate Glass Company several months earlier to take another job, and he believed that his change of employment and our inability to pay the full charges at the center without PPG's help were the real reasons for my termination.

I was dismayed. I had loved every minute at Crotched Mountain. If somebody had asked me how long I expected to stay there, I would have answered, "Forever." So sure had we been of my return to the center that we had left behind a special wooden relaxation chair, a gift that Father had made for me.

Being at home with my family helped soften the blow, but I still became very depressed. For the first time I began to indulge in self-pity. It wasn't just the fact that I couldn't return to Crotched Mountain that bothered me, but also my emerging realization, even when I was at the center, that my dreams of walking and talking would never come true.

No one at home was treating me like a cripple, and I tried not to let anyone know how morose I felt. But I'm sure that Mother had some inkling of it. I was a highly motivated young girl whose most cherished dreams had just been crushed, and I felt lost and helpless. Try as I might to make the best of things, I had lots of free time on my hands to ask myself why I had been chosen to suffer.

.MARIE.WATER.DRESS.

The first few months I was home after Crotched Mountain, Marie showered a lot of attention on me. We shared a bedroom upstairs, and one of her jobs was to help me during the night, by turning me over or fetching Mother for a trip to the bathroom.

At first Marie couldn't pamper me enough. She treated me like her baby sister, a cherished plaything, even though I was three years older than she was. Every morning she would brush my hair and help me select an outfit to wear. She was eager to fulfill any wish for me.

But after a few months the novelty wore off. After all, I was not the easiest person in the world to have for a roommate. Often I roused Marie out of bed in the middle of the night to get me a drink of water or to replace the pillow under my head.

Sometimes I was very whimsical with her. One night, when it was very late and everyone else was in bed, Marie was tossing and turning. I made some noises to tell her that I wanted something. When she asked me what I needed, I looked over at my doll, which was on the floor near the night-light, and made my sound for the bathroom.

"Do you want me to take your dolly to the bathroom, Ruth?" asked Marie.

I raised my eyes to say yes, following quickly with a curled lip, the way I usually indicated no. Putting these two expressions together was my way of saying "maybe" or "sort of."

"Does the dolly have to go?"

No.

"What do you want me to do with the dolly in the bathroom, Ruth?"

Then Marie guessed a number of things, such as brushing the

doll's teeth or giving her some medicine. When she asked if I wanted her to wash the doll's hands, I repeated the "maybe" expression, but this time with a lot of enthusiasm.

"You want me to wash the dolly, but not the dolly's hands. Something else on the dolly? Her face?"

No.

"Her clothes?"

Yes.

I smiled and made a high-pitched sound to tell Marie that she had almost guessed it.

Marie got out of bed and picked the dolly up from where it was lying next to my bed. "Oh, I see. Her dress is dirty. You want me to wash her dress, don't you, Ruth?"

I laughed with excitement and raised my eyes strongly to say, "Yes, that's it exactly."

Marie thought for a moment, and then replied, "Ruth, that's the dumbest thing I've ever heard. I'm going back to sleep."

But I wasn't so easily put off. I kept making sounds to tell Marie that I wanted my doll's dress washed and I wanted it washed *now*. If I could have done it myself, I would have, but since I couldn't, she had to do it for me. Besides, I was her older sister.

She resisted for a few more minutes, but finally realized that she wouldn't be able to sleep until my doll's dress was washed. Reluctantly, Marie trudged off to the bathroom and did it.

The next day Marie told Mother the whole story. Was Mother ever angry! When Father came home from work that night, she told him all about it, and he spanked me and put me to bed early. He told my sisters that I'd been spanked because I couldn't be treated any differently from any of the other kids when I did something wrong.

After this incident Marie began to change her attitude toward me. By the end of the summer I no longer was a princess in her eyes. I was okay to have around for a while, but I also could be a pain in the neck. I understood Marie's feelings toward me, and she was never unkind or mean. But we never struck up a special relationship again.

Despite our age difference, Marie and I wore the same size clothes back then. Since neither of us was possessive about her things, we shared a wardrobe. Marie also never objected to letting me hang around with her friends. When the weather permitted, she usually took me out to play with the other kids on our street.

Once, during the first summer I was home after Crotched Mountain, Marie and I were down the street in front of a friend's house when we heard Mother calling us home for lunch. Marie began to wheel me along the sidewalk, much faster than usual so we could get home quickly. All of a sudden my chair hit a crack and I went flying. I remember how the ground seemed to jump up into my face when I fell. *Splat!* It was my first serious spill. I crashed face first on the cement, with my front teeth acting as shock absorbers. In seconds my face was a bloody mess.

Marie didn't know what to do, so she started to cry. Then I realized that my face hurt and I tasted the blood, so I started to cry too. Before we knew it, half the neighborhood was there. Then Mother came running out to see what all the fuss was about. She immediately calmed everybody down, sat me back in my wheelchair, brought us home, dressed my wounds, and took account of the damage. To Marie's great relief, Mother pronounced that I would live, although my front teeth had been loosened by the fall.

Marie felt terrible about the accident and apologized to me profusely. I knew that she hadn't done it intentionally, and I forgave her on the spot. The whole thing would have been avoided if I had been wearing a seat belt, but they weren't in vogue back in 1960.

About a month later, Marie was pushing me and my wheelchair down the driveway of our house. She let my chair go down the incline too quickly, and it turned over when it hit the side-walk. Once again I went flying, and once again my face hit the concrete. This time I got a black eye, accompanied by similar histrionics from Marie and me. The second spill also was unintentional, but after this one I became wary of Marie's bad luck. She felt awful about the accidents, but I was the one who was taking the lumps.

By autumn Marie was becoming increasingly impatient with me. On more than one occasion when she turned me over in bed at night, she wrenched me around in her haste to go back to sleep. In fact, I had a sore knee that Christmas because Marie picked me up too roughly on Christmas Eve. Not that she bore any malice toward me, but it soon became obvious to both of us that she shouldn't tend to my needs so frequently and that I should make fewer demands on her.

I began to use a tactic of laughing whenever Marie started to lift me or help me with something that I preferred to have someone else do. My laughter usually befuddled her, diverting her attention from what she was about to do to the question of why I was laughing. This approach worked much better than telling her directly that I didn't trust her hands anymore.

.SHARI.GRETL.SOAP.

My relationship with Shari was quite different. Shari was four years old when I finished at Crotched Mountain. From the moment I came home she gravitated to me, and we soon developed a wonderful understanding of one another. Since she was too young for school the first year I was home, we spent a lot of time together. And as Marie and I drifted apart, Shari became my special assistant. In September 1960, right around my tenth birthday, Shari began switching off with Marie, sometimes sleeping in my room. Within six months Marie moved out and Shari became my permanent roommate.

Early on I put Shari to a test similar to the one I had tried with

Marie. Once again, everyone had fallen asleep when I woke Shari up with some quiet sounds.

"What is it, Ruthie? The door—are you lookin' at the door? Want me to get Mommy so you can go potty?"

No.

"You're still lookin' at the door, right? Is it the bathroom, something about the bathroom?"

Yes.

"But you don't have to go, right? You really don't have to go?"

No.

"Is there something you need in the bathroom, Ruthie?"

Yes.

Shari jumped out of bed and came over beside me.

"What do you need from the bathroom, Ruthie? Tell me what. Hey, why are you hitting Gretel, Ruthie?"

Gretel was my favorite doll, a recent birthday present from my best friend in our neighborhood, Karen Foley. Gretel had bright blond hair, and as my very best doll was granted the privilege of coming to bed with me every night.

"Is something wrong with Gretel?"

No.

I nudged Gretel again with my hand and repeated my bathroom sound.

"Does Gretel have to go potty?"

No.

I repeated my negative frown, but I smiled when I nudged Gretel's head again and sounded for the bathroom.

Shari pondered my clue. Then she asked, "Does Gretel have a headache?"

No.

I started laughing, but continued to hit Gretel's head and sound for the bathroom.

"Is it her ear? Does she have an earache, Ruthie?"

No.

"Does Gretel want to put on Mommy's makeup?"

No.

I laughed at Shari's silly suggestion.

"I know, that's silly. But you're still hitting her head — no, her hair, are you hitting her hair, Ruthie?"

Yes. Yes.

"Does Gretel want me to comb her hair?"

No. Yes. Sort of.

"I'm getting warm, right, Ruthie?"

Yes. Yes.

"Does Gretel need to go to the bathroom, not for potty, but for something else?"

Yes.

"Is it a bath? Does Gretel need a bath?"

Yes. No. Almost.

"Sort of maybe, right? Oh, I know, I know, Ruthie. Gretel needs her hair washed. Right?"

Exactly.

By now Shari was giggling, and I was shrieking with laughter.

"Ruthie, you're funny. Okay, I'll wash Gretel's hair. Does she like the soap or the shampoo?"

I laughed the whole time the water was running in the bathroom. A few minutes later Shari came back with Gretel tucked under her arm, the doll's blond hair dripping wet from the beauty treatment. We must have been up half the night giggling about it. Even better, Shari never told anybody.

From then on, I never made Shari do any crazy things for me in the middle of the night. That is not to say, however, that she needed much prompting to do wacky things.

There was an attic fan in the house. On several occasions, usually when Father turned on that fan on the first hot day of the year, a couple of bats came swooping down the stairs and into our room, which was directly across the hall from the doorway to the attic. I remember watching Father catch the bats in bedsheets in our room and take them outside to be released.

There's a family story that when Shari was a little girl, one very smart bat eluded my father's detection and flew back and forth between our room and the attic, hiding behind a curtain in our room whenever an adult came in. Shari swore that "Mr. Birdy" kept her company for a whole summer, but I don't remember having any bat for a roommate. I was terrified of the things. All Shari had to do was say "Ruth, there's Mr. Birdy," and I would nearly jump out of my bed.

Years later Shari had a real pet in her room, a guinea pig named Pierre. Although Pierre usually stayed in his cage, Shari liked to shut the door and set him free to scurry around on the floor. One morning she almost scared me out of my wits by letting Pierre loose when I was still in bed. Although he was harmless, I was utterly helpless to move away from him. I screamed in terror while that guinea pig crawled around in my bed, but Shari and I enjoyed a good laugh—after she had put Pierre back in his cage.

Perhaps it was because Shari was offbeat that we got along so well. I recall one very special time in the fall of 1961. I was eleven years old and Shari was five. We were both in bed, and I was sleeping on my back as I usually did. Somehow my leg got wrapped up in the blanket, and it made me very uncomfortable. I called out to Shari for some help. She woke up, saw the problem, and straightened it out easily. But instead of going back to bed, she began to tell me how glad she was that I was home, how she was proud of me, how I was the bravest person she knew. She told me how she wished that I could walk and talk, and she described all the adventures we could have together, exciting things like running away to join the circus or going off to live with a band of wild Indians.

We both knew that this would never be, but it was fun to pretend. All of a sudden, Shari came over and squeezed my hand and whispered, "Ruthie, I love you."

I almost burst from not being able to tell her that I loved her very much too. There were a thousand things I wanted to tell her, and I started to cry. But I knew that she understood what my eyes were saying and the soft, cooing sounds I was making. Shari didn't need to hear the words.

We stayed up for a while longer, holding hands and smiling at each other. Shari and I have been best friends ever since.

.10.
.FATHER.TRIP.BAG.DINNER.RED.

Our house was in an old-fashioned neighborhood where everybody knew everyone else on the block and all of the kids trooped around together. I was included in the local activities as much as possible. Fortunately, all of the other kids in the neighborhood accepted me. I guess that because Marie and Shari treated me like a regular kid who just happened to be in a wheelchair, the other children followed suit. Nobody ignored the fact that I was in a wheelchair—that would have been pretty hard to do—but with my sisters' help, I was able to join in the fun most of the time.

My tenth birthday party, on September 22, 1960, provides a good illustration. Mother invited some of our friends over for cake and ice cream after dinner. My neighborhood friends, Edith and Emily Steinhauer and Karen Foley, were there, along with our cousins Sue Armstrong and Joanne Case. Mother baked a cake, which had beautiful white frosting and fancy pink decorations surrounding "Happy Birthday Ruth 10." The girls helped me blow out the candles and we sang the birthday song. Everybody said how pretty the cake was, and we all had seconds. Of course I got lots of presents; that's when Karen gave me Gretel, my doll.

Father came home in the middle of the ice cream. Marie, Shari, and I were excited to see him, because he'd been away for his job all week up in Maine. Mother hadn't been sure whether he would be back in time for the party. He was singing "Happy Birthday" very loudly as he walked in the door, and he kept singing it while he dropped his suitcase on the floor in the hallway, walked into the dining room, and scooped me up in his arms. He made up some funny words to the song that made everybody laugh.

After he put me back into my chair and Shari and Marie got their hugs, I noticed that he was holding a brown paper bag. He walked into the kitchen and put the paper bag on the counter. Shari ran in and asked him what was in it.

"It's my dinner," Father said. But he said it too loudly, and started laughing. I knew something was up; there was something funny in that bag.

Shari didn't catch on right away.

"Is it a hamburger?" she asked. "A hot dog? Mashed potatoes?"

Everyone ran into the kitchen and started guessing what was in the bag. They left me behind in the dining room, so I yelled out and Mother came back from the kitchen to get me. By then Father was laughing so hard that he couldn't even say no to the girls' guesses about what he was having for dinner.

Suddenly the bag moved a little — by itself. I saw it, and Marie saw it. Then it moved again and everybody saw it. That stopped the guessing, and everyone stared at the bag. When it moved again and toppled over on the counter, the girls all screamed and ran back into the dining room — except for Shari and me. Shari started to climb up on the counter to look in the bag, but she couldn't make it because she was too little. Father pushed a chair over for her and said, "Go on, Shari, show Ruthie what Daddy's having for supper."

Shari climbed up on the chair, opened the bag a tiny bit, and looked in. Then she screamed, jumped off the chair, and ran into the dining room. That got all the other girls yelling and jumping up and down, even though nobody understood a word Shari was saying. Father and Mother followed Shari into the dining room and halfheartedly tried to calm everyone down.

I was left alone in the kitchen, two feet away from a paper bag that was wriggling around on the counter by itself. The bag rustled some more, and then toppled over on its other side. My heart was pounding like crazy. I tried to scream but couldn't muster up enough breath for a whimper. Then two skinny black wires popped out from the open end of the bag, and an ugly claw began to follow.

Eyes clamped shut, I screamed as loudly as a fire alarm. Mother ran back into the kitchen to rescue me, giggling like one of the little girls. She laughed even harder when Father asked me if I wanted to eat some of his lobster. I replied with a horrified "No!"

It took ten minutes before my teeth stopped chattering, although I was laughing along with everyone else. Father actually ate that icky thing, or so we heard. When he announced that he was going to drop the lobster into a pot of boiling water, he lost his audience. Not even Shari stuck around.

That was the best birthday I ever had.

.KARN.

I mentioned that Karen Foley was at my birthday party. Karen was a year older than I was and lived down the street. She was one of my best friends. Quite often she dropped by after school and took me out for a walk around the neighborhood. She even babysat for us when my parents went out for a while.

One time when Karen was staying with us, Marie suggested that we bake a cake. This sounded like a fine idea to everyone but me. I made noises to tell them to stop before they blew up the oven or got us into trouble by messing up the kitchen. Despite my protests, the girls took a cake mix out of the cupboard and mixed up the ingredients. Karen was the head baker, Marie and Shari her assistants. I was lost in the shuffle.

That time, Karen was the leader of the pack. This would have been my role with my sisters if my physical condition had been different. My frustration over this fact increased as Marie and

Shari grew older and I was left out of the action more and more often.

Mother knew that I liked to be included in everything. She customarily brought me into the kitchen when she was cooking dinner and set me up at the table with a cup of water, a wooden spoon, and a bowl. She encouraged me to stir the water in the bowl, and in this way I symbolically helped her prepare dinner. Much as I appreciated the gesture, I hated the fact that this was all I could do in the kitchen.

I experienced similarly mixed feelings when I played with "normal" kids. In the warm weather, Mother would spread out paper and crayons on the picnic table in our back yard and Shari, I, and whoever else was around would draw pictures. Of course, I could only make dots and attempt to draw crude lines, but it was another way of keeping me involved. As with other things, I was happy to play as regular a part as possible, yet frustrated that I couldn't join in more fully.

.DOL.SANDY.

One winter day I was over at Emily Steinhauer's house with Shari and Marie. Emily was a year older than me. Her sister, Edith, was my age, as was another friend who was there, Judy Kimberly. Also present were Karen Foley and her two younger sisters, Joanie and Sue, and my friend Sandy Dayton, so we had quite a crew.

We were playing hospital with our dolls, nursing them for a variety of imagined illnesses. One of the girls' dolls had a broken leg, one had the measles, one had chicken pox. I was treating Gretel for a fever. With Shari's help, I fed my doll some make-believe ice cream, which fixed her right up. The doll with the broken leg was cured with a Band-Aid, and the dolls with the "germs" were quarantined for several minutes, then returned to the others in perfect health.

I was enjoying playing with the other girls, but I remember

wishing that a cure for my malady could come as easily as it did for our dolls. My melancholy thoughts were interrupted when Sandy put her doll in a doll chair and pretended that it was a wheelchair. Then she remarked, "Look, my dolly is sick like Ruthie."

The other girls looked at me. I saw that Shari and Marie were about to get mad at Sandy. But I laughed, so everybody else laughed too. I knew that Sandy meant no harm by what she had said. Sandy acted slower than the other girls because she was mentally retarded. Often she would stay near me when the gang was out playing, and we got along just fine.

.FATHER.HURT.

Something that really frightened me was when Father was involved in minor accidents.

With all the traveling he did for his job, he rarely was home for dinner with the family during the week. Frequently he was away on sales trips for several days. When he was home, usually on weekends, he loved to cook for everyone. One summer evening he was cooking steaks for dinner, along with squash and a salad. While slicing up the vegetables for the salad, he cut his hand badly. I don't remember whether he needed stitches, but the fact that Father had been injured at all really bothered me.

Another time, during the second winter I was home after Crotched Mountain, we had just returned from a ride in the car. Father was carrying me up the stairs to the house when he slipped on an icy step and crunched his knee. He limped around for about a month as a result.

These accidents were trivial, but at the time they caused me considerable concern. Father was a big, strong, gentle man, and I simply couldn't imagine him getting hurt. He liked to sit me on his knee and bounce me up and down, which I always loved. He also liked to kid me, and I recall laughing at his corny jokes much more than feeling bad from his rare reprimands.

Sunday was usually my big day with Father, especially in the morning, when Mother took Marie, Shari, and Howard to church. I looked forward to having him all to myself on Sunday mornings. Once the rest of the family returned home, we usually went out for a ride in the car, either to visit relatives or just to take in some sights.

.SCHOOL.

As I've already mentioned, Mother took care of most of my personal needs. She was always sensitive to my physical condition without being overprotective. Like Father, she tried very hard to give me every chance of being a "normal" kid. But caring for me was almost a full-time job, and Mother was being worn to a frazzle. She did get some help from Gramma Ruth and Aunt Jane, but the burden remained on her shoulders — or, more literally, on her weakened back. All the lifting and carrying was ruining her health.

By early 1962, I had been home for nearly two years. I loved my family and I appreciated what they were doing for me, but I also missed Crotched Mountain. I was bored with too much sitting around with nothing to do. I longed to move forward again, to meet new people and try to push my own development. Seeing Shari come home every day from school and complain about how crummy it was only increased my desire to return to school myself.

Even more important, I was aware of how hard Mother was struggling to meet my needs and the needs of the rest of our family. There wasn't enough of her to go around, and I knew that if I left home it would ease the situation. When my parents began to discuss the possibility of my attending another institution, I was very receptive to the idea.

My parents tried to get me back into Lakeville. Father took me for some psychological testing by a Dr. Scherer in Springfield. At first Dr. Scherer had no idea of how I communicated, or even that I was capable of communicating. Then Father got involved and showed him how I said yes and no, and the tests seemed to go a little better. Unfortunately, they didn't go better enough. Mother told me later that Dr. Scherer concluded that I had an IQ of 50, which once again ruled out Lakeville.

Owing to our family's lack of financial resources, this left only one institution for me: the Belchertown State School in Belchertown, Massachusetts. My parents visited the institution in late March, and reported to me that it was not as good as Crotched Mountain. It provided care for many mentally retarded residents, some of whom were also physically handicapped. It was not as modern as Crotched Mountain, and was shorter on staff and specialized facilities. But my parents also told me that the people at Belchertown said they could provide me with much of the physical therapy and individualized educational training I needed. Moreover, Belchertown was less than an hour's drive from home, so my family could visit me more often than they had at Crotched Mountain.

Based on this account, I was all set to go and give it a try. Although it didn't sound perfect, I envisioned it as a run-down version of Crotched Mountain. I presumed that no matter what, I would accomplish more at Belchertown than at home. If it didn't work out, I always could come back home and we could look for another school.

My parents weren't very happy about the place, though. In fact, I overheard them arguing about it a couple of times, which was very rare for Mother and Father. Mother was reluctant for me to go there, and she seemed quite upset about it. Father kept saying that it was the best thing for the family. When I heard them arguing about this, I wanted to run away.

At separate times, both Gramma Ruth and Nana Christine told me they didn't want me to go to Belchertown, but neither told me why. In the end, the whole family crossed their fingers and hoped for the best. We applied for admission in March. After some paperwork mix-ups, I was accepted, and was scheduled to arrive in May 1962. Gramma Ruth spent hours sewing name tags into my clothes.

At the time, my parents failed to mention a comment that one of the officials at Belchertown had made during their initial visit. He told them that I might have to wait for quite some time before I could attend the State School, because new admissions were made only when one of the current residents died. I think that Mother and Father were alarmed when my application was approved in such short order.

My parents also neglected to tell me that an absolute condition for admission to Belchertown was certification by a licensed physician that the applicant was mentally retarded.

4

.NUMBER.4774.

When my parents took me to live at the Belchertown State School on May 14, 1962, I was four months shy of my twelfth birthday. I had been cautioned that Belchertown was different from Crotched Mountain, but I was determined to make the best of whatever I encountered. After all, how bad could a place be that was devoted to serving the needs of disabled people?

As we drove up that first day, I was oblivious of everything but my excitement about coming to a new place and my nervous anticipation of meeting the people who lived and worked there.

The State School was much bigger than I had pictured it, with several large brick buildings and a number of smaller ones spread out on a spacious setting, surrounded by grass and trees. After we got out of our car, Father put me into my wheelchair (the one he had made for me) and we entered the administration building. There my parents signed papers and talked to some people in an office for a few minutes. When they were finished, a lady came out and took Mother and me down the corridor to have my picture taken.

From there we went back to the car for a quick drive to another large brick building, the Infirmary, which was to be my new home. This time Father took my two suitcases with us into the building. I expected that we would be given a tour of the grounds, or at least of the building. I wanted to get a feel for the place and meet the people who were going to work with me. But nothing of the kind occurred. If we had been given a tour, I would have begged Mother and Father to take me home immediately.

Just inside the building, a man and a woman dressed in white hospital clothing were waiting for us. Mother and Father spoke to them for a few minutes. Then Father came over and kissed me goodbye. Mother gave me a long, long hug and whispered in my ear, "I love you, sweetheart, remember that." She was crying.

Then they were gone.

I was taken into an office and examined by the man who had been waiting for us, whom I will call Dr. Soong. Dr. Soong spoke English with a very thick accent. With the nurse's assistance, he placed me on a table, undressed me, removed my leg and back braces, slapped me into diapers and a hospital johnny, weighed me, measured my height, and moved my arms and legs around. He talked while this was going on, but I didn't understand a word he said.

Dr. Soong was the staff doctor at the Infirmary. Many years later I learned that the brief examination I have just described also included a "psychological evaluation." In that evaluation, Dr. Soong concluded that I was an imbecile. His method of evaluating me consisted of looking me over during the physical exam and deciding that since I didn't talk and apparently couldn't understand what he was saying, I must be an imbecile.

Although Mother and Father told Dr. Soong how I communicated before they left, I doubt whether he was aware of my facial signals. It wouldn't have mattered anyway. When he examined me, he mumbled unintelligibly. I couldn't tell whether he was talking to me, the nurse, or himself. Since I couldn't ask him to speak up or repeat what he said, he assumed I was a moron.

After all, the Lakeville report indicated that I was "severely re-tarded," and the records from Crotched Mountain said that I had made very little progress there.

It would have been difficult for anyone, even a trained expert in speech pathology, to assess my intelligence accurately in so brief a time. But with Dr. Soong's apparent lack of expertise in this area, not to mention the language barrier, I didn't have a chance.

Anyway, he didn't spend much time trying to figure me out. He was a physician, not a psychologist or a speech therapist, and he was the only physician on duty to service the entire popula-tion of 1600 residents at Belchertown.

The Infirmary served as the State School's hospital. It was also the only building on the grounds at that time that was in any way adapted for handicapped people. As a result, all of the phys-ically handicapped residents were thrown into the Infirmary, along with severely retarded individuals who were prone to hurt-ing themselves and needed special care.

My intake evaluation labeled me an imbecile, and thus deter-mined how the nurses and attendants were to treat me for the next few years. Since everyone assumed that I couldn't under-stand what was going on around me, they ignored any and all evidence that I could present to the contrary. I cannot view this label as an understandable mistake, because it took nearly ten years before it was officially changed.

After Dr. Soong completed the examination, the nurse put me back in my wheelchair and took me down the hall to a small room with a hospital bed in it. She did not bring along my braces and clothes, or my suitcases. Without saying a word, she put me in the bed, took my wheelchair, and walked out, shutting the door behind her. I was left in that room without one personal item, and with no explanation of what was happening. I never saw any of my things again, including my doll, Gretel, which Mother had packed for safekeeping in one of the suitcases.

At some point I learned that I had to stay in that room by myself for a week before I could meet any of the other residents. The staff didn't want me to bring in any communicable diseases. After the week was over, I was to be moved in with everyone else, and presumably I would get my clothes back. This procedure didn't please me at all, but there was nothing I could do about it.

There I was, alone and flat on my back in a small room with the door shut tight. Although I suspected nothing of what was to follow, I became very apprehensive about Belchertown. To begin with, I didn't appreciate being placed in diapers and hospital bedclothes. I had been toilet-trained at an early age, years before I left for Crotched Mountain, and needed only physical assistance to and from the bathroom. I gathered from the around-the-clock diapering that either nobody was going to pay close enough attention to me to make diapering unnecessary or the staff was unaware of my ability to control my bodily functions. Either way, I didn't like what it told me.

.HEAR.SCREAM.

Lying in that bed and trying to figure out what to make of the diaper question, I became aware of very strange sounds coming through the walls and ceiling. These noises — groaning, moaning, screaming — were being made by people, that much I could tell. But I couldn't imagine what kind of people were making them. The possibilities scared me, and I tried to block the noises out. Try as I might to ignore them, however, they kept me on edge the whole time I was stuck in that room.

.FOOD.LIKE.SHIT.

Later that first day I was treated to yet another surprise when a nurse came in to check my diaper and feed me. Bored and scared, I desperately wanted the woman to talk to me, to tell me what I could expect. Instead she handled me like a sack of flour.

She changed and fed me as if I couldn't even tell what she was doing. I wasn't a particularly finicky eater, but there was a necessary art to feeding me because I had great difficulty in chewing and swallowing. At home I ate everything. All Mother had to do was cut my food into small pieces and feed me slowly. She was very patient, always aware that I was doing my best, even when food popped out of my mouth involuntarily. To her credit, Mother never scolded me on an emotional basis for what was essentially a physical problem. At Crotched Mountain the staff had taken the same care to make my meals as enjoyable as possible. But at Belchertown the attendants shoved globs of food into my mouth and expected me to swallow them in big gulps while I was flat on my back, not even propped up in a sitting position.

The food itself was awful, the worst I had ever tasted. They fed me either boiled vegetables or steamed meat, ground into a tasteless pulp. Most of the time the food was so bad that I couldn't tell what it was. From the outset, eating at the State School was a painful experience, and I had a terrible time of it. To make matters worse, whenever I choked while they were shoveling the food down my throat, the attendants became angry. They thought I was being uncooperative.

After several of these sessions and two days in that room, I was absolutely despondent. It was obvious that the attendants didn't understand me at all, and they were making little effort to do so. They talked disparagingly about me right to my face, as if I couldn't understand a word they were saying. They handled me roughly, and they couldn't get out of that room fast enough.

It didn't take me long to become hostile toward these people, which I think was understandable under the circumstances. The diapers, the solitary confinement, the weird noises, all rattled my nerves. The callous treatment from the attendants transformed my anxiety into anger.

I wanted to know why they were being so harsh with me, why

they were talking about me like I was a moron. I made hundreds of sounds and facial expressions in the hope of generating a response, any response, but they continued to ignore me. They thought that my yes-and-no signals were mindless gesticulations, and I had no way of telling them anything different. As long as these people considered my brain useless and my facial expressions and sounds meaningless, I was doomed to remain "voiceless."

I had learned that I would have to stay in that room for a week. But nobody bothered to tell me that I wouldn't be allowed to see my parents or have any telephone contact with them for a whole month! This was done to facilitate my "acclimation" to the State School. I believed at the time that it saved my parents a quick return trip to Belchertown to pick me up.

.NO.EAT.

I had come to Belchertown prepared to make the best of whatever I encountered, but after a few days of solitary confinement and inexplicable abuse, I couldn't take it any longer. I decided that the whole venture was a mistake and that the fastest way to get out was to refuse to cooperate at all — to go on strike. That way the attendants would become so exasperated with me that they would have no choice but to call my parents and beg them to take this little troublemaker off their hands.

Or so I thought. I didn't consider that these people encountered troublesome behavior all the time, that this was what they expected from me. When I closed my mouth and refused to eat, it only reinforced the image that Dr. Soong's evaluation had established. The attendants responded by prying my mouth open and forcing the food down my throat. I fought them all the way, but they had strength, numbers, and ultimately my hunger on their side. When I realized that my strategy wasn't working, I reluctantly gave in.

It was all I could do to get through the week. I kept hoping that once I was moved in with the other residents, things would improve. Counting the hours until then, miserable and lonely, I literally cried my way through the week.

The one bright spot was that Mother wrote nearly every day, and her letters were read to me. Although I was thrilled when any of the staff spoke to me at all, the attendants read Mother's letters as if they were talking to a wall. Nonetheless, the letters helped quiet my fear that I would never see my family again. It was reassuring to know that everyone at home was concerned about my well-being. While I was in that room, I felt like an animal in a cage. For all I knew, they were going to keep me there longer than a week just to punish me. Mother's letters were the only contact I had with the outside world. Without them, I would have felt completely abandoned.

.HAPPY.NERVOUS.BAD.SAD.SCARED.SICK.

I breathed a great big sigh of relief when my week of confinement ended. It happened without any explanation. An attendant came in after breakfast, put me in a wheelchair, and rolled me off to the other end of the building, to a place called Ward 1.

Ward 1 was a large, open area with about thirty beds arranged in rows. Each bed contained a female resident. It was on Ward 1 that I learned that the building I was in was called the Infirmary and that it was the only place at the State School for physically handicapped residents.

The Infirmary had eight wards on two floors, with females in Wards 1 through 4 on the first floor and males in Wards 5 through 8 on the second floor. In 1962 very different types of people were thrown together at the Infirmary — residents who were physically handicapped, retarded people who were apt to injure themselves, and residents who were temporarily ill. It was as progressive a place as a medieval madhouse. All of the residents at Belchertown suffered from overcrowding, lack of proper staffing, and indifference from what little staff there was. But the

Infirmary was in many ways the institution's chamber of horrors. It was here that I would spend the next thirteen years of my life.

Ward 1 was actually the model ward of the female floor of the Infirmary. Of the thirty adult women who lived there, half were mentally competent and half suffered from mild degrees of mental retardation. All of the mentally competent women, and most of the retarded ones, had severe physical handicaps and were confined either to wheelchairs or to their beds. There were six ambulators, all of them older retarded women in failing health.

Every woman on the ward, except for two who were bedridden, wore clothes, as opposed to johnnies and diapers. Many fed themselves, and those who couldn't were fed by those who could. Many of the residents helped with the daily tasks of caring for themselves, and at the very least they were able to assist the staff with feeding and cleaning. Some were even permitted to leave the ward and wheel themselves down the hall to watch television in the lounge.

Since so many of the women were mentally competent and most spent at least part of their time in wheelchairs, there was much less chaos and despair on Ward 1 than on the other wards, where people's mental and physical conditions were much, much worse. But Ward 1 was allotted only one attendant per eight-hour shift, instead of the three who worked the shifts on the other wards — not because the women couldn't have used the additional staff, but because there was more drastic need for services on the other wards.

Upon arriving at Ward 1, I was stunned. Although I was relieved to be with other people at last, the ward was unlike anything I had ever seen. The odor was sickening, the air was stale, and the atmosphere was lifeless. I was nervous about what to expect from this group of people, all of whom looked like they were suffering and miserable. I wondered whether I looked as bad to them.

My only previous experience with mentally retarded people

had been with Sandy Dayton, the girl who lived in my neighborhood in Springfield. As I said earlier, we used to play together
once in a while. I had realized that Sandy was a little slow in
thought, but she was always friendly to me and we got along
well. Until I went to Belchertown, I never looked on Sandy as
being "mentally retarded."

It was quite different to see a dozen or more women on Ward
1 who were obviously "slow." All of them looked and acted
much worse than Sandy. But I overcame my initial apprehension
when I saw that there was nothing threatening or scary about
them. The general atmosphere on the ward was dictated by the
mentally competent women, from whom the retarded women
took their cues for most of their behavior.

.MONTH.TERRY.FRIENDS.

I soon noticed that there were some very special relationships
among the residents on Ward 1. For example, two ladies named
April and Theresa were inseparable companions, spending almost every minute in each other's company. April was in her
forties, and walked with the help of a cane, but with great difficulty. She was mildly retarded, and extremely pleasant. She usually had a good grasp on what was going on around her. Her
friend, Theresa, was older, in her sixties, and was confined to a
wheelchair. Theresa was fine mentally and she spoke perfectly,
but her body wasn't in very good shape. I don't remember what
her specific physical problem was, but I do remember that she
couldn't do much by herself. This was where April came in. She
helped Theresa by dressing and feeding her. In turn, Theresa
acted like a mother to April, constantly advising and instructing
her with gentle, understanding firmness.

They were quite a pair, April and Theresa, and the spirit of
their relationship was not unusual on Ward 1. Other residents
engaged in the same kind of mutual assistance. It was this spirit
of cooperation that prevented people from going off the deep

end on the ward, and it went a long way toward softening the negative effect of the institution.

I was eager to make friends, but several obstacles stood in my way. The first one was my age. At eleven, I was easily the youngest person there; the next youngest resident was in her late teens. It didn't help that I always have looked much younger than my age. When I came to Ward 1, I was clothed in diapers and a johnny and was never taken out of bed. I must have looked like an infant to many of the women on the ward, and it was understandable that some of them remarked that I looked like a little girl in a crib. This was very frustrating, especially since I could have spent my days in a wheelchair like the other residents, as I had at home. But my wheelchair, back brace, leg braces, and clothes were consigned to storage, and I never got a chance to use them.

Some of the attendants did make an attempt to put my leg braces on me soon after I arrived, but they couldn't figure out how to work them, so I never wore leg braces at Belchertown. Dr. Soong made a note in my records several months later, in August 1962, explaining that my leg braces weren't being used because they were "too small." As a result, and because of the lack of any physical therapy, my physical condition deteriorated terribly during my first year at Belchertown.

Mother was extremely worried that all of our hard work with the exercises at home was being undone, but when she asked about this, the staff at the State School lied. I remember receiving letters from her saying that she had heard from the staff that I was wearing my braces every day. The superintendent, Dr. Lawrence Bowser, indicated in a letter to Mother in November 1963 that I was wearing my leg braces and sitting in a wheelchair *every day*. Whether he knew it or not, this statement was totally false. I am sure that someone fabricated this for my record so they would have a response to Mother's inquiries on the subject.

It wasn't until 1965 that my parents became sure that I was *not* wearing leg braces. At this time they offered to buy a new set for me, but their offer was declined.

.LITTLE.BIRD.

In addition to being younger than everybody else on the ward, and looking even younger than I was, I suffered from being considered severely retarded. Since I required a lot of physical assistance and was unable to speak, this assessment was accepted without question by nearly all of the women.

Some of the retarded women liked to play with dolls, and several of them viewed me as a little doll. The word on the ward was that I was a lost little bird with broken wings. The attendants saw to the necessities, changing my diapers and managing to force some of that disgusting food down my throat. But I was still treated as if I had no mind, and nobody on the staff took the time to talk to me or get to know me.

When I did get some attention, it usually came in the form of a remark from one of the residents, like "poor little girl" or "poor birdy" or "isn't that sad." Talk about making a good first impression! It was bad enough that I had to lie flat on my back in diapers all day, without everyone thinking that I was a helpless little cripple lost in my own world. Any sound or expression I made to attract attention, or to vent my frustration, was perceived as a nuisance and nothing more.

.FRIEND.HAIR.YELLOW.

Ward 1 was no great shakes for anyone. For the mentally competent women who were trapped there in wheelchairs, it was horrible. Nobody left the building, even to go out for some fresh air, unless the whole ward went out, and that happened only two or three times all summer. The same problems affected the retarded women, but the psychological toll was much greater on the mentally competent residents.

Yet many of the women were trying to make the best of their

environment and themselves, and I liked them for that reason. As a little girl suddenly dropped into this new world, I was filled with fears and uncertainties. I desperately wanted to be accepted into the mainstream of life on the ward. When I found myself being treated like a mindless infant by the other residents, it hurt me much more than all of the shock and insult of my first week of isolation.

After several days on Ward 1, I was a wreck. I was emotionally overwrought, and weak from vomiting repeatedly and not eating. But then I ran into my first bit of luck, in the form of an elderly resident who had been consigned to the Infirmary because of failing health. Goldy was in her sixties, and she walked around very slowly with the help of a cane. She seemed to be mildly retarded, which might explain why she ignored the staff's evaluation of my intellectual capacity. Or maybe she noticed something about the way I responded to people. For whatever reason, Goldy perceived that I was in fact tuned in to what was going on and that I did have a personality after all. Intuitively realizing that I was frightened and upset by the way I was being treated, Goldy became my ally and guardian angel. Because of her age and her maternal attitude, she reminded me at times of my Nana Christine and Gramma Ruth.

Goldy was friends with Theresa and April, the inseparable ones. When she started spending time with me, Theresa and April came around too. Maybe Goldy envied their special relationship, for she really threw herself into seeing that my lot improved. She talked to me for hours, telling me about the various people on the ward and encouraging me to eat.

Goldy provided me with the first kindness I encountered at Belchertown. It was a wonderful relief to hear someone talk to me like I actually understood what she was saying. For a brief interval, it made me believe that it was only a matter of time until others took notice and the prevailing attitude toward me changed.

.WARD.4.

After three weeks, and before I had fully adjusted to Ward 1, I was moved abruptly to the other end of the building and Ward 4. I had been scared, angry, and frustrated during my first month at the State School. But by comparison with what I was about to experience, that first month had been a picnic.

Like Ward 1, Ward 4 housed about thirty females. That is where the similarity ended. Ward 4 had a younger population, with teenagers comprising about a third of its residents. I became the youngest girl on the ward when I arrived, but over the summer several girls who were four or five years younger than me joined us. Everyone on Ward 4 wore johnnies and diapers. Although some residents could walk, most were confined to their beds, and only two or three spent any time at all in wheelchairs.

Almost all of the residents on Ward 4 suffered from some combination of a physical handicap *and* mental retardation. Several of them were mentally competent, but all had a physical handicap as bad as or worse than my own. When someone was physically "normal," as were the half-dozen or so ambulators on the ward, she was severely retarded. The ambulators lived there because they were likely to inflict physical harm on themselves. About half of the residents of Ward 4 fell somewhere between these two extremes.

Ward 1 had been dominated by frustration and boredom. Many of the women there would have been able to take advantage of a wide variety of therapeutic and educational programs if they had been offered. But Ward 4 seemed a human wasteland. It presented a staggering array of crippled bodies and damaged minds, a living picture of pain and madness.

.SHIT.EAT.MAKE.WEAR.JACKET.

There were many people on Ward 4 whom I will never forget because their behavior nearly drove me crazy. One of these was a girl I'll call Valerie, one of the ambulatory people on the ward. She was about a year older than me, and was very small. Valerie's bed was near mine and always smelled awful because of a particularly repulsive habit of hers: she liked to stick her hands into her diapers, extract her own excrement, and smear it all over herself, her bed, and whatever else she could reach. She also liked to eat soap. It was this habit that usually caught the attention of the staff, especially when she began to choke on it.

Another girl, "Carla," who was in her late twenties and also an ambulator, was also fond of reaching into her diapers and spreading whatever she found there all over herself. I distinguished between Valerie and Carla because Carla had very skinny legs. And there was another girl like them, a girl I'll call Patty. She was an ambulator about Carla's age, prone to the same kind of fumbling in her diapers. But Patty had developed a trick of her own: she vomited all over herself nearly every day. Patty was affectionately called "the Puker" by the staff.

These three very sick girls were placed in straitjackets in the fall of 1962, about four months after I came to Ward 4. They were still wearing them when I left the ward in June 1963. I can't say I was happy to see them restrained, but I was relieved by it. Although none of them ever harmed me or anyone else on the ward that I knew of, I would have been an easy target if they ever got the urge to come visit. Lying on my back in bed, I was defenseless. The straitjackets offered at least a measure of safety for these girls, as well as for potential victims like me. The mere fact that they no longer were doing such terrible things eliminated one nightmare from the ward.

.GLOVES.HIT.HEAD.

Two little girls with similar problems entered the ward during that first summer. They were nine years old, and engaged in the same diaper games as Valerie, Carla, and Patty. Additionally, these two practiced the dangerous activity of repeatedly banging their heads against the walls. Unable even to attempt to curb this behavior in any psychological way, the staff had to find some method of preventing them from seriously hurting themselves. So they placed boxing gloves on their hands to keep them from going into their diapers, and they strapped hockey helmets on their heads to prevent them from cracking their skulls open.

I heard later that it took about three years of the gloves and helmets to cure these girls of their diaper fumbling and head banging. In this instance, the ingenuity of some of the staff overcame the shortcomings of the institution's facilities and programs. Such successes, however, came few and far between.

.GRAY.HAIR.BROOM.BACK.

Another person from Ward 4 stands out in my memory, a severely retarded woman who was about fifty years old. She spent some of her time in a wheelchair, but I distinctly remember her bent over a cane, shuffling slowly around the ward, mumbling incoherently to herself. This woman had a very pronounced hunchback, and her scary appearance was accentuated by long, straggly gray hair which she tugged at quite violently. She reminded me of the mean old witch of whom I had heard so often in fairy tales. I was deathly afraid of her.

The hunchbacked witch quickly became a symbol of Ward 4, and the contrast between her and sweet old Goldy of Ward 1 reflected the difference in the quality of life on the two wards.

.NOISES.

The sights I observed on Ward 4 were truly bizarre. So were the sounds. Almost all of the residents produced some kind of characteristic noise throughout the day, either as a result of their mental aberrations or for lack of anything better to do. After spending a few hours on the ward, I discovered who had been making those strange sounds that had so mystified me when I was cooped up in solitary during my first week. You literally had

to be there to believe that some of those noises actually were
produced by human beings.

.IMAGINE.VOMIT.

"The Retch" was a retarded thirty-year-old paraplegic who
continually made vomiting noises. She never really vomited; she
just made the noises.

.CLOCK.MILK.

Another retarded woman, an ambulator, was nicknamed
Daisy. She was a short, fat woman with heavy hips and large
breasts. She liked to moo at regular intervals throughout the day.
Every half hour she let go a *moo-ooo-oo* that would have fooled a
farmer. Daisy's mooing was so regular that the staff used to call
her the alarm cow.

I didn't have a watch, so I relied on Daisy.

.CAR.POLICEMAN.SOUND.

One ambulatory woman can only be called "the Siren." She
was about five years older than I. Like Daisy, she was severely
retarded, short, and fat. The Siren was the most accomplished
of the ward's sizable contingent of screamers. Without any particular pattern or frequency, she would suddenly rip off high-
pitched, ear-piercing screams.

Quite often one of the Siren's blasts woke me up in the middle
of the night. In case I somehow managed to sleep through it, the
subsequent glare of the ward lights and flurry of activity around
her bed were guaranteed to ruin my sleep. The Siren's screams
in the middle of the night always drew an immediate response
from the attendants, who definitely did not want her to continue
to sound off and wake up the whole ward. If more than a few
residents were roused, the whole ward was bound to follow.
When that happened, it took a few hours to quiet the place

down. Needless to say, the Siren wasn't one of the more popular people on Ward 4.

.I.CALL.DAD.REPEAT.

About half of the people on Ward 4 talked to themselves, mumbling semi-intelligible comments to nobody in particular. "I am called Dad, I am called Dad" was what one woman said to herself all day long, day in and day out. Since some of the other residents were prone to echolalia — repeating what they had just heard someone else say — an "I am called Dad" chorus sometimes would bounce around the ward like some crazy version of "Row, Row, Row Your Boat." On other days I heard "Hello, goodbye, hello, goodbye" being repeated for hours on end.

Usually three or four radios were blaring away at any given time during the day. It might sound like a good thing that the residents were allowed to operate their own radios, and occasionally it was. I liked to listen to the music, and I also appreciated the contact with the outside world that the news and commercials provided. But more often than not the radios were turned up to full volume and tuned in to different stations, providing a confusing soundtrack for the sorry sights around me. On a loud day, all of the noises on the ward combined to create a truly maddening din.

The noise situation was something I couldn't escape simply by closing my eyes, so I attempted to block out the sound by concentrating on other things. This was not always possible, however, especially when the moon was full.

One incident will give you a good idea of what I mean. A girl named Debbie, who was extremely tiny, even though she was sixteen years old, was quite disturbed mentally. Debbie usually was silent. When she did make a sound, it always was very soft and very brief. One night during a full moon, Debbie began to scream loudly, for no apparent reason. She continued for hours, and kept all of us awake. Finally she petered out from sheer exhaustion, but an attendant had to rock Debbie in her arms like a baby for over an hour until she quieted down completely. Such a thing had never happened before with Debbie, and as far as I know it never happened again. Nobody ever figured it out, but the staff and residents agreed that it must have had something to do with the full moon.

.MONKEY.PANTS.

Each of the women on Ward 4 was unique, but there were two who were more unusual than anyone I have mentioned so far. One was in her early twenties, a woman with dark hair, very tiny and painfully thin. She never left her bed and showed no signs of being aware of what was going on around her. This woman used to wrap her legs around her neck, literally tying herself up in knots as if her limbs were made of rubber. She was always dressed in pants. The staff called her the Monkey, and she was known by this name throughout the building. This itself is something to consider, for notoriety at the Infirmary did not come easily.

A girl named Laurie, who lived on another ward in the Infirmary, was also unique. I heard a great deal about her from the staff and the other residents. Laurie was hydrocephalic. Excess fluid had enlarged her head to several times the normal size. She could not sit in a wheelchair, because at the time there were no specially adapted wheelchairs that would support her head without tipping over. Amazingly, although her head was the size of a medicine ball, Laurie wasn't retarded.

Unfortunately, these two unlucky girls were considered "freaks" even at the State School, the one place where they should have received empathy and understanding.

I have described some of the more extraordinary characters I encountered on Ward 4, but it was these people who set the tone for the place. Ward 4 was a mess. There were only three attendants on every eight-hour shift. They were responsible for feeding, diapering, and bathing all thirty residents, as well as changing bedlinens and seeing that the ward remained clean. With a staff-client ratio of one to ten, the attendants had their hands full performing the custodial duties. They had little time to spare for engaging the residents in pleasant conversation or providing us with any kind of recreation. It was all they could do to tend to their daily chores and keep the residents from hurting themselves or each other.

Many of the residents of Ward 4 were mentally competent but, like me, severely handicapped and therefore incapable of tending to their own needs without help. The staff couldn't spare the time to do this, so we all had to suffer the indignity of diapering. The ambulatory people were physically capable of seeing to their own needs, but they wore diapers too; the staff didn't want to risk "accidents." Of course, as long as these people wore diapers, they didn't become toilet-trained, and abandoned whatever bathroom discipline they once had known. This was one of many self-perpetuating woes at the Infirmary.

Ward 4 was run according to a fixed schedule. The morning shift arrived at seven A.M. and proceeded to wake everyone up, give baths, and change dirty johnnies, diapers, and sheets. All meals were delivered from a central kitchen in another building and served in bed. Breakfast usually was finished by about ten o'clock. Changed and fed, the residents were left to their own devices while the staff prepared for lunch, which usually came around noon. After lunch we were changed again, then we waited for the next shift change, at three P.M.

This new shift started slowly, with the attendants taking care of odds and ends as they prepared for dinner. During the late afternoon hours the residents again had nothing to do but stare at the walls and each other. Dinner was served around six o'clock. After another mass diaper change, anyone who was not already in bed was put there. Lights went out at ten, and the attendants squared things away before the night shift came on at eleven.

On some nights the late shift had it easy. But when somebody woke up and made a disturbance, they jumped into action to quiet things down as quickly as possible. If a problem arose, the main floor lights were switched on to help the staff deal with the incident. Unfortunately, the sudden glare of lights often woke up more people than the disturbance did. So it was hit or miss for the night staff. On a good shift things were quiet, but when one of the residents got going, it usually developed into a real nightmare.

.TIME.GO.SLOW.

The days were enough like nightmares for me, however. I had nothing to do. Flat on my back, day in and day out, I passed the time by studying the physical and mental condition of those around me. This activity was interesting at first, but after the initial surprise wore off, I lost all interest in observing my wardmates. To my relief, the other residents either were incapable of taking any interest in me or chose not to do so.

I retreated into my own private world of memory and imagination. Time was slower than slow, with the usual measures of seconds, minutes, hours, and even days suspended in a blur of frightful sounds and pitiful sights. I marked the passage of time by feedings and diaper changes. Since every day was the same, that period is a fog of people and behavior that I tried very hard to forget.

Occasionally, on warm days, some of us were wheeled out onto a large, screened-in porch that adjoined the ward. Since the wall-length screens were made of a thick mesh, we breathed some fresh air but couldn't see much of what was happening outside. I spent most of my time on that porch staring at the brick walls, feeling like I was trapped in a ventilated dungeon.

During my first summer at the State School, we were taken out of the building only three times — a wild group of thirty wheelchairs and rolling beds, the prisoners of Ward 4, outside just long enough to remember what we were missing. We must have given the squirrels and birds quite an eyeful! My lasting impression of those trips outside is that I returned to the ward and forgot that I had ever left.

Inside the ward, I was lost in a sea of white — not the bright, clean white of puffy clouds or freshly fallen snow, but the dingy gray-white of hospital clothes and bedsheets. The only interruption of the bland color scheme was the shiny chrome of the serving trays. When I focused my eyes on those metallic objects, confusing reflections of pale flesh usually sent me reeling back into my dream world.

It would be an understatement to say that I was depressed on Ward 4. I felt hopelessly alone and deserted there. In order to maintain my sanity, I retreated into a state of self-induced numbness, occupying my mind with recollections of the past and dreams of the future. The present was simply too repulsive. Every time I let myself recognize how dismal it was, I was overpowered by bewilderment. How long would I have to stay in this place?

The food didn't help. I was still being fed by the attendants' mechanical hands, and their insensitive techniques made it quite difficult to eat the baby food or mashed vegetables they poured down my throat. Occasionally I received a "treat" of mushed meat or fish, but since all of the flavor had been steamed out, it was hard to tell what I was eating anyway. My emotional doldrums didn't do much for my appetite, nor did the fact that I was being fed liquids through a long-spouted metal watering can.

When I checked into Belchertown, I measured four feet tall and weighed almost forty pounds. After several months I was down to thirty pounds. Over the next few years, a pitiful diet and total lack of exercise considerably weakened my limbs, severely constricting the arm and leg movement I had developed with so much hard work at Crotched Mountain and at home.

.DRINK.EGGS.

My weight loss was one sign of the failure of my acclimation to my new home. This became evident to Dr. Soong when he examined me after I had spent several weeks on Ward 4. He gave me a quick once-over and put me on a scale that looked like it belonged in a butcher shop. He noted that I had lost a lot of weight, and I overheard him asking one of the attendants whether she could suggest a dietary supplement for me. The attendant told him that they sometimes used eggnog for this purpose. Accordingly, I was served eggnog the next day at breakfast, and at every meal thereafter.

Since I liked eggnog, this prescription worked pretty well. It continued until a new doctor, an Indian man named Dr. Kaswani, came along two years later. He thought he was doing me a favor by switching my dietary supplement from eggnog to ice cream, but he was wrong. I love ice cream, but it loses its magic when you eat it at every meal, especially breakfast. Eggnog, in contrast, holds up pretty well around the clock. Ice cream did the job, but I preferred Dr. Soong's prescription.

.DOCTOR.HATE.

The eggnog was the only good thing I can recall about Dr. Soong. He struck me as a pushy, obnoxious person who talked quickly and unintelligibly. I hated not being able to understand him, because he was the doctor and what he said influenced the staff's attitude toward me. If I couldn't understand him, how could he understand me?

I used to have a recurring daydream about Dr. Soong, in which he broke his leg. I was his doctor, and I had to operate on him. This was feasible because I was not handicapped in the dream, and could walk and talk normally. After the operation I put a cast on Dr. Soong's leg. The action then skipped to my removing the cast and studying the leg's progress. I determined that the operation had failed, that Dr. Soong's leg would never heal and he would have to spend the rest of his life in a wheelchair. On my orders, he was moved to the Infirmary, the only place where he could be cared for "properly."

I indulged in many fantasies in order to take leave of my surroundings. Nevertheless, my brightest rays of light weren't fantasies but the letters Mother wrote almost daily. Mother sent me cheerful, chatty notes about what was happening with the family and the kids in the neighborhood, and with our numerous relatives. For the few moments that one of the attendants was reading the letter to me, I imagined that I was hearing Mother's voice. In this way I was able to "go home" nearly every day, which helped me retain some degree of sanity. Unfortunately, when the letter ended and the spell was broken, I always found myself back on the ward.

Mother's letters were both wonderful and horrible: wonderful for transporting me home for a few moments, horrible for reminding me of what I had left behind. Still, I cherished every letter, as well as the sweet notes that Shari and Marie occasionally sent along. As the year wore on, Mother began to write to me several times a week, after which she settled into sending one long letter every week. She kept this up faithfully for the next thirteen years.

In the middle of June 1962, I had been at Belchertown for about a month. I was just starting to emerge from the initial shock of living on Ward 4. As I began to appreciate how completely off the wall most of my wardmates were, I slipped into an ever-deepening state of depression about my presence among these poor people. My mood later alternated between anger, sadness, self-pity, empathy, frustration, and numbness. But in those first weeks, it was a real battle to find some way of dealing with my unhappy surroundings and not go crazy in the process.

It was at this time that Mother paid her first visit.

.VISIT.MOTHER.

The only contact I had been allowed with my family during my first month at the State School was Mother's letters. I was very anxious to see my parents, and was extremely upset that I had no way of communicating with them to tell them about my unhappiness.

One morning in June I was dressed in clothes and taken outside in a wheelchair—the only time I had been out since my arrival at Belchertown, and all without any explanation. Then, standing before me was Mother. I was overjoyed to see her, but soon was overcome by frustration in not being able to tell her much of what I had experienced in the past month.

Since I could "talk" no more than my facial expressions and sounds permitted, I was forced to rely on Mother's questions in order to communicate specific information. When she asked me about the food, I let her know in no uncertain terms that it was dreadful. When she asked me how the staff was treating me, I gave her an emphatic "no" face with a nasty sound to express my displeasure. I was unable to tell her, however, that I was being fed on my back through a watering can, or that the attendants preferred it when I cried during feeding because this made it easier for them to shove food down my throat. I also couldn't tell her that most of the people around me on Ward 4 were mentally disabled.

Mother got the message that I was unhappy, but she did not understand how bad things were. She had learned from a phone call with Dr. Soong that I had been kept in isolation during the first week; evidently no one had bothered to tell Mother and Father about this procedure when they had brought me to the State School. I tried to tell Mother that I was being kept in bed all day, but I couldn't get the whole message across to her. She thought I was telling her that I wasn't getting off the ward much.

Putting on her best face, Mother urged me to hang in there, saying that things were bound to improve. I had no choice but to hope she was right.

.PICNIC.

About a month later my family came by the State School and took me to Nana Christine's house in nearby Northampton for an extended Sienkiewicz family picnic. This included a cousins' swim in the little wading pool set up in the back yard. It was also the first time I had seen Shari, Marie, Howard, and Father since I'd gone to Belchertown. I was thrilled.

When Mother changed me into a swimsuit that day, the physical evidence that I was deteriorating at the State School was revealed to everyone. The previous summer that bathing suit had fit snugly; now it hung on me like a sack. I watched Mother do her best to hide her tears. Any further questions about how I was faring were unnecessary.

According to Mother, this marked the beginning of what were to be years of sorrow and anguish over her inability to come to the State School on a regular basis to see that I received at least a minimal program of physical therapy. If she had lived nearby, or if transportation had been available, Mother would have been there every day. As it was, she felt that there was nothing she could do but cry and write me letters.

At some point during that family picnic, someone asked me about the other residents at Belchertown. I gave a very confusing answer. I had met some people on Ward 1 whom I liked, and a lot of people on Ward 4 whom I either pitied or feared. But it was impossible to make this kind of distinction with my facial expressions and sounds. Although everyone knew just by looking at me that I was very unhappy, I couldn't tell them that my only form of entertainment was listening to the rantings of a ward full of retarded people, or that I didn't know how long I could last if I wasn't moved to another ward.

My parents may have realized that I was wearing diapers all the time, but they did not know that I never wore clothes and was never taken out of bed. They could tell that I wasn't getting any exercise, but they had been told by the staff that I was wearing my leg braces and sitting in a wheelchair daily.

If anyone had asked me if I wanted to come home, I would have given an unmistakable answer. But nobody asked, and I could find no way to make such a statement spontaneously.

Mother and Father again encouraged me to be patient and give the State School "a chance." I gathered from this, and from what they didn't say, that their assessment of the situation hadn't changed. Father felt that because it was impossible for me to live at home, nothing could be gained by discussing the matter. Of course, seeing me in such a miserable state had a strong effect on the whole family. I know that Mother and my grandmothers were heartbroken.

Since I hoped that I might be moved soon to another ward and that this would bring some improvement, I managed to keep up my courage. Still, I soaked up all the encouragement my family could give me. When the visit was over and my family took me back to Belchertown, I almost burst at the seams from wanting to go home with them.

I returned to the ward a very sad girl. Like Mother's letters, the visit had both encouraged and discouraged me. It left me more homesick than ever. I tried to soothe my nerves by telling myself over and over that things had to get better, but lying flat on your back all day surrounded by people who behave crazily does not foster calm nerves.

My daily range of sights consisted of the people in the beds adjacent to mine, the half-dozen or so ambulators on the ward, and the changing shifts of attendants. It frightened me when one of the ambulators came anywhere near my bed, because I never knew what she might do. Quite possibly, one of these women would think that I was a broken little doll and try to take me out of my "crib" to "fix" me. It never happened, but I lived in constant fear of such an incident.

The staff offered little relief, coming and going as quickly as they could to deliver the basic services. They seemed to have little use for me, and I soon abandoned any hope of establishing meaningful relationships with any of them. Since the bedridden residents were mentally impaired, I gained little cheer from my neighbors.

.THERESA.EYES.UP.SAY.YES.

There was one wonderful exception, however. The woman who lived in the bed next to me on the right had caught my eye the first day I came to Ward 4. As the days passed, I spent more and more time watching her. She was about sixteen years older than I, her facial characteristics were different from mine, and she was taller. But in other ways she was my physical duplicate. Her name was Theresa Ladue.

Theresa, too, was a victim of cerebral palsy. Like me, she could make sounds but couldn't speak, and had limited movement of her arms and legs. The first time I saw her, I knew that inside Theresa's crippled body there was a sharp, alert person. I saw it in her eyes and heard it in her voice. Within a day or two, I realized that lying next to me was the first person I had ever seen who matched me closely in abilities and disabilities. Watching Theresa showed me how I must look to other people. But what fascinated me most was the challenge of discovering what kind of person lived behind those unmistakably intelligent eyes.

My first clue that Theresa was unlike the others on the ward was that she constantly studied what went on around her. Along with this, I noticed that her sounds weren't just random noises; they indicated her moods and responses. Since this was precisely how I used my own sounds, I picked up on it right away. As I watched her more carefully, I saw that Theresa was watching me too. In fact, she was directing many of her sounds at me, looking for a response in kind.

After several days Theresa and I let our defenses down and stopped sneaking looks at each other. We began to gaze steadily at one another, making sounds to enhance the process of becoming acquainted. I would watch Theresa and she would watch me right back—not in a hostile way, but with friendly curiosity. As we became more comfortable, we began to "talk" to each other more and more through sounds and facial expressions. Before long we were sharing our opinions and feelings about living on the ward.

Late one night during my second week there, Theresa and I were engaged in a silent conversation with our eyes. Most of the residents were asleep, and it was quiet. Although the ward lights were off, we could see each other's faces from the light in the hall.

Suddenly a remarkable spark passed between us, something that no one watching us would have been able to perceive. Theresa and I experienced it simultaneously: a riveting, deeply moving flash of complete understanding. At that moment we became aware of the extraordinary insight we shared, knowledge that no one who was not just like us could possess. Both of us were painfully aware of what it was like to be trapped inside a body that followed few directions of its mind and ignored the simple commands of speech and movement that nearly everyone takes for granted. We knew what it was like to be unable to express even one thousandth of the thoughts whirling inside our minds; what it was like to be unable to walk, or even feed ourselves; what it was like to be treated by most people as an oddity, a quirk of nature to be gawked at and given a wide berth; and what it was like to live on Ward 4 of the Infirmary at the Belchertown State School in 1962.

We both knew what all of this was like — completely.

As our mutual recognition of that knowledge emerged, our souls embraced. Our eyes locked for several exhilarating, magnetic, timeless moments. Then Theresa turned her head and nudged the yellow teddy bear lying beside her pillow. Making quiet, gentle sounds, Theresa repeated this gesture several times until she was certain I understood. By indicating her teddy, the only object of affection around her, she was telling me that she liked me very much, that she was beginning to develop a profound understanding of me.

At this, my face lit up in delighted verification. I responded with loving sounds of my own, and raised my eyes in an emphatic "Yes!" to make sure Theresa understood that I felt the same way about her. At that instant Theresa figured out what none of the staff would decipher for several years: that I raised my eyes to say yes.

From that moment on, Theresa and I were close friends. We took advantage of every occurrence on the ward—movements, feedings, changings, noises, outbursts, periods of total boredom —to exchange glances, facial expressions, and sounds. In this way we developed our own special language, evolving it slowly over a period of three or four months. After countless hours of careful study, we were able to fashion a basic, yet effective, system of communication.

Whenever something screwy or annoying happened, we sounded off about it, as much to inform each other of what a particular sound was supposed to mean as to comment on the event itself. We became attuned to every change of tone and pitch in each other's repertoire of sounds, familiarizing ourselves with what each sound meant in terms of emotion, opinion, or thought. To demonstrate the significance of our expressions, we studied each other's face while repeating our sounds over and over. When someone on the ward cried or screamed, Theresa and I remarked, in our own way, "Poor girl, she's having a rough time today," or "Damn, there goes the loudmouth again." When an unfriendly attendant came around, one of us made an ugly face and a nasty sound to indicate something like "Uh-oh, here comes old Stone Hands again." But the message that we established first, and communicated to each other so many times that we wore it out, was "God, please get us out of here before we fall over the edge!"

Our favorite time to talk was at night, after the ward had been put to bed and the lights dimmed. We each had a sharp sense of hearing, probably to compensate for our limitations, so we didn't have to make sounds very loudly to communicate. This eliminated the potential problem of bothersome attention from the night staff. In the early stages of our friendship, Theresa and I used this time to improve our techniques. As we progressed, we used it to review the day's events, if there had been any, and to share our feelings.

I recall one such conversation after I received a letter from my little sister Shari. One of the attendants had read the letter to me after lunch. Since Theresa was lying only a few feet away, she couldn't help but overhear. She noticed that I pursed my lips the whole time the letter was being read. During our conversation that night, Theresa raised the subject of Shari by pursing her own lips and imitating the soft cooing sound I had made that afternoon. This puzzled me at first, but then I caught on and broke into laughter over Theresa's impersonation of me. I answered her inquisitive looks by indicating with sounds that I loved Shari very much. Since Theresa had gathered from the letter that Shari was my sister and that we were very close, I used this as a starting point for elaborating about my relationship with Shari. From then on, pursed lips indicated "Shari," "love," or "home" in my private language with Theresa.

We used a similar approach to name various residents and attendants. When somebody came by, or when Theresa and I were both looking at the same person, one of us made a sound or face to characterize that person. The sound or expression then became our name for her. If we wanted to discuss someone when she wasn't in sight and we couldn't glance at her to indicate our subject, we made the sound or expression that had been established as her name, just as a speaking person might say "Ruth." We then utilized our facial and vocal signals to talk about her.

For example, one day a new attendant came around to feed me. I didn't like the rough way she was going about it, so I made some hostile faces and growled at her. As a newcomer to the Infirmary, unaccustomed to such modes of expression, the startled attendant was set back on her heels by my outburst. Then Theresa piped up and joined in the assault with a vocal attack of her own. For a few seconds the two of us vented all of our frustrations on this unsuspecting woman. We drove her away in tears.

Without a doubt, this was one of my finer moments on Ward 4. The attendant returned later, but with a markedly more cautious and respectful attitude toward Theresa and me.

Almost without realizing it, Theresa and I advanced our system by developing a few simple hand signals. Neither of us could do much with our fingers, but we could both raise and lower our hands and arms a little. This enabled us to adopt the following system of signals: a sideways movement of the hand and forearm indicated that the subject of discussion involved emotions; an up-and-down movement indicated that the subject was a person; an upward movement alone meant "man," a downward movement alone meant "woman"; raising the hand toward the face meant "I"; an abbreviated movement of the hand toward the face meant "who?"; a more rapid movement of the hand toward the body meant "I'm mad at myself."

To complement these signals, we specified a couple of facial expressions: closing our eyes meant either "why?" or "I wish I hadn't seen what just happened," and an open mouth meant "I don't like it." Together with our facial expressions, vocal tones and pitches, and system of names, these simple signals enabled us to converse with each other pretty effectively.

A typical conversation might go something like this: I would raise my arm to show that I wanted to talk about a man, then purse my lips to show that I loved this person. After Theresa answered with an affirmative sound, I would go on, perhaps following up with a babyish cry or gurgle. This might confuse Theresa, because I had just identified the subject as a man I liked. To clarify the point, I would look over at Theresa's teddy bear. Once she caught the object of my gaze, she would understand, I hoped, that I was talking about a baby boy.

If all went well, Theresa would give me a positive signal at this point, perhaps making a baby sound of her own to show that she understood. Then I would purse my lips again and look her squarely in the eye. This was the crucial part of the exchange, where we used repetition and a little ESP to drive the message home. In this instance, the message was that I wanted to talk about my baby brother, Howard.

It might take several repetitions of the whole sequence to make the point. Whoever was "speaking" would carry on with it patiently until the other person's face lit up with a look of understanding. Once this happened, we could move on to the next stage of our conversation.

Sometimes I couldn't produce the sounds I wanted because of my unreliable breath control. Theresa was better in this department, so whenever she noticed that I was having trouble producing a noise, she would run through a selection of messages until I signaled to her that she had hit the one I wanted. In all, we used about eight noises to indicate moods, and another five or six for names. Eventually we limited the noise-names to staff people, because we could usually glance over at the appropriate bed to indicate a resident.

Often we failed in our attempts to communicate. By the very nature of our conversations, Theresa and I couldn't always tell whether a message had been interpreted correctly. Even when one of us signaled that we got the point, it was still difficult to be sure. We relied on eye contact and intuition to confirm our messages. Sometimes an unmistakable sixth sense told us that the communication had been successful, but there were many times when, after endlessly repeating a message, one of us could tell that the other one didn't know what the hell we were talking about!

Half the battle was to keep the topic of conversation within the limits of what we reasonably could expect to tell each other. For example, it would have been impossible for me to tell Theresa exactly what had happened with the lobster at my tenth birthday party. But if Mother mentioned something in a letter about

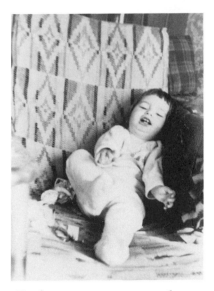

Ruth at seventeen months

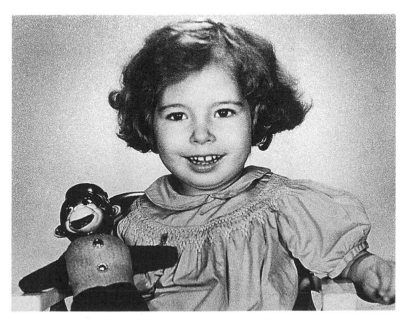

At home, circa 1955

Crotched Mountain, 1957

The family at home, circa 1960.
Shari is beside Ruth; Marie is behind her.

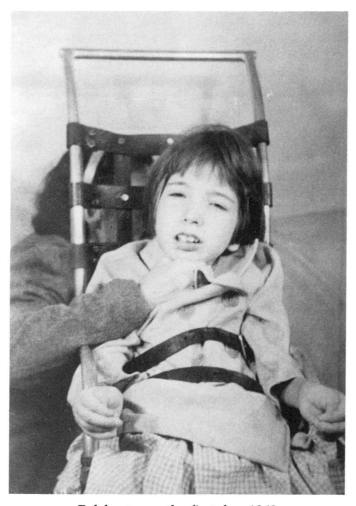

Belchertown: the first day, 1962

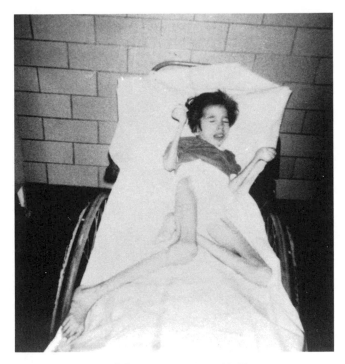

Belchertown, circa 1965

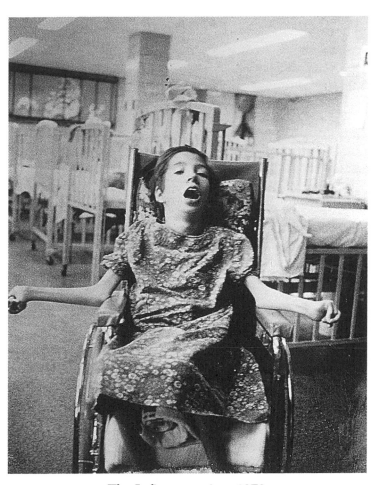

The Infirmary, circa 1970

I/ME	MY/MINE	PEOPLE	AUNT/UNCLE	FAMILY	NAM...
HE	HIM/HIS	MAN/WOMAN	COUSIN	SHARI	HOWA.../SHAN...
SHE	HER/HERS	DAD/MOM	WIFE/HUSBAND	JASON	VERON...
YOU	YOUR/YOURS	NEPHEW	FRIEND/ENEMY	HOWARD	BET...
THEY	THEM/THEIR	SISTER	P.C.A.	MARIE	JOH...
WE/IT	US/OUR	BROTHER	TEACHER	NORMAN	BOB...
THIS/THAT	THESE/THOSE	SON/DAUGHTER	THERA-PIST	SHELLY	JUD...
AM	WANT TO	PAST	ASK	I FEEL/FEEL	LISTE...
IS	HAVE TO	PRESENT	BRING	FORGET/FIND	LOV...
ARE	GOING TO	FUTURE	BUY	GET	NEE...
WAS/WERE	WILL/WOULD	NOT	CALL	GO	PIC...
HAS	CAN/COULD	-ING	CHANGE	HELP	PU...
DO/DOES	SHOULD	-ED	DRINK	HURT	REME.../REM...

A portion of one of Ruth's word boards, 1980

RROL			ROSEY	SHAW-ANA		WHO
BBIE	HEATHER	PAT	STEVE	DIANE		WHAT
E DEE	KATHY	PAUL	SUSAN	LINDA		WHEN
N/NA	MARK	RICK	JEFF	JODIE		WHERE
VID	MARY	ROMA	SHEILA	WESSIE		WHY
FLYN	DIERDRA		THERESA	HALI		HOW
EN	MAUREEN	ROSE	VAL	ANNE		HOW MANY / HOW MUCH
OP	USE	TILT MY CHAIR	BATH-ROOM	I DON'T UNDER-STAND	I AM PISSED OFF!	I HAVE AN APP
GGEST	VISIT	CHARGE MY BATTERY	THANK YOU	I'M CONFUS-ED	PLEASE EX-PLAIN	PLEASE CALL
KE	WASH	FIX MY CHAIR	SORRY	I'M HUNG-RY		GIVE A MESSA TO
LK	WEAR	TURN MY HEAD SWITCH ON/OFF	PLEASE	I'M THIRSTY		I GOT TOUCH WITH
LL	WORK	ADJUST MY BELT	YOU'RE WELCOME	I'M HOT		PLEASE CALL M AT 536-645
CH	WRITE	ADJUST MY CHAIR	EXCUSE ME	I'M COLD		DO YOU HAVE TIME T

Ruth and Norman, 1985

Steve Kaplan and Ruth, working with a word board, 1989

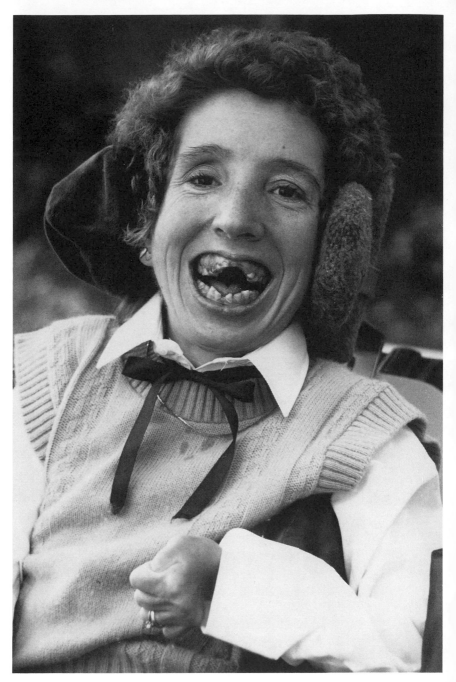

Ruth Sienkiewicz Mercer

my birthday, I could tag that with an expression or sound and comment later on the general subject of birthday celebrations at home.

Another factor to consider was that the more we talked to one another, the more we honed our understanding. Call it intuition, nonverbal communication, ESP, or whatever, but there were occasions when we stared into each other's eyes and communicated messages without making any sounds, expressions, or signals of any kind. In these instances our eyes did all the talking . . . and all the listening too.

Theresa had lived at the State School for eight years when I arrived, and she helped me through the initial shock of the woeful scene on Ward 4. In return, I eased her pain and frustration by sharing the experience of being abandoned among thirty confused and suffering women while denied the opportunity to speak, move, or be recognized as possessing even a shred of intelligence. Together, we at least attempted to overcome the fear and frustration that filled our days. It didn't matter that sometimes we couldn't understand each other's messages, or that there were some things we could never tell each other. What mattered was that we each had someone who was trying to understand, someone deeply interested in our feelings and willing to share those feelings totally.

Goldy had helped me by convincing me to eat. Theresa helped me by encouraging me to push my powers of expression to the fullest. Simply knowing that she was there next to me, watching the same things from a remarkably similar perspective, kept me sane in the midst of an irrational environment.

.BIRTHDAY.12.

My morale was boosted in late September by a one-day trip home to celebrate my twelfth birthday. It was great medicine to see my parents, Shari, Marie, and Howard, get a bunch of presents, and have a big fuss made over me. But as with the family picnic in the summer, the birthday party hurt as much as it helped. Much as I enjoyed seeing my family, it was extremely painful to return to Belchertown at the end of the visit.

Once again my parents didn't raise the issue of my coming home. Although there was no hiding the fact that I was faring poorly at the State School, Mother and Father still felt that they couldn't care for me. They paid the Commonwealth of Massachusetts fifty cents a day for my room and board at Belchertown; Crotched Mountain would have cost $105 per week. Unless Father's financial situation or Mother's health improved dramatically, they believed, there was no alternative to the State School.

I still clung to the hope that once my parents discovered what I had been encountering, they would take me out of Belchertown for good. Perhaps if they spent a few hours on the ward, observing the daily routine and the people, they would appreciate what it was like for me to live there. But this was the wish of a twelve-year-old girl trying desperately to find a way out of a no-exit situation. My folks were never given the chance to see Ward 4. Even if they had been, it probably wouldn't have changed anything.

Although unrealistic, my hope did sustain me by giving me some basis for optimism. The dream of somehow getting the message across, and then returning home, softened the blow of living on the ward.

Sometimes, however, my despondency over remaining at Belchertown simply got the better of me. On occasion it prompted physical illness. The first time this happened was shortly after my twelfth birthday visit home. The early shock of Belchertown had worn off, the exultation of meeting Theresa and devising our system of communication had diminished, the immediate hope of returning home had faded, and the full effect of living on the ward had taken hold.

I looked around one day and it suddenly hit me full force that I was stuck in this awful place! My spirits plummeted. I woke up in the middle of the night running a high fever, and then vomited repeatedly. Before then I had experienced trouble eating, but now I could barely hold down any food at all. This illness lasted about two weeks, and it marked the completion of my "acclimation" to the Infirmary.

My illness didn't change anything, and I wasn't treated any better by the staff as a result. All it accomplished was to take my mind off being on the ward for a while. Once I recovered and again could take full measure of my life, I wished that I was still sick! At least when I was ill, I could look forward to getting better.

The remainder of 1962 passed in dreadful monotony. As the autumn came and went, I became increasingly anxious about the approach of winter, and with it the week-long Christmas vacation. This would bring my first opportunity to leave the State School for longer than a day. I was never told why, but none of the residents were allowed to go home for Thanksgiving.

When I went home for Christmas, I felt like I had been released from the worst prison on earth. I never wanted to go back, ever. Being home and not having to return to Belchertown in a few hours was wonderful. As we went through our holiday routine of selecting a tree and doing some last-minute shopping, I almost forgot that I had ever been away.

The best thing about being home was getting to know my baby brother, Howard, again. I had seen him for only a few minutes since I had left. During that time he had really grown up. He was getting into everything, and acting adorable as he did so. Only seven months had elapsed since I had gone to Belchertown, but it seemed more like seven years.

Although I enjoyed this stay at home very much, I noticed that things had changed. The family had become accustomed to my absence. I felt like an intruder, throwing the household into disarray and disrupting everybody's routines so they could accommodate my special needs. As before, Shari roomed with me and helped me during the night if I needed it. Mother devoted much of her time to tending to me, and the whole family went out of their way to make me feel comfortable. But that was part of the problem: they were trying too hard. And there was the unstated but ever-present awareness that I soon would return to Belchertown. For the family, this was an unpleasant thought; for me, it was like a death sentence.

Most of the burden of caring for me fell on Mother's shoulders. Nonetheless, she had strongly opposed my going to Belchertown, and now she opposed my staying there. She knew that I wasn't a spoiled child, that I adjusted well to new situations. If I was miserable at the State School, it must be a bad place.

Father viewed things differently. He had watched Mother's health decline rapidly after I came home from Crotched Mountain. He had seen how much pressure my presence put on the rest of the family, and he had decided that sending me to Belchertown best served the interests of the entire family. Father was not happy with this decision, but he believed that he had no choice. Once he was convinced that the State School would provide me with minimally adequate care — which it didn't, but he didn't know that yet — he accepted the inevitability of sending me there.

Father may have convinced Mother of the logic of his decision, but he never won her heart as to its absolute necessity. If it had been left up to Mother, she would have worked herself onto the operating table, or worse, before sending me to the State School.

I knew all along who was the driving force behind my going to and remaining at Belchertown. As that first Christmas vacation came to a close, I could scarcely hide my resentment toward Father. I was angry at him, and he knew it. I felt that I had given the place a long enough try and it had failed miserably. The idea of leaving home wasn't the issue, either, for I knew from experience that a proper facility could provide me with decent care and take a great strain off my family. I understood why Father wanted me to give Belchertown a fair chance. What I couldn't accept was that he would allow me to stay there any longer.

So far, my parents had avoided any discussion of my leaving Belchertown. But by the end of that first Christmas vacation, my resentment toward Father was so obvious that he was forced to explain his position to me.

He talked to me alone. He encouraged me to give the State School more of a chance. I tried to show him from my response that more time wouldn't do any good; I was miserable there and it was the institution's fault. When Father repeated his belief that he was doing what he thought was best for everyone in our family, I tried to make him understand that Belchertown was so bad that it couldn't possibly be good for anyone.

My father has always been a stubborn man. Once he makes a decision, he sticks to it. But I am a chip off his block and can be quite stubborn myself. I was determined to convince him that I could no longer remain at the State School. Father couldn't read my mind, and since I could express my emotions only nonverbally, he couldn't always tell what points raised my anger, despair, anguish, or frustration. But he knew, or sensed, what I was trying to tell him. Our discussion ended in a heart-wrenching stalemate. Father pleaded, "What else can I do?" I responded with tears, overcome by all of my emotions.

I have always believed that my parents could have worked out a way to care for me at home. They could have solicited help from my grandmothers and our other relatives. Mother could have hired someone to assist her during the day so that she could do more telephone work and make enough extra money to pay for the help. As my sisters grew older, they could have assumed more of the workload. Certainly there was no easy solution, and I would have spent many idle hours at home. But boredom at home was a thousand times better than boredom at the Belchertown State School!

The key factors were Mother's health and satisfactory care for me. Father was caught in an exasperating dilemma: he believed that what was best for me and what was best for the family were mutually exclusive. He didn't send me to Belchertown to rot away into oblivion; he set a minimum level of acceptable care in light of the overall picture. Unfortunately, his minimum was much lower than what was acceptable to Mother, or for that matter, to me.

The new year came, and I returned to Belchertown a confused young girl. I had gone home expecting to convince my parents that the State School was a horrible place and that my stay there must end immediately. I had failed. I had always looked up to Father as a pillar of strength and wisdom, relying on his word as the last word, but now my faith in him was severely shaken. I didn't want to believe that he knowingly would permit me to suffer at Belchertown, and I desperately wanted to believe that he simply misunderstood what my life at Belchertown was really like. I had to cling to some hope of leaving the place, so I continued to hope that I would be able to enlighten Father about Belchertown and thereby gain my ticket home. But deep down, I already sensed that the truth was otherwise.

Some months after my return, in the summer of 1963, I was moved to another ward in the Infirmary, a children's ward, which provided me with more considerate and understanding personal care than I had been receiving on Ward 4. My parents visited this ward shortly after I was moved there, and they were allowed free access to it on their subsequent visits. Based on their first-hand observations, they were satisfied that I was receiving acceptable, if minimal, care. At the same time, Mother and Father knew that I was not being offered any kind of educational or social program, and they realized that I was regressing both physically and emotionally.

By the end of my second Christmas vacation at home, in 1963, a year and a half after I was first taken to Belchertown, I no longer blamed my continued presence at the State School on my parents' lack of information or awareness. A few details may have been missing, but the basic picture was painfully clear to both Mother and Father. Father had made the decision, and he was sticking to it. My personal development had been sacrificed for the benefit of the rest of my family.

This was a harsh fact of life over which I had no control. Eventually I came to understand it, but I have never been able to accept it.

5

Back on Ward 4, I was faced with a basic choice: to let myself go down the drain, or to fight to preserve my dignity and sanity. I chose the latter, but it was a difficult struggle all the way, and sometimes I had no idea whether I was winning or losing.

Even though my parents couldn't take me home, they remained deeply concerned about my welfare. At times the knowledge that my family was rooting for me was the only thing that kept me from giving up.

Theresa Ladue provided me with invaluable friendship and compassion, and that helped enormously. Although Theresa was the only person who related to me with any proper regard for my intelligence, my everyday life grew more tolerable as the staff learned how to deal with my physical difficulties in eating and other basic functions. As the months passed, creature comforts became less of a problem. Yet the essential features of my world went unchanged — confusion, frustration, pitiful sights and sounds, and sick behavior. I was surrounded by many people whose minds were severely impaired, and my caretakers treated me like them. My environment continually threatened to turn my mind into mush.

As I mentioned, I inherited a mulish stubbornness from my

father that helped me to tough it out. And although I was physically trapped on the ward, there were no limitations on my imagination. By focusing my mental energy, I was able to escape the real-life nightmares of the ward with frequent flights of fancy.

As I noted earlier, the atmosphere of the ward was dominated by random, irrational noises produced by the residents. In an occasional moment of weakness, or just to let off some steam, I allowed myself to join the chaos with a yell or a shriek. But it became a point of pride to avoid making this a habit. Whenever possible, I blocked out the ward by filling my mind with images of home, such as my family talking around the dinner table on a Sunday afternoon or the neighborhood gang playing with dolls in our living room. I cherished my daydreams and found great comfort in replaying fond memories over and over in my mind. I often visited my friends and relatives by conjuring up mental pictures of them, imagining that I was enjoying their company somewhere far away from the institution.

When these daydreams didn't occur spontaneously, I willed them into my head. I didn't limit myself to actual, or even plausible, events. Instead, I took experiences from Crotched Mountain or home and altered them, populating familiar scenes with familiar characters doing unfamiliar things. I mixed handicapped kids with nonhandicapped kids, so that children from Crotched Mountain were singing, talking, cooking, running, skating, playing with dolls, and building snowmen alongside my "normal" friends from Springfield. Nobody was the least bit handicapped in my daydreams, including me.

One of my favorite tricks was to reconstruct activities from Crotched Mountain. Whether it was swimming, musical chairs, "Mother, may I?" or giant steps, I swept away all of the wheelchairs and damaged bodies. The faces remained the same, but crippled limbs were replaced by strong, healthy arms and nimble legs. We even danced on *American Bandstand*, performing all the steps that the real world only permitted us to watch from our wheelchairs.

In the spring of 1963 I developed a technique that rarely failed when I needed to escape from the scene on the ward. I had always loved having stories read to me, and my special favorite was the Nancy Drew detective series. As a regular diversion, I elaborated on some of the basic Nancy Drew plots and fashioned my own fantasy versions. I played the lead, of course, as Ruth Drew, Private Eye.

One case that I solved at least a hundred times began with me on the trail of the thieves who had robbed the Foleys' house in our neighborhood in Springfield. I tracked the villains all over town in a hot-rod version of my father's car, and finally managed to corner them and call in the police to make the arrest. In that particular episode, I recovered the priceless antique clock that the crooks had stolen from the Foleys. No such clock existed in real life, but that was of no concern to my story.

Anyone who has read the Nancy Drew books knows that the only thing that could pull Nancy away from her detective work was her boyfriend, Ned. The same was true of Ruth Drew. At the age of twelve, I spent a tremendous amount of time lost in romantic fantasy, the usual object of my affection being *my* boyfriend Ned. I guess it was rather ordinary material for a girl my age, with much hand-holding and some kissing to underscore the fact that Ned and I were going steady.

When it came to the crunch between the horrible realities of the ward and the wonderful adventures of my imagination, the world of Ruth Drew won out enough times to keep me afloat. Unfortunately, the balance sometimes tipped the wrong way. Such was the case when one of Mother's letters in the spring of 1963 informed me that our dog, Prince, had been put to sleep. This did not come as a total surprise, for Mother had written earlier to tell me that he was worn out. Still, I was quite upset. At times I had felt that Prince understood me better than any other creature in the world. He knew what it was like not to be able to talk, and he was always happy to accept me on my own terms. The fact that I couldn't run or talk had never bothered Prince.

I continued to rely on my memories of home and Crotched Mountain to get me through the days at Belchertown. But I was beginning to realize that the world of those memories was gone forever.

.WARD.3.

One morning in June 1963, the attendants put me in a wheel-chair and rolled me next door to Ward 3. No explanation, no discussion, not even a chance to say goodbye to Theresa — just a quick ride around the corner and into a whole new world.

In some ways Ward 3 resembled Ward 4. About thirty females, most of them suffering from some combination of physical and mental handicaps, lived in close quarters. I think that Ward 3 had only three handicapped residents who *weren't* retarded. The major difference between the two wards was age. Ward 3 was the children's ward, inhabited by girls between seven and nineteen; in this respect, I was right in the middle of the pack. Physically, many of the residents were as bad, or worse, than me; with few exceptions, they were all far behind me in mental abilities. Although I had found some girls my own age, I didn't feel like I was in any kind of a peer group. Rather, I was taken aback by the sight of so many people whose minds *and* bodies were so devastated.

I had made many friends at Crotched Mountain and I suffered no illusions as to the extent of my own physical handicap. But I had problems dealing with the girls I encountered on Ward 3. They weren't just handicapped. Most of them were totally incapable of interacting in any way with the world around them. The average condition of the residents on Ward 3 wasn't that much worse than of those on Ward 4, but the fact that they were children, not grown women, really set me back. I had never seen kids like this!

When I had first encountered the women on Ward 4, I had been scared and shocked by their condition and behavior. When I saw the children on Ward 3, I was overcome by pity. I felt lucky in comparison, for even though I didn't have much going for me physically, I did have a sound mind and a good set of eyes and ears to keep me in tune with things. Most of my new wardmates were not so blessed. Almost all of them were lifelong veterans of the State School, which affected their behavior terribly.

Most parents make a valiant effort to keep their handicapped children at home as long as possible. Often it is not until the child has grown and come to present a totally new set of problems that the necessity for institutionalization overcomes the natural ties, or the material resources, of the family. The fact that the point of desperation and abandonment had come so early in these girls' lives indicates how difficult it was to care for them. By the same token, I had a lot of trouble getting used to being looked on as one of them.

It is hard for me to recall more than a few of the girls from Ward 3, despite the fact that I lived there for eleven years. I made several close friends, but most of the faces faded into a blur, a nameless group of immobilized people lying in rows of beds and cribs. Their mental condition cut them off from the world, and there was little I could do to get to know them.

Aside from the few girls who became my friends, I remember only those whose condition was so bad that they stood out even at the Infirmary. A girl named Marcia was one of the few who was all right physically, but she was lost in a world of her own. Marcia was one of the "echo people"; if she spoke at all, it was to repeat randomly the words spoken around her. Another girl, S. J., was a head banger. Like the ones I had encountered on Ward 4, she was equipped with a helmet to keep her from bashing in her skull. Then there was Darlene, who used to shove her hand so far down her throat that it looked like she was going to swallow her arm. Before too long, Darlene was wearing a strait-jacket. She never talked, except when the moon was full. Then she screamed all night, and there was nothing the staff could do to quiet her down. The rest of the girls on Ward 3 simply blended into the background of depressing sights and sounds.

But "depressing" can be a relative term. Once I adjusted to it, Ward 3 turned out to be something of an improvement over Ward 4. True, I missed Theresa Ladue very much, and it was discouraging to be surrounded by so many messed-up kids, but when I found a few girls whose minds were intact, things began to improve considerably. After all, this was the children's ward. There is something about handicapped children that usu-ally brings out the gentleness in everyone, and the attendants on Ward 3 were more sensitive to the needs of the residents than those on the other wards. It was a qualitative, not a quantitative, difference; the staff-resident ratio still was about one to ten. But the attendants were a little more patient and considerate in feed-ing and changing us.

Although it might have been the result of the improved at-mosphere I found on Ward 3, I was also encouraged by what I viewed as the staff's increased willingness to credit me with pos-sessing some intelligence. It wasn't a drastic change, but a few of the attendants did begin to see from my reactions to things that I was aware of at least some of what was happening. They even spoke to me as if I might be able to understand what they were saying. This was a very welcome change from being looked on as one of the "veggies."

.C.A.R.L.

My first and closest friend on Ward 3 was a girl named Carol Muse. Carol occupied the bed next to mine and we hit it off right away. She was about six years younger than I, the same age as my sister Shari, and at first I looked on her as a little sister. She was friendly and chubby, with brown hair and smiling brown eyes. Carol suffered from spina bifida.

Carol was lucky in being paralyzed only from the waist down. She didn't suffer significantly from the problem of hydrocephalia, which often affects people with her disease. Her main problem was with her digestive organs, for which she required limited medical supervision.

Looking at Carol, you could see that her legs and feet were short, fat, and of little use. Otherwise she looked fine, enjoying the full use of her arms, hands, mind, and voice — especially her voice. Carol was a real gabber. Whenever I was unable to fill in my share of a conversation, Carol was more than happy to make up for it. She was not retarded, and she was the only girl to use a wheelchair regularly when I arrived. Since she had full use of her arms, Carol moved around the ward under her own power. She went all over the place, socializing with people on the other wards and returning to report all of the gossip so that I could keep up on the latest events in our self-contained little world.

Carol had arrived at Belchertown a couple of months before I joined her on Ward 3. She had spent her earlier years at home with her family in Tewksbury, and had been forced to come to the State School because of family problems. With her sharp mind and other abilities, she did not belong at Belchertown, but there simply was nowhere else for her to go.

Having been raised in somewhat normal environments outside the institution, both Carol and I knew very well what we were missing outside the State School. This set us apart from the other girls, most of whom were "lifers," and it served as a bond that drew us together very quickly.

With the keen eyes of a seven-year-old, Carol immediately gathered that I was intelligent and observant. We spent countless hours together, but even so, it took her several months to appreciate the extent of my ability to communicate. It took even longer for her to pick up on the subtler aspects of my communication techniques. She missed many of the comments I tried to make with my face and sounds; after all, she was still a little girl. Since she could talk and move herself around in a wheelchair, we didn't share identical perspectives in life. Carol and I did not spend all day staring into each other's eyes, as Theresa and I had done. Nonetheless, we became close friends rather quickly. Once she became aware of the fact that I could comment on any given subject, she started to watch closely for my reactions.

As I said, Carol loved to talk. Since I was a captive audience, as well as an appreciative one, we were glad to have each other's company—although I would have settled for a bit less of it at times. But listening to Carol certainly beat staring at the ceiling or watching the other girls. Until she began to understand me better, the only way I could get a "word" in was to sound off as loudly as possible with whatever chirps, giggles, cries, or sighs I could manage.

Everyone knows at least one person who can make them laugh no matter what the situation. Carol Muse was that person for me, and I couldn't have found her at a better time. All Carol had to do was make a funny face or crack a joke about an attendant or one of the girls on the ward and I was giggling. Carol knew the way to my funnybone better than anybody I had ever met, and I loved her because of it.

Typical of Carol was a routine she pulled one evening after dinner. The staff was going around changing some of the girls' diapers. I was lying in bed, spacing out. All of a sudden I imagined that somebody was yelling my name.

"Ruth! Ruth!" cried the voice, sounding terribly lifelike. When I heard it again, I realized that it was Carol's voice. She was sitting up in her bed, screaming my name as she hopped up and down on her haunches.

When Carol saw that my mind had returned to the ward, she

began shaking invisible bars. "Let me out of here! I'm cracking up!" she yelled.

At first I thought she had gone completely crazy. But when she started laughing at the astonished look on my face, I broke up.

This kind of thing went on between us quite a lot, especially when we first met. But horsing around wasn't Carol's only strong point. She also had a lovely singing voice. Sometimes she sang to herself; sometimes she sang along with the popular songs we heard on the radio. Either way, I loved to hear her sing.

Even in her quieter moments, Carol was good company. On countless occasions we boosted each other's sagging spirits by commiserating over our common plight. As that first year on Ward 3 crawled along and the thrill of our new friendship wore off, Carol and I came to value each other's mere presence as much, if not more, than all of the joking and fun. This was a good thing, for as time went on, Carol lost a lot of her spunk. There was no place like the State School to wear down somebody's spirit.

.J.F.K.

Where were you when President Kennedy was shot?

On November 22, 1963, I was lying on my back in Ward 3 of the Infirmary at the Belchertown State School. My head was propped up on a couple of pillows and I was listening to a radio hanging on a kid's bed nearby. It was tuned in to WHYN, the pop station in Springfield. I liked to listen to the music, but I also liked the news and commercials because it felt good to hear about names and places from my hometown.

I had been living at home when President Kennedy had been elected. Since my parents were among his staunch supporters, I was quite familiar with the president and proud that he came from my state. When the program was interrupted by a news bulletin saying that he had been shot, I was very concerned. I wanted to find out more, but someone turned down the volume on the radio and I couldn't make out all of the bulletins. I tried to get one of the attendants to fill me in on the news from Dallas, but she didn't understand why I was making faces at the radio. I was left in the dark, except for what I managed to overhear from the staff's conversations.

Looking back on it now, I have ample reason to forget where I was when JFK was shot, and in the years that followed I tried hard to do just that. At times it has seemed strange that in order to write this book, I have strained to recall details of those intentionally lost memories; very few events of those days seem worth remembering.

For about a year and a half, my routine on Ward 3 was quite similar to that on Ward 4. Time passed in a succession of diaper changes and tasteless meals, and I kept my mind occupied with dreams and reminiscences. Carol helped, but I continued to encounter the same everyday problems of misunderstanding and insensitive treatment by attendants who couldn't, or didn't care to, evaluate my intelligence correctly. I had moved up a notch in the eyes of the staff, progressing to "mildly retarded," but there was a long way to go.

Despite my ongoing frustration, I did appreciate the small gains I had made. I was particularly happy that I had befriended Carol Muse, and I was cheered further in late 1963 when I made two more friends.

.DOG.LIKE.

One of my new friends was Bob, a student intern in his early twenties. Bob was working as a physical therapist at the Infirmary, and he helped some of the girls on our ward. The State School's physical therapy program was very limited in both staff and resources, and Bob couldn't have been paid much, if anything, for the long hours he put in. Yet he was the most caring, gentle, and genuinely pleasant staff person I had encountered at Belchertown until then. In my subsequent years there, I met very few people who measured up to him.

I first saw Bob in October 1963, when he first came onto our ward. Even though I wasn't in the physical therapy program at the time, he introduced himself to me. He always said hello to everyone, but after he saw how responsive I was, he made a point of coming by to chat whenever he could spare a few minutes.

Bob had a terrific personality, naturally cheerful and upbeat, and his presence never failed to perk everyone up — at least those of us who could appreciate him. With dark hair and warm brown eyes, he was quite handsome. It was no wonder that I fell in love the first time I saw him! As a matter of fact, I had a crush on him the whole time he worked at the State School. I was usually a little shy when he stopped by, but I thought I knew him intimately from watching him interact with the other girls. He seemed to have a magic touch, and he brought happiness to many of the residents. My life took on a whole new slant when Bob was around, although my feelings were only puppy love.

The second new person in my life was Diane Skorupski, who came with Bob to our ward a few weeks after I met him. Diane was a resident of Ward 1, where I had encountered Goldy, and I remembered seeing her during my brief stay there. Diane was sixteen — three years older than me — when she started coming to Ward 3, and she had spina bifida. Like Carol, she was affected from the waist down, but she had stronger legs than Carol and sometimes used crutches to get around. Diane's upper body was perfectly sound, and she was very intelligent; a little quieter than Carol, but very friendly.

After Bob brought Diane to our ward, she continued to visit on a daily basis to help out. Along with two other women from Ward 1, she fed a few of the girls, or just talked to them to provide some company. Although she didn't work directly with me, Diane and I became acquainted in the course of her visits, and we soon became good friends. Carol had a hand in this, because she kept telling Diane that I was "really smart" and understood what people were saying. Unlike most of the staff, Diane didn't write Carol off as a dumb little kid. She paid enough attention to Carol's evaluation of me to find out for herself that it was accurate.

During my brief stay on Ward 1, I hadn't gotten to know Diane at all, but I remembered her as being extremely quiet and introverted, totally lacking in energy or drive. When she started visiting Ward 3 a year and a half later, she was a changed person. She came by every day without fail, either struggling onto the ward on crutches or wheeling herself in by wheelchair.

Bob had suggested that Diane assist on our ward when he was helping her learn how to use the crutches. Although she couldn't stay up on them for long stretches, she used them as much as possible on Ward 3. It was hard work for her to haul herself over to work with us, but these visits were important to her: for the first time in the four years she had been at Belchertown, Diane was doing something constructive. This marked a turning point for her. Years later she told me that Bob had inspired her to break out of her shell. All she needed was a little encouragement to fight back against the crippling environment of the institution.

Diane showed me that self-improvement at the Infirmary was possible — difficult, yes, but possible. As I got to know her, I saw how painful it was for her just to be at the State School, let alone to struggle to better herself. Without exception, I met no one who had less reason to be a resident at Belchertown than Diane Skorupski. Sure, she had some physical problems, but none of these warranted her confinement in any institution. She was the victim of unfortunate family circumstances and societal ignorance. As things turned out, she spent fourteen years trapped at Belchertown because she too had nowhere else to go.

Although she suffered terribly in spirit, Diane never burdened me with her problems. She was always reluctant to speak about things that were bothering her, and never indulged in self-pity, especially around people who had enough problems of their own. Rather, she poured her energy into improving the lives of her friends at the Infirmary. I can vouch for her success in that respect.

In no time, Diane, Carol, and I formed our own little social group, and we remained constant companions for several years. This came about because Diane didn't get hung up on Carol's youth or my inability to speak. She was wise enough to realize that even though Carol was very young and I was severely limited physically, we still could interact meaningfully. Besides, we desperately needed each other's support.

I can't count how many times I've wished that I could speak, but I never desired it more than when I was with Diane in those early days of our friendship. I developed a deep respect and admiration for her shortly after we met, and I wanted to tell her so out loud. I was grateful that she understood the gist of my feelings through my facial expressions and sounds, but I was frustrated that I couldn't express my thoughts as clearly and strongly as I wished.

In the early stage of our friendship, there was another important reason why I wanted to talk to Diane: Bob. She spent a lot of time with him in her physical therapy sessions, and since she knew I had a crush on him, she talked to me about him frequently. I was dying to jump into these conversations, to gush out my impressions and ask Diane all sorts of questions about him. It was exasperating to have all of those adolescent feelings bottled up inside. After all, most of the fun of a crush is sharing it with your friends. I couldn't do that very well, but Diane knew how I felt, and she indulged my appetite for gossip as much as her patience would permit.

.DIANE.WATER.COLD.

For months all I wanted to hear about was Bob, Bob, Bob. Finally it got on Diane's nerves. She figured that I was getting carried away with the whole thing, so she told Bob about my crush on him, hoping that a little reality would throw cold water on my feelings.

At first I was angry, mostly out of embarrassment. But once I saw how Bob reacted, I was glad. He handled it perfectly, acknowledging my crush without hurting my feelings. He made a point of talking to me more often, greeting me with "Hi, beautiful!" or "How's my sweetheart today?" in a way that told me it was perfectly all right, and harmless, for me to adore him. I was thrilled that he paid more attention to me, but at the same time I sensed that he didn't want to encourage my imagination. That was fine with me, because I didn't need any encouragement.

.DREAM.TOWN.RED.

My relationship with Bob had a dramatic impact on my fantasy life. In my dreams Bob whisked me off to some exotic place like Hawaii or Paris, where we got married, raised a family, and lived happily ever after.

Another Bob fantasy was set in Springfield. I was living at home with my parents, and he was my steady boyfriend. One evening he came over to take me out on a date, arriving at the door in a snazzy-looking tuxedo. I walked downstairs wearing a chic red dress, complete with matching sequined purse and red high-heeled shoes. My sister Marie had helped do up my hair, and I looked dazzling. Bob looked great in his tux, and we made a striking couple. We were all set to paint the town red when my mother asked us if we would change our plans. She hadn't been able to find a babysitter for Marie and wanted to know if we could cover for a few hours. Bob looked at me for an answer. After a few seconds of silence, I told Mother to find someone else, and Bob and I went out for a great time.

I cooked up other daydreams about Bob which I ran over and over in my mind to pass the time, but they were all similar. Either I was Mrs. Bob, living in perfect domestic bliss, or Bob and I went out on dates, dancing, swimming, or doing something athletic.

There's no doubt that I went overboard in my fantasies, but they served a worthwhile purpose at the time. By age and circumstance, I was ripe for romantic departures from reality. My real world on Ward 3 was not a very pleasant place, and I relished any chance to fly off into my private dream world. All the moments of laughter with Carol, the hours of friendly conversation with Diane, were very real and wonderful, but they made up only a small part of the endless, boring weeks and months that dragged by. All the talk, all the fantasizing, at best neutralized the day-to-day drudgery of the ward. And as Prince's death had done earlier, certain events added to the miserableness of the place, tipping the precarious balance between my comforting fantasies and a harsh reality.

.HEAD.BIG.

The arrival of a new girl on the ward in early 1964 disrupted my emotional status quo. She was severely hydrocephalic, with a head as big as a watermelon set atop a tiny body. It seemed that she was always in great pain, and only the sheer grotesqueness of her appearance kept me from being completely overwhelmed by pity for her.

This poor girl spent three years in the bed across from mine. In all that time, she never exhibited any behavior to indicate that she was aware of anything going on around her. She only made horrible noises and thrashed about, hurting herself with uncontrolled body movements. The attendants had to tie down her hands because she kept sticking her fingers into her open eyes. She was taken away in the summer of 1967, and I overheard some of the attendants saying that she died a few weeks later.

Many people would feel that this girl was probably better off dead. Although I can understand this sentiment, I am cautious about forming such opinions. I'm sure that a lot of people would look on me just as I viewed that girl, believing that life couldn't possibly offer me anything worthwhile on account of my "pathetic" physical condition. I know far too many people who are enjoying their lives fully, yet appear to others as pitiful.

.TERRY.

Terry, a blind girl, also lived on Ward 3. She was about twelve years old when she arrived in the summer of 1965, and she stayed with us until 1973, when she was moved to another part of the Infirmary. I'm not sure about the cause of her physical problems, but she was small for her age and had little muscular strength or ability to move around. She was unable to speak, although she made very strong vocal sounds.

Along with the sadness of her situation, there was an element of mystery about this girl. From her reactions to sound and touch, it was obvious that Terry was attuned to voices and the presence of people around her. Her face was truly beautiful, despite her eyes, and her soft brown hair set off a creamy complexion. For all I knew she was just like me, except for her blindness. At the time, nobody at the State School could measure her intelligence.

Soon after Terry arrived, Diane Skorupski started working with her, and she quickly became Diane's "baby." Diane fed Terry every day and talked to her for hours and hours, trying to stimulate and soothe her with sensitive human contact. Diane kept up this intense level of attention for all of the eight years that Terry lived on our ward. Although she was cut off from everything but sound and touch, Terry responded to Diane's presence in a way that differed significantly from how she reacted to everyone else. She recognized Diane by her voice, perhaps even by her "vibes," and I am convinced that she would have been absolutely lost without Diane's selfless devotion to her.

Were it not for her blindness, Terry might have been able to find ways to communicate with people. I'm sure that if I had been born blind along with my other infirmities, I could not communicate as I do today. I probably would be as cut off from people as Terry was. Whenever I think of her, I recall the story of Helen Keller and how she was able to overcome her physical limitations in learning how to speak. What chance do you think Helen Keller would have had if she had been bedridden from birth? It's a pretty safe bet that she would have ended up somewhere like the Infirmary, and that her wonderful mind and spirit would have been lost to the world. I'm not trying to compare Terry to Helen Keller, or Diane Skorupski to Annie Sullivan; unfortunately, Diane wasn't able to work any miracles with her friend. But I did see Diane touch Terry's life in a very real and special way; they interacted on a level that very few people would have thought possible.

When you've spent as much time as I have with people who have been totally rejected by society, when you have been written off by nearly everyone around you, it becomes very difficult to draw the line at which life is no longer worthwhile. I choose not to draw that line at all.

Bob stopped working at the State School in June 1964 and left to pursue his interests elsewhere. I was crushed. My dream world came crashing down around my head. Most of my relationship with Bob had existed in my mind, but as long as he worked at the Infirmary, I could count on seeing him a few times a week and talking to Diane about him. His departure hit me as strongly as if all my fantasies had been true.

I had become increasingly dependent on my Bob dreams to escape my troubles, and his departure set off a chain reaction, unraveling my other sanity-saving daydreams as well. It seemed like all of my self-generated optimism walked out the door with Bob. I had experienced more than my share of frustration and disappointment in my fourteen years, but this was the first time I had watched a person dear to my heart walk out of my life forever. It made me feel absolutely helpless, to the point that I lost the spirit that had enabled me to dream up my self-preserving fantasies in the first place. I didn't have the energy even to try to escape the ward anymore.

Diane had good reasons to become upset over Bob's departure as well. She had enjoyed a close working relationship with him, and he had inspired her to take great strides in improving herself. Yet she accepted the loss in a very mature, reasonable way, and didn't let herself lose any ground over it. I was a different story. Except for Diane and Carol, nobody on the ward knew what had come over me. I didn't eat, I didn't smile, I didn't get enthusiastic about anything.

When Bob left, I weighed forty-three pounds, which might not sound like a lot, but it was an increase of eight pounds from the previous summer. For my size, about four feet tall, that weight wasn't all that bad. But in the twelve months after Bob left, I lost eleven pounds — one quarter of my total body weight! It never had taken much for me to reject the food served at the Infirmary. With my spirits plummeting to an all-time low, I simply did not feel like eating.

.EAT.CRY.

I can't attribute all of my decline to Bob's departure, though. During the summer other staff people left, people whom I liked, and I wasn't happy with their replacements. Moreover, after a year the novelty of the children's ward had worn off completely. Bob's departure, the collapse of my fantasy world, and the loss of my favorite attendants all occurred during the summer of 1964. Each time I came into contact with the new recruits, which was every day, I felt terrible.

Two of these new attendants were especially incompetent. They were lazy, disorganized, insensitive, impatient. They yelled at me about aspects of my handicap over which I had no control, such as my difficulty in eating. During my first year on Ward 3, I usually had been propped up on pillows, especially when I was being fed. When these attendants came on the scene, they decided that it would be easier to feed me while I was lying flat on my back. This only made it harder for me to eat. It was also particularly boring to spend my whole day staring up at the ceiling, when I at least could have been sitting up and checking out what was going on.

You'd think that these people would have noticed that there was something wrong with their approach, but they never did. Their disregard for my well-being typified the attendants' attitudes toward the other residents on the ward as well. From mid-1964 through mid-1965, my basic activities consisted of crying and not eating.

My friend Carol didn't fare well during this period either. Although she didn't share my reaction to Bob's departure, she sympathized with me and did all she could to cheer me up. Carol attempted to tell the staff what was bothering me, just as she tried to tell them that they weren't feeding me correctly and they weren't giving me enough credit for intelligence. But the attendants didn't listen; they probably didn't care enough about me to have made any changes even if they had believed Carol. It was just as easy for them, if not easier, if I didn't eat. It wasn't easy for Carol, though, and watching me deteriorate affected her deeply. The staff's rough hands and coarse attitudes took their toll on her too, and she lost a lot of her spunk as the year wore on.

During that summer Carol was almost as depressed as I was. It didn't help when she came down with a cold and couldn't keep any food down for almost two weeks. One night I woke up at about two A.M. and heard some awful sounds coming from her bed. At first I thought I was having a nightmare, but in fact I had been awakened by the sounds of Carol vomiting. As was customary when somebody was ill, the lights on the ward were kept on all night so the staff could keep an eye on the sick person. After the attendants cleaned things up, I stayed awake for a while to watch Carol. She looked miserable, and not just because of her illness.

I made a soft sound to attract her attention. When she looked over at me, I encouraged her with a look to speak to me. We talked for a long time that night. Carol told me how depressed she was about being sick and how lousy she felt about the way things were going on the ward. I answered her with sounds, looks, and telepathic messages, telling her that I understood her. It had been hard enough from the beginning for the two of us to keep our spirits up; with recent events, we both felt like all the starch had been taken out of us. Our conversation didn't lead to any revelations, but it did help for Carol to vent her frustrations and to see that I shared her unhappiness.

Later that summer Carol was involved in another incident, one that really frightened me. It was a cool August night and everyone was sleeping soundly when an electrical storm struck, at midnight. The thunder was deafening, but something else woke up most of the girls on the ward before they saw any lightning or heard any thunder: terrifying screams. I quickly realized that Carol had ruined another one of my pleasant dreams.

But this time she wasn't fooling around. Carol had been the first person to hear the thunder, and the storm triggered a hysterical outburst. She was screaming her head off, which took me completely by surprise because Carol wasn't even afraid of thunder. She carried on for over an hour, keeping everybody up until she wore herself out and fell asleep.

The storm hadn't frightened Carol. Rather, it had pushed her worn-out nerves too far. The past year had taken its toll on her, gradually sapping the energy she used for generating laughter and happy conversation. It was impossible for the institutional surroundings *not* to affect someone as sensitive and intelligent as Carol. Try as she might to fend it off, the inevitable effect of living at the Infirmary had overwhelmed her. Carol didn't all of a sudden stop laughing; her jokes just came less often, and her laughter lost some of its infectious appeal. It was rare for her to let go as she did the night of that storm, and it was a scary thing to see.

BOX.

One of the most annoying aspects of Ward 3 was the Box. This was a long table with one-foot wooden sides around the outside edge and a mattress set inside. Starting in the fall of 1963 and continuing for the next four years, two of these contraptions were used on the ward. Three or four girls were placed inside, side by side, for "socialization."

I think that the Box was an early response by the State School to growing outside pressures against keeping the residents of the Infirmary in their beds all day long. Some of the girls on our ward — Carol Muse at one end of the spectrum, and the medically unmovables at the other end — never spent any time in the Box. But most of my wardmates logged many hours on those mattresses, and I spent three or four afternoons a week there for the next three years.

Since I had just fallen into a depressed state after adjusting to my surroundings on Ward 3, the last thing I needed was to lie around in the Box. Nobody cared to ask my opinion, however, and into the Box I went. I suppose that it wouldn't have been that bad if I had been able to sleep in it, or at least rest comfortably. But this proved impossible, for I was laid flat on my back in the company of three girls whose behavior ranged from tolerable to downright dangerous.

One of these girls, Donna Highland, occupied a bed on the other side of the ward. Although I had never met her, Diane told me some good things about her. Diane had been working with her since she had first started visiting our ward, and she fed Donna lunch and kept her company almost every day. From what Diane told me, I liked Donna before I met her. Unfortunately, the circumstances in the Box left a lot to be desired for developing a mutual friendship. Like myself, Donna was a victim of cerebral palsy and was quadraplegic, unable to talk or do much with her arms and legs. She was about eight years old when I met her, five years younger than me to the day, almost — her birthday was on September 22, the day before mine.

During our first weeks together in the Box, Donna didn't seem to be clued in to very much. She didn't appear to be in total control of herself, and I guessed that she was mildly retarded. Once I got to know her better, I corrected my mistake. Not only was she *not* retarded, she was actually pretty smart. Donna had spent almost her whole life at Belchertown, and because of the overall lack of stimulation, the absence of contact with "normal" children, and the misguided attitudes of the staff, her upbringing had severely retarded her emotional growth. Donna just didn't know what it was like to play with children her age, or to go to the beach, or to bake cookies at her grandma's house, or to go to a movie.

Donna's confinement at the State School had also stifled her development of communication skills. Combined with her physical disabilities, this made her incapable of interacting with other people. Diane had told me that she possessed a healthy mind, but it took me a while to accept this because Donna acted like a baby. She had no idea how to respond to my attempts to communicate with her. Eventually we figured out how to reach each other, but on first meeting Donna, I wasn't very pleased with the prospect of spending my afternoons lying next to her in the Box.

Aside from my initial impressions, there were two good reasons why Donna and I didn't hit it off right away: the two other girls with us in the Box. They nearly drove me crazy! One of them was Debbie Dearborn, an East Indian girl with jet black hair, very dark eyes, and ruddy brown skin. Debbie was about my age but she was tiny, and she looked like she was five years old. She was a quadraplegic too and moved around somewhat, but she also was severely retarded and rarely made a sound. You could tell just by looking at her that she was a lost soul, although she was sort of sweet in her own way.

Debbie wasn't much fun as a constant companion in the Box, especially when she moved around and got tangled up with Donna and me. But I preferred her to the fourth member of our "play group." I forget this girl's name; she was severely handicapped and profoundly retarded, totally out of control mentally. This girl could be described as "the Rolling Screamer," for she combined two particularly annoying traits, under the circumstances: she liked to roll around and wrap herself up in a bundle with our arms and legs, and she screamed all the while at the rest of us, who were powerless to fend her off or get out of her way. What a nightmare!

After three days of this, the attendants grew tired of untangling our limbs and listening to us yell at each other. To solve the problem, they put Donna and me on one side of the Box and Debbie and the Rolling Screamer on the other side. A barricade of pillows was erected between us and the other two, and Debbie was separated from the Rolling Screamer in like fashion. That way, Donna and I were able to get acquainted without having to worry about being assaulted by those two poor kids playing rolypoly with their bodies. I'm not sure which attendant devised the simple but effective trick with the pillows, but I'm glad she came up with it as quickly as she did. I heard from other people who were put in the Box that some of the residents actually fought in there, going at it with whatever flailing movements their arms and legs could muster.

The Box didn't exactly thrill me, even after the situation with Debbie and the Rolling Screamer was straightened out. I was able to put up with it, but I would have preferred physical therapy, not to mention the comfortable privacy of my own bed, to the "socialization" of the Box. I did get to see Diane Skorupski more often, because she continued to visit Donna at lunchtime, when the two of us usually were in the Box together. Carol paid us regular visits too, but for the most part the Box was a pain in the neck. Being stuck in there got on my nerves. It made me feel like a helpless little baby trapped inside a big, clunky crib with three other babies. As such, the Box magnified the effect of wearing diapers at the age of thirteen.

But the worst part of this "therapy" was the timing. It started when I was at a low point in my self-esteem and overall emotional level. Good old Belchertown! The institution had found yet one more way to strip me of what little dignity and individualism I was struggling to preserve for myself. Coming on the heels of my terrible first year, a couple of weeks in the Box sent my spirits plummeting.

.BROOM.

The situation on the ward stayed pretty bad for the next year or so, and I lay in bed wasting away to skin and bones. My weak windpipe prevented me from blowing off steam the way Carol had, but I screamed a lot internally; my temper tantrums were just more discreet.

Depressed as Carol was, however, if it had not been for her (and Diane), I never would have made it through that awful time. The facilities at the Infirmary were woefully inadequate and terribly overcrowded, but even so, it was the staff that made my life truly miserable. They viewed me as a helpless little creature whom they were supposed to keep alive, and nothing more. Since an attendant's job was thankless, few people stayed on for very long. I never got a chance to get to know many of the women who worked with me before they quit, so there wasn't much I could do to change their impression of me.

Our ward supervisor, an Irish woman, was one of the few fixtures in my life during my first few years at Belchertown. Short, fat, ugly, loud, and bossy, she richly deserved the name the staff called her behind her back: the Witch.

I didn't take much notice of the Witch during my first year on Ward 3, because I was too busy getting used to the place and striking up friendships. Besides, Bob was still around and I had more pleasant things to occupy my mind. As 1964 came and went and things fell apart for me, though, the Witch emerged as the one nasty constant. Ward 3 was her show, and she ran the place very much like Nurse Ratched in *One Flew Over the Cuckoo's*

Nest (one of my favorite movies). She was indifferent toward the staff and insensitive to the real needs of the residents. Under her command, the attendants provided us with custodial care of the most basic kind, and any attempt to treat us as individuals was severely discouraged.

Few residents died on our ward, so in that sense the Witch met her objectives, especially when one considers how she over-worked the attendants. But that was no excuse for how she viewed us. We weren't people with physical *and* emotional needs; we were objects that had to be fed, cleaned, and changed, fed, cleaned, and changed, and so on. If an attendant took a few minutes out from her chores to talk to me, she risked being yelled at by the Witch. No wonder nobody wanted to stay at that job! Who would want to work with a bunch of crazy crippled kids in a run-down, crowded institution, under the command of a whip-cracking sourpuss? During my first year on that ward, more di-rect-care staff shuffled in and out than you could shake a broom at.

Things improved a little during the summer of 1965. A contin-gent of college girls worked on the ward, most of them students from the University of Massachusetts, and a few of the gutsy ones stuck it out until September. On account of their youth and open-mindedness, most of them approached us as handicapped human beings rather than semivegetables. But the working en-vironment and presence of superiors like the Witch smothered their good intentions. It was much easier for these girls to bail out and return to college than it was for them to overthrow the institutional system.

Two of these students did stay on past the fall, choosing to work on the ward for a couple of years rather than return to school. One was named Karen, and she was the only attendant I really liked in the summer of '65, possibly because she re-minded me of Shari. Karen was tall and thin, with long, beauti-ful, honey-brown hair. Like Shari, she had an offbeat sense of humor and was very quick to laugh. Karen liked to joke around with the other attendants on the job, which was unusual back then. She was also a very gentle person, and treated me with tenderness and kindness. Unfortunately, she had been informed that I was severely retarded, and her attitude toward me reflected this belief. I was a "poor little thing" in her eyes.

Karen came to work with a friend. As cheerful and attractive as Karen was, her friend was obnoxious, unpleasant, insensitive, and gossipy. She sniped about her co-workers behind their backs and treated the residents like dirt. I could never understand what Karen saw in this girl, but maybe my unique perspective gave me special insight into her personality. You can tell an awful lot about a person from how she picks you up or feeds you, as well as from what she says about people behind their backs when she doesn't suspect you're listening and comprehending.

6

PCA.GOOD.

The fall of 1965 marked the beginning of some crucial changes on the ward. A group of new attendants replaced the departing college girls and summer workers. Among them were five women who effectively put a stop to the turnstile-like arrival and departure of our attendants. One lasted seven years; the other four were still working at Belchertown fifteen years later. These women stuck with a job that offered them the worst of working conditions. Improvements in staffing and reduction of the resident population didn't begin until a good five years later, so their tenacity was no small achievement. The mere fact that they stayed around provided consistency, which was an improvement in itself, but they also were responsible for a host of other developments that made my life better almost as soon as they arrived.

These five women — Lydia Weston (Wessie), Hazel Ritter, Alice Dupell, Rita Cormier, and a woman named Rosa — never met one another until they started working at the Infirmary. Fortunately, it didn't take long for them to strike up good working relationships that eventually turned into friendships. This picked up the general atmosphere of the place quite a bit.

All of these women were central figures in my life from 1965 to 1975 (although Rita left the State School in 1972), but two of them, Wessie and Hazel, were especially important to me. For whatever reason, these two women were drawn to me right away. They spent more time with me than any of the other attendants, new or old, did, and as they got to know me better they came to realize that the way I was being treated by the staff was grossly unfair. It didn't take them long to do something about it, either.

Wessie was in her late thirties when I met her. She was of medium height and build, and was very strong, both physically and emotionally. I felt that strength in her hands, saw that strength in her face and in the way she dealt with the staff and residents. Her face was plain and pleasant, with sharply drawn features and quiet, observant brown eyes. I always received an honest answer when I looked into Wessie's eyes, and she always got the same from me. She was like a mother to me through many dreadful years at the Infirmary, and she reminded me a lot of my own mother: down-to-earth, practical, ready to deal with people on their own terms, and willing to say what was on her mind when she was unhappy with a situation. Wessie was always very outgoing and upbeat with the residents, but she was also a no-nonsense lady. She was never satisfied when a co-worker gave her an evasive answer to a straightforward question.

Hazel was about five years older than Wessie. Although she was extroverted around me, she was very quiet around the other attendants. She tended to follow Wessie's lead in pushing for changes on the ward, but like Wessie, she acted on her own instincts and observations in forming opinions about the residents. Hazel was short and not particularly stout, but she too was a strong woman, with firm, gentle hands that cared for each and every resident as if that person were her daughter. Whereas Wessie was like a mother to me, Hazel was like a maternal aunt.

She took it upon herself, along with Wessie, to see that I was treated as something more than a mindless cripple.

.TALK.COUNTRY.

Alice Dupell also was in her late thirties and was a quiet person, inclined more to work in the background than to hassle with supervisors over how best to care for us. She didn't spend as much time working directly with me as Wessie and Hazel did, but she was around constantly, and all three women exchanged observations about me. I liked Alice's sweet disposition very much. She was low-key and had a very soft touch that reflected her personality.

What stands out most in my mind about Alice is that she frequently spoke French on the ward with Rita Cormier, who was French Canadian and didn't speak much English. (Aptly enough, Rita was nicknamed "Frenchy.") Although Alice was an American, she was of French descent and spoke the language fluently. Sometimes she served as Rita's interpreter and filled her in on what was happening. At other times Alice and Rita spoke French because they wanted to gossip about somebody nearby without that person's knowing about it. Frequently that somebody was the Witch.

I liked both Alice and Rita apart from their conversations in French, but I loved to hear the delicate sounds of that language. It was like a vacation for my ears from the harsh, grating noises of the ward. When I eavesdropped on them, I sometimes thought I understood what they were saying from their inflections and tones of voice. On one occasion there was no question that I understood them. It was on Saint Patrick's Day in 1966. Alice and Rita were talking to each other in English when the Witch walked in at the other end of the ward, dressed from head to toe in green. All of a sudden Alice and Rita began speaking in animated French. I knew they were making fun of the Witch from how they tried, unsuccessfully, to stifle their laughter. I figured that they must be getting in some good shots, so I joined in the laughter, feeling as if I had understood every word they had spoken.

There were many times when I overheard Alice and Rita talking that I wished I really could understand French. I would have loved to have been able to speak the beautiful sounds of that language. But I wasn't choosy—I would have settled for any language, even Latin.

.SPAGHETTI.FLOWER.RED.

The last member of the group was Rosa. She was about thirty in 1965 and thus was younger than the others. But she stood out from the rest for other reasons as well. Rosa was of Italian descent, and she was tall, thin, and had very dark hair. She was also very loud, and came on strong, mixing in a lot of profanity with her everyday speech. At first this scared me, and made me very wary of her. I had grown up in a home where profanity was reserved for the expression of anger or strong emotion, especially when children were nearby. By talking like a sailor, Rosa intimidated me. Her rough hands did nothing to ease my fears; I didn't appreciate being tossed around like a sack of potatoes. Luckily, Rosa softened up a little as she grew more accustomed to caring for me and the other residents.

One thing that all of these women brought with them to the ward was a strong desire to provide the residents with the best care possible under the circumstances. This was no easy task, for upon their arrival they found thirty-two handicapped and/or retarded girls, ranging in age from five to seventeen, who had been left to rot in crowded rows of cribs and beds. Three attendants worked each shift, and their duties included total care of the residents: changing, bathing, feeding, mopping floors, and washing bedclothes. There was little supplementary staff to assist with any of these chores.

A few of the girls on our ward were taken out of their beds during the day and put into "wheelchairs." They weren't real wheelchairs as we think of them today, but wooden reclining chairs — chairbeds — with wheels and adjustable backs, similar to old-fashioned patio furniture. These girls spent a few hours each day in their chairs, which enabled the attendants to wheel them about so that they could do nothing in a different part of the ward. The chairs were in short supply, and I was denied even this limited mobility at the time.

Another method that was used to get some of the residents out of their beds was to place bottomless playpens on the floor, forming little enclosures in which a few girls could "play." This didn't work too well when it was cold outside, because the tile floors became chilly and drafty. Owing to the lack of sweaters and extra blankets and the overall absence of clothing, we all had to stay in bed so we wouldn't catch colds.

There was no question that the Infirmary was poorly equipped to care for its residents. The situation was no different on the other wards, nor was it substantially different in other buildings at the State School: the quality of care received by the residents depended totally on the staff. Given the shortage of attendants and their heavy workload, I understood why the Witch cracked her whip to get things done on our ward. But she could have demanded hard work without forcing the attendants to look on us as a bunch of dumb animals.

Despite the Witch's approach, Wessie, Hazel, Alice, and Rita, and Rosa too, made a difference, even while they were still learning the ropes. There was something in the way that Wessie picked me up, or Hazel flicked the hair out of my eyes as she hurried past my bed to do some task at the other end of the ward. I sensed that my life would take a major turn for the better if these women stayed for a while, and I was right — the longer they stayed, the better things got.

.WESSIE.

Wessie was the first one to question how things were being done, and I think that her observations about me had a lot to do with it. The staff kept me flat on my back all day long. Wessie challenged the necessity for this, especially while I was being fed. The rough attendant I mentioned earlier told her that I was kept on my back for feeding so I wouldn't let so much food fall out of my mouth. According to her, I was uncooperative and refused to learn how to eat properly. Her sentiments were shared by some of the other attendants. I usually cried when one of them fed me, and one attendant told Wessie that she liked this because it was easier to feed me when my mouth was open.

What she neglected to tell Wessie was that the reason I cried was that she was feeding me. It was a real struggle for me to keep from choking to death while one of these thugs shoveled food down my throat. Although Wessie's first impression of me was that I was "cute, thin, and didn't seem to know anything," it was clear to her that this treatment was terribly wrong. It took her several weeks to work up the nerve, but she finally asked one of the Infirmary nurses about it. The nurse told her that there was no reason that I shouldn't sit up while I was eating. Rather than argue about it with the attendants, Wessie simply took over the job of feeding me. She propped me up with a couple of pillows and gave me all the time I needed to swallow my food at my own pace. She perceived immediately that there was quite a difference for me between eating "properly" and doing the best I could.

I never cried when Wessie fed me.

Wessie also managed to find one of those wooden chairbeds for me. It was more comfortable to sit in the chairbed than in a hospital bed, because of the adjustable back. Finding the chairbed took some extra effort, but more than anything it involved Wessie's desire to improve my living situation as much as possible. Changing the method of feeding me and finding the adjustable chairbed were relatively easy, common-sense improvements, yet they were like miracles for me. In less than a month Wessie had dramatically improved my life.

When Wessie took me under her wing, she received a lot of help from Hazel. Even though they were under constant pressure from the Witch to complete their numerous tasks, they spent enough time with me to notice that I was more than just a "cute little thing who didn't know anything." The Witch bawled them out because she didn't like the attendants spending too much time with one resident, which was why I had never been evaluated fairly by attendants in the past. But Wessie and Hazel drew the line at feeding me. They knew that I needed extra time, and they simply ignored the Witch's repeated outbursts over the issue of "playing favorites."

Meanwhile, I was beginning to develop deep affection for these two women. I tried to show them my appreciation whenever and however I could. But in addition to expressing my gratitude, I wanted to show Hazel and Wessie that a good mind was at work behind my big brown eyes. The official tag for me was "severely retarded," yet Wessie and Hazel noticed that I was trying desperately to communicate with them. After several weeks they realized that the label was incorrect. Since I looked like a rather intelligent seven-year-old (I was fifteen at the time), that's how they treated me.

Hazel and Wessie were willing to give me an honest chance to show them my stuff. This was a terrific development, and I was thrilled. But I also was anxious to raise their opinion of me another notch.

All of the new attendants liked to joke around with each other while they were on the job. Everybody enjoyed taking pot shots at the Witch, usually when she was out of hearing range. One afternoon in early October 1965, I overheard Wessie wisecracking to Alice about the Witch and I broke up. Lately I had come to dislike the Witch intensely, and it felt great to laugh at her expense. But my laughter startled Wessie and Alice, for they didn't think that I was capable of appreciating their sarcastic humor.

You should have seen the astonished expressions on their faces! First they looked at each other, then they looked at me, then they asked each other whether I could possibly be laughing at what they had said. This prompted me to gesture excitedly with facial expressions and sounds, to tell them, "Yes indeed, I was laughing at your joke." Then one of them asked me directly if I had been laughing at their remark about the Witch. After some additional raising of my eyes, I convinced them that it was time to revise their opinion of me again.

This incident was an ice-breaker. Once Alice and Wessie discovered that I appreciated adult humor, they started to direct comments to me instead of talking about me. For a while the question "Just how smart is Ruthie?" was of considerable interest on the ward. Wessie and Alice told other people about my laughter, and I received a little more attention from some of the other attendants, especially those who had already credited me with some intelligence. More important, these new attitudes altered the very nature of the attention I received. The outward signs were hard to detect — a sympathetic look here, a friendly comment there, a bit more patience in the way someone handled me. But a few people were paying more attention to how I responded to various things. This gave me a greater opportunity to prove that I possessed a personality, that I was more than just a poor little bird with broken wings.

Laughter continued to be my best way of interacting with my new friends, for that was one thing I could do as well as anybody else. I pushed it, too, forcing out at least a chuckle whenever I heard somebody make a comment that was even close to funny. It was my way of telling the ward staff that I really was tuned in to what was going on. This might have done the trick even earlier at the Infirmary, but nobody on the staff except Bob had given me much to laugh about, until Wessie and her group came along.

.EYES.UP.YES.

After the laughter episode, I redoubled my efforts to communicate with my new friends. Since Wessie worked in the morning, she usually fed me breakfast and lunch. As the weeks passed, she began to talk to me more and more while she was feeding me. Almost without knowing it, she started to pause after she said something, as if she was anticipating a response.

During lunch one day in early December 1965, Wessie said something to me like "Too bad the food at this place is so lousy."

I laughed, and raised my eyes toward the ceiling in an exaggerated way to draw her attention.

As she brought the next spoonful of food up to my mouth, she noticed that I was doing something funny with my eyes, obviously in reaction to what she had just said. I kept looking up at the ceiling, but Wessie couldn't figure out why I was doing that. She put the spoon down and thought for a few seconds, then asked, "Ruthie, are you trying to tell me something?"

With a broad grin on my face, I looked at her squarely. Then I raised my eyes up to the ceiling again with such exaggeration that I thought my eyes would pop up through the top of my head.

Wessie knew she was onto something, but she wasn't sure just what. She pondered for a few more seconds . . . then it clicked! A silent conversation flashed between us as loud and clear as any spoken words. Even before she asked me a dozen times over, and before I exuberantly answered a dozen times with my eyes raised skyward, Wessie knew. And I knew that she knew.

I was raising my eyes to say yes.

We both started laughing. Then I started laughing really hard, and before I knew it I was crying so uncontrollably that I couldn't see because of the tears. They were tears of pure joy, the kind of tears a person sheds on being released from prison after serving three years of what she had feared would be a life sentence.

None of the staff at Belchertown had noticed my yes-and-no signals until that day, when Wessie discovered them. For more than three years I hadn't been able to communicate any of my thoughts or feelings to the people on whom I depended for my survival. Back when my parents first brought me to Belchertown, they made a point of telling Dr. Soong and others about my facial signals, but no one paid any attention to what they said. Everyone just assumed that I was a helpless cripple, and with the constant turnover of staff, the very suggestion that I could communicate was soon lost. During visits or vacations, my folks never thought of specifically asking me whether my signals were being used at the Infirmary. They just assumed that they were, so they didn't follow up with anyone at the State School to make sure. Before Wessie came along, only one other person at Belchertown ever took advantage of my signals: Theresa Ladue. But Theresa couldn't communicate this to the staff any better than I could, so it had remained our unwanted but well-kept secret.

Between my laughter and tears, I somehow managed to show Wessie my no signal: curling my upper lip and frowning. During the next few days, Wessie spread the word around the Infirmary, and once again I became a point of interest for some of the attendants. A few people, mostly those women I've mentioned who were genuinely interested in the residents, came over and asked me simple questions to check out my signals for themselves. I was so excited about this development that I was glad to show off for them.

In the years since, I have had to repeat this kind of demonstration hundreds of times. I always cringe a little when I have to go through my paces like a well-trained dog doing its tricks. But this is the small price I pay for the ability to communicate with people, so I don't get too upset about it.

Unfortunately, once the novelty of Wessie's discovery wore off, only my closest attendants made any effort to read my facial signals for regular communication. As usual, Wessie and Hazel, and to some extent Alice, were the ones who pushed ahead. They made a point of asking me simple questions about all sorts of basic stuff, like "Are you hungry?" or "Does that taste all right?" Limited though it was, this process seemed wonderful. It made me feel like a human being again, after being on the shelf for so long. Not only did these women ask me how I felt about things, they even looked for my answers! But I hadn't suddenly been granted the gift of speech. Far from it. A major problem remained, for even though Wessie and the others could now discover whether I liked something, it was still impossible for me to state anything that involved more than a simple yes, no, or maybe. When someone asked me a direct question, I could answer it adequately. But when I wanted to answer a question that hadn't been asked, I was out of luck. If I had something to say and nobody had any idea of what it was, the interview process turned into a frustrating guessing game. Hazel and Wessie always were interested in whatever I wanted to tell them, but they rarely had the time to ask me the necessary range of questions until they hit on the right one. Countless times they were unable to figure out what I wanted to talk about and they had to let it go until "later" — meaning they forgot about it, I forgot about it, or we just dropped it.

To avoid going crazy with frustration, I became very selective in choosing the messages I even attempted to communicate. For example, if someone was talking about a particular person or thing, I could make some kind of comment because the subject was already established. If somebody wanted to know why I felt that way, she could usually figure out what questions to ask in order to find out. Likewise, I did all right when I was able to draw my listener's attention to a person or thing within view; the astute listener could then ask me questions about the object of my gaze. But even when the subject had been identified, I remained completely dependent on my listener's intuition and the amount of time available for conversation.

A few weeks after Wessie discovered my facial signals and we began using them on a regular basis, we had a conversation that illustrates these problems. She was taking a quick break from her chores to talk to me when she noticed that I kept looking over at Rosa, who was tending to something on the other side of the ward. From the way I glanced at Rosa and then made a face at Wessie, she knew that Rosa was on my mind. She asked me if I wanted her to call Rosa over.

I replied no by frowning, pursing my lips for emphasis. But I continued to look at Rosa and then back at Wessie again.

Wessie asked me if I wanted to tell her something about Rosa.

I raised my eyes and smiled to say yes.

"What do you want to tell me about Rosa?" Wessie asked. She realized that I couldn't answer this question directly, but she looked into my eyes, concentrating intently to pick up some kind of a clue.

I curled my lips and scrunched my whole face into an exaggerated frown, trying to float the message from my mind to hers. I wanted to tell Wessie that although I knew Rosa meant well, she was too rough and gruff with me. I wanted Wessie to give Rosa a few pointers on how to lighten her touch, to ease up a little. But this was too much to say with a no signal, and all Wessie could make of it was that I was annoyed with Rosa for some reason.

"Do you like Rosa?" Wessie asked, determined to follow it up.

I responded with a combination of raised eyes and pinched-together lips — my version of "maybe." I couldn't choose a simple yes or no because I wanted to tell her, "Yes, I like Rosa, but no, I don't like the way she treats me."

Understandably, Wessie was confused. Again she asked me, "Do you like Rosa?"

I raised my eyes for yes, and followed immediately with a frowning no.

This didn't do the trick either. After asking me a few more questions that yielded similar results, Wessie reluctantly gave up. She realized that something about Rosa was bothering me, but she couldn't figure out the rest. The conversation was partly successful, but it was very frustrating for both of us to reach a dead end.

As it turned out, my luck improved with Rosa. She developed a close relationship with Carol Muse, and through Carol, she came to understand me better and stopped being so rough with me.

As time went on, Wessie developed a routine approach for finding out what I wanted to say, and our conversations became increasingly fruitful. Nonetheless, many of my attempts at communication didn't meet with even the limited success of that early one about Rosa.

During this period, while Wessie and the others were experimenting with my newly discovered ability to communicate, other changes took place on the ward. One of these was caused by a letter that Mother wrote to the administrators of the State School.

The previous summer, in 1965, I spent a week with my family at Crystal Lake in Connecticut. (Father had planned his vacation so he could spend time with me, as he did for the next five or six years.) During the week, Mother became extremely upset about my overall poor state of health. She finally discovered that contrary to what the people at Belchertown had been telling her, I was in fact *not* wearing my leg braces and had never worn them at the institution. She found out about this because she finally thought to ask me!

When she discovered the truth and realized that the officials had lied to her, Mother was furious. She wrote to the State School and offered to buy a new set of braces for me, seeing as I had "outgrown" the other set. The people at Belchertown never took her up on her offer, but her letter must have gotten someone's attention, because a physical therapist started visiting me a few weeks later.

Twice a week a lady picked me up and wheeled my wooden chairbed down the hall into an open room. In the center of the room was a large table with a mat on it. The lady would take me out of the chairbed, place me on the table, and put me through the paces. The physical therapy sessions were short, lasting about half an hour. They consisted of the same passive stretching and arm-and-leg flexing I had done at home as a little girl. These sessions made me feel much, much better, for they provided the first exercise I had received in years. They were also my only chance to get away from the ward.

Once the sessions started, I noticed how much strength and flexibility I had lost as a result of the years of inactivity at Belchertown. My limbs had stiffened terribly, and my muscles were very weak. (I'm sure that my drastic weight loss over the previous year didn't help.) When I had lived at home, I had been able to roll myself around on the floor with my legs. I even used to tumble off my bed and roll myself down the hall to surprise my parents. At Crotched Mountain, my arms and hands had been flexible enough that the people there thought I might be able to feed myself.

After three years at Belchertown, however, my body was literally as stiff as a board. I found it difficult to do even the slightest stretching motions with the help of the therapist. But this didn't upset me too much, for I knew that my health had declined. I figured that now I had resumed a physical therapy program, it wouldn't take me too long to get back into the shape I was in when I first arrived at the State School.

As was so often the case at Belchertown, my hopes were dashed shortly after things started to look up. In late November, about eight weeks after the physical therapy sessions began, they abruptly ended. True to form, nobody told me in advance that they were going to end; no one provided me with any explanation. The therapist just stopped coming around one day, and that was that. Under the circumstances, I would have preferred that the sessions had never begun, because I had started to invest a lot of emotional energy in them. Stopping them so suddenly let me down very hard. I felt helpless and insignificant all over again, just like I had felt when Bob left. But I always reacted badly when an important change took place in my life and I was given no say in the matter.

In her diary, Mother noted that my Christmas visit in 1965 was a miserable one for the whole family. When I had come home before for vacations in the summer and at Christmas, my parents had noticed that I didn't look like I was doing very well. This upset them terribly, but they intentionally avoided talking to me about it because they believed that since we had no alternatives, the best they could do was to cheer me up by showing me a good time. They also prayed that conditions at the State School would improve. But this time they found it impossible to carry on their well-intentioned charade any longer. I looked so emaciated and morose that they couldn't hide their displeasure with how I was faring.

My parents knew I was trying to adjust to Belchertown, so they wanted to know what was happening to me there. In the course of their exhaustive questioning, a few things came out. They learned that my physical therapy sessions had ended, and they correctly guessed that this had a lot to do with my unhappiness. But I had no way of telling them about things like the Box and my ongoing frustration in not being able to communicate my thoughts to people. Since they never asked, those parts of the puzzle were missing.

Mother and Father couldn't learn every detail, but they saw that I was a bag of bones. They knew that I wasn't eating, and that I wouldn't be so depressed unless things weren't going well. To me, the fact that I couldn't even receive basic physical therapy at the State School demonstrated more conclusively than ever that I should leave Belchertown and come home for good. It broke my parents' hearts, but they were still handicapped by their recurring dilemma: they didn't think they could care for me at home, and there was no place for me to go but Belchertown.

Once again I returned to the State School, crying my eyes out the whole ride. As on previous trips, Mother and Father could only hide their tears from me and hope against hope that my life would take a turn for the better.

Amid all the unhappiness, there were two items that captured at least some of the spirit of the season. The first one was a very special Christmas gift I received from my parents: a beautiful powder-blue dress with lace ruffles and satin trim. Even though it was too big for me — I had lost eleven pounds since the last Christmas — and even though I knew that I would never wear that dress at the State School, I loved it. As things turned out, I took the dress back to Belchertown and it promptly disappeared. But that didn't spoil the significance of the gift. In my parents' eyes, I deserved a fancy party dress, regardless of how much I actually needed it. It might have been only a gesture, but it meant the world to me.

I still consider that dress the best Christmas present I've ever received. It represented my parents' unwavering belief that I could and should lead the same kind of life as any "normal" girl. Even when I was spending my days in diapers, in the Box, or in a bed on Ward 3 of the Infirmary, my parents envisioned me wearing a blue satin dress.

The second special item was a "holiday greeting" that Mother wrote to the State School after I returned. In a letter to the superintendent, Dr. Bowser, she described my poor physical shape and utterly depressed emotional condition. As in her letter of the previous summer, in which she had pointedly noted that I had "outgrown" my leg braces, Mother explained that this was the "first time" I appeared to be genuinely unhappy on a visit home. She attributed this completely to the cancellation of my physical therapy, but she did note in passing that it was obvious from my weight loss that I wasn't eating. She also noted that I could no longer move about the floor at home under my own power. Her strong displeasure was very clear between the lines.

For the second time, Mother's restrained yet firm approach got results. In early February my physical therapy was resumed. It consisted of only a few minutes of stretching exercises in my bed several times a week, but at least it was something—a step in the right direction, and a reason for encouragement.

When the physical therapy started again, I was having trouble with stiffness in the muscles of my arms. Even after only a very light stretching routine, my arms cramped terribly, probably because of the years of neglect, inactivity, and atrophy. The physical therapist spoke to the nurse about this, and I was given muscle relaxers to alleviate the cramps. This was one of the only times that I received appropriate medical attention for a problem at the State School.

At about this same time, in early 1966, my opinion of the Box changed from reluctant toleration to occasional enjoyment. This occurred as I began to develop a worthwhile relationship with my neighbor, Donna Highland. It took a lot of hard work, but it was definitely worth it.

The first obstacle I had to overcome was getting Donna to realize that my facial expressions and sounds were not just random, that I was "talking" to her, that these were my words. There was no magic trick to this; I just kept repeating basic expressions to her, communicating simple messages about how I felt about a particular person, or a meal, or anything else around us. Eventually Donna started to catch on. Once she understood the basic function of my sounds and expressions, things began to take off. The changes were subtle, and I'm sure that none of the attendants noticed them, but I watched Donna's perception and overall awareness continually sharpen as I lay next to her in the Box. We never came close to establishing the sophisticated system of communication that Theresa Ladue and I had worked out, mostly because of Donna's youth and her inhibited development, but she did become fairly adept at understanding my basic messages.

I encouraged Donna to express herself to me in a similar fashion. She was able to do this successfully when she started slowing down her random sounds and facial expressions. She concentrated very hard on studying my sounds and faces, often mimicking me like a little kid. This enabled her to develop her own set of responses. I guess there was something of a younger sister–older sister relationship between Donna and me. I know that I put a lot of effort into teaching her my approach to communicating.

The tools that Donna and I had to work with were very limited. Accordingly, the gist of my message to her was "use what you have!" This meant eye movements, hand movements, sounds of all kinds, facial expressions, mental telepathy, and anything else that would get a message across. To show Donna what she could do with her eye movements, I played a game: I would look around the ward until I focused on a particular person or thing; then it was up to Donna to guess who or what I was looking at by following the direction of my gaze. Since we were propped up on pillows and the Box was higher than the beds on the ward, we had a pretty good vantage point for this exercise. It not only helped pass the time, but it also taught Donna how to use her eyes like someone else might use her finger: to point to something. Sometimes we swapped roles and Donna led me to the target, but either way, it was good practice for her and fun for both of us.

Another game we played was "echo." This came about when I was mimicking Donna's sounds in the hope of getting her to bring them under control for selective communication. This was what led her to mimic my sounds. I wanted to go from there and begin to formulate a vocabulary of sounds, as Theresa and I had done, but it was a difficult concept for me to get across. We never got beyond the mimicry.

Aside from these instructional activities, Donna and I spent a lot of time laughing with each other. She was very good-natured, and like me, she preferred laughter to anything else. Sometimes it was a weird noise made by a girl on the ward, or maybe an attendant whom we didn't like was walking by — whatever the case, we tried to giggle at the slightest provocation. This never failed to perplex some of the staff, who couldn't figure out why we were laughing. But some of these people believed we weren't playing with a full deck anyway.

One constant source of entertainment was eavesdropping on the attendants' conversations. Since they didn't believe that we were capable of understanding what they were saying, we caught a juicy tidbit of gossip every now and then. One time Donna and I got a huge laugh out of a nearby card game involving two attendants on their coffee break. In the course of their short game of gin, the two women teased each other in a friendly but not altogether genteel manner. Actually, they cursed each other up and down. Donna and I almost split our sides laughing, and we also learned a few new words. The women must have heard us screeching and howling like two loonies but it didn't bother them a bit. Such behavior was to be expected on Ward 3.

At times I almost envied Donna for never having lived anywhere but the State School — she didn't know what she was missing. But just when I was starting to wish that I could share in her blissful ignorance, a good daydream would come along and make me glad I had memories of a better life. Our mutual suffering helped to cement our relationship, and by March 1966, Donna and I had become good friends. When something was bothering one of us, the other was usually the first, and perhaps the only, one to know about it.

One night after everyone else had fallen asleep, Donna started crying. She made a real racket, and since she had recently been moved to a bed near mine, I was one of the first to be awakened. I was in a good position to watch when the attendants turned on the lights to find out what was happening. Since Donna wasn't the crybaby type, they assumed that her trouble was physical, like an upset stomach or a diaper pin sticking into her leg.

But I knew better. I realized from the sound of her cries that

Donna was depressed. Maybe she was beginning to sense that there was more to life, even for a handicapped girl, than lying in the Box on Ward 3.

The attendants fussed and fumbled around for a while, but they didn't find any way to stop Donna from crying. She eventually petered out, and everything quieted down.

When I saw her the next day, Donna was still distraught. I gave her some sympathetic looks and sounds to show her that I understood what was going on. She read my message perfectly. What's more, she indicated as much to me with the look on her face and a particular kind of sound.

This incident stands out because it was the first time that Donna and I ever communicated something important to each other. It would not have been possible six months earlier.

Looking back, I can see why the staff at the Infirmary had so much trouble understanding people like Donna and me. If I was surprised at the depth of Donna's personality and intelligence, how could a "normal" person be expected to understand her? It took me months of lying next to her for hour after hour, trying my hardest to communicate with her, before I could develop a fairly accurate sense of what she was all about. I was probably more sensitive to her than most people because of our similar physical attributes, yet I still had problems understanding her.

These same kinds of problems existed for me with the people to whom I was attempting to "speak." In the absence of communication boards and electronic communication devices, I was left to my own ingenuity in finding ways to reach them. My basic problem, however, was the same one that Donna encountered, the same one I've encountered through my whole life: when you can't talk, and people believe that your mind is as handicapped as your body, it's awfully difficult to change their opinion.

My best stretch of time at Belchertown started in the spring of 1966 and lasted about a year. Although my living conditions and treatment remained much worse than anything I had experienced before the State School, the institution hadn't totally numbed me yet. Several improvements on the ward made this an upbeat, almost happy time in my life.

First, the Witch called it quits that spring, and nobody was sorry to see her go. The atmosphere on the ward relaxed considerably once the attendants didn't have to look over their shoulders every two seconds to see if she was about to yell at them. And with the Witch gone, Wessie and Hazel were free to care for me as best as they could.

Whether by coincidence or as a result of the Witch's departure, another nemesis soon disappeared — the Box. Throughout the spring, I spent fewer and fewer afternoons on the big mattress in the Box; by June, nobody was put in it anymore. As with the Witch, I heard no complaints when the Box was wheeled off the ward for good.

Without it, however, the staff had to come up with another alternative to keeping us in bed all the time. Starting that summer, about half the girls on the ward spent their entire day in chairbeds. This development meant two things: a little bit of increased mobility, and a lot of painful screaming.

Most of the chairbeds had small wheels in the back and large, spoked sidewheels that rose about a foot over the bed at the knee. Although this made them easy to move around, the attendants just wheeled us to one end of the ward and parked us there for hours at a stretch. Worse yet, those sidewheels were dangerous. The first time Wessie put me in a chairbed, my knees got all chopped up because I couldn't keep them from sliding into the sidewheels. Fortunately, she stuffed some pillows around my knees before they were completely shredded.

When the other girls on the ward landed in chairbeds, similar mishaps occurred. Hands, legs, and feet repeatedly were nicked and bruised — accompanied by screams of pain — whenever people were moved around the ward. For a while those chairbeds were like so many torture chambers. It took several black-and-blue weeks for the attendants to figure out who needed a pillow here and a strap there to prevent serious injury.

Another big event coincided with the departure of the Witch and the Box and the arrival of chairbeds: *clothes!* Pants, blouses, sweaters, skirts, and even an occasional dress replaced most of the hospital johnnies on the ward. Also, the girls who needed the least assistance in toileting were taken out of diapers. Over the next few years, diapers were phased out for many of the others as well. Unfortunately, and through no fault of my own, I had to wait a while before I finally lost that particular badge of institutional degradation.

Nonetheless, I was ecstatic when I first started wearing real clothes again. With the exception of visits from my family and summer vacations at home, I hadn't been out of a johnny in four years. It didn't bother me that my new clothes were faded and ill-fitting, or that they were as stylish as what you would find at a Salvation Army store.

The clothes came from a general supply that had been gathered from charitable contributions and the personal belongings of the residents over the years. I'm sure that's what happened to the suitcases full of clothes that I brought to Belchertown in 1962 and the various new things Mother sent back with me after my visits home — except, of course, for the blue Christmas dress. An attendant with a young daughter or niece probably took that home.

At first the residents on Ward 3 wore whatever found its way onto their bodies. The attendants couldn't spare the time to co-ordinate our outfits or let us choose for ourselves. Particular items did get sorted out for each resident's use, but we never had individual dressers at the Infirmary. Since everybody's stuff was thrown together in common storage, it was impossible for the attendants to keep our things separate for very long. As a result, I wore something a few times and then it disappeared. This was very frustrating, especially when I lost something that Mother had sent from home.

By the end of the summer, the novelty of wearing clothes began to fade. The ragtag nature of the clothing bothered me more and more. Everything looked, smelled, and felt like the institution, from the "Belchertown State School" stamp on each piece to the hideous colors and combinations of our outfits. Eventually this institutional uniform became almost as exasperating as the johnnies had been.

And there was the annual Thanksgiving ritual. We were dressed up in our institutional Sunday best, and the Commonwealth of Massachusetts treated us to turkey dinner with all the trimmings. It was the best meal of the year, but I never understood why I couldn't go home for Thanksgiving. My parents wrote for permission year after year, but they were refused without explanation every time. Getting all dressed up for turkey day at the State School only reminded me of the good time I was missing at home.

But Thanksgiving 1966 was an exception. The year had gone well, and some good people had entered my life. I became friends with a woman named Roseanne Wroblicki, a registered nurse who had just begun working at the Infirmary. Roseanne was in her early twenties and was very pretty, tall and slender with long, dark, silky hair. She visited our ward daily to check up on the residents. In the course of her rounds, she took an active interest in my health, particularly my diet.

Even though I was eating better after Hazel and Wessie took over feeding me, I was still hovering at a perilously thin thirty-two pounds. Roseanne checked with both Wessie and me about the foods I liked, then made it clear to the new ward supervisor that it was a medical requirement for me to go on a special diet and get plenty of time to eat my meals.

From that point on, Roseanne and I really hit it off, especially after she started to feed me herself a few times a week. Since she was smart enough to take her cues from Wessie, Roseanne picked up on my facial signals and basic communication techniques right away. In a month, she knew me as well as anyone at Belchertown.

Like Wessie, Hazel, Rita, and Carol, Roseanne spoke to me as if I was more than just a heap of flesh and bones. Whenever I saw her, even if only for a quick "Hi, Ruthie" and a smile, Roseanne seemed like a visit from the outside world. She was one of the very few people I encountered at the State School who made me forget where I was just by talking to me. Roseanne didn't limit our conversations to the institution, and she never spoke to me like I was her patient. Hazel and Wessie treated me like a daughter, and they were my Rocks of Gibraltar. But Roseanne, who was only five or six years older than me, treated me like a sister. She improved my health by fattening me up to thirty-nine pounds in her first year at the Infirmary, and as my friend, she boosted my spirits infinitely more.

Throughout 1966 and into 1967, I continued the biweekly sessions of simple stretching exercises. In order even to try them, I needed a steady dosage of muscle relaxants. The pills were crushed and dissolved in a drink, usually pineapple juice, to kill the bitter taste and to make it possible for me to swallow. Fortunately, they worked without any side effects; when my muscles began returning to life, the prescription was ended.

I'm sure that Roseanne's monitoring had a lot to do with my relative success with the drugs. A carefully administered program of medication was by far the exception, not the rule, at the State School. Hundreds of residents were kept drugged so they could be controlled more easily by an overworked staff. I did not see much of this at the Infirmary, however, because almost all of the people there were physically handicapped and fairly immobile. Also, we had medical personnel at the Infirmary, and a much better attendant-resident ratio than most of the other units.

*

The summer of 1966 passed pleasantly, at least by comparison to my prior ones at Belchertown. I made another new friend, a young woman named Mary who was doing volunteer work on the ward. Like Roseanne, Mary was in her early twenties. She worked on the ward for about two years, changing bedsheets, dressing and feeding residents, mopping floors, and doing other routine chores. She frequently fed me and tended to my other physical needs.

It wasn't too long before Mary adopted me as a sort of baby sister. I say "baby" because Mary treated me like I was eight years old, which was about how old I looked. Even so, I appreciated her attention. She treated me like a normal eight-year-old, as opposed to a mindless infant. I couldn't be too picky, because the handful of attendants who treated me like a normal teenager had no spare time to socialize.

One thing about Mary: she was a resident of the State School. There was absolutely nothing wrong with her, mentally or physically. She suffered the misfortune of having been committed to Belchertown by her parents as a "problem child." Mary worked as a "volunteer" to offset the cost of room and board, something that scores of residents were forced to do in order to reimburse the commonwealth for their maintenance.

Some of these "volunteers" were children like Mary who had been dumped at Belchertown because they had emotional problems or their parents couldn't take care of them. Others were borderline retarded people who could, and in many cases later did, function in society with a little assistance and support. Still others were normal adults who grew up at Belchertown because they had been abandoned as children. For them, the State School served as a poorhouse. These "volunteers" constituted what in some ways was a slave labor force for the institution. My friend Mary was fortunate to leave a few years later, and I suspect that she did well on the outside because she was a resilient person. But many others like her never left Belchertown.

There were other positive developments that summer. For the first time since my arrival, I was taken outside for a simple stroll around the grounds. Unfortunately, there weren't enough attendants to make this a regular routine, but I did go out in my chairbed a few times. This may not sound like much, but aside from my annual summer visits home, admiring a blue sky and green grass was a memory of better days. For the past four years, my landscape had consisted of hospital beds, dingy johnnies, diapers, linoleum floors, chairbeds, blank walls, and suffering, neglected faces. The stale air on the ward was loaded with an awful stench and a maddening clatter. Trapped in such an environment, I relished those few moments when I could gaze at the trees waving in the breeze or watch the squirrels run across the grass.

I had been taken outside in previous summers, but never alone. On those occasions, the whole ward had spilled out onto the lawn for the afternoon. All the commotion of coming and going didn't afford much relief for anyone. That's why a solitary stroll outside, even for a few minutes, was a real treat. Once I did get out, I never wanted to return to the ward, but that wasn't an available option.

During this time I made unqualified progress in two areas. One was communication. Even small breakthroughs, like befriending Roseanne and Mary and providing them with a receptive audience for their chitchat and corny jokes, were significant victories.

I also made solid gains with my stretching exercises. My body grew a little stronger with every week of therapy. Unfortunately, I was healthier the day I came to Belchertown than at any time thereafter. But with regular, although limited, exercise, I did regain some muscle tone and flexibility. The better I felt physically, the more my spirits improved.

In March 1967 I got a big lift when the exercise lady said that I might be fitted for leg braces over the summer if my progress continued. Leg braces!

I had spent so many hours with Mother on the floor of our living room, my legs strapped in those heavy metal braces. Long before Belchertown, I realized that I would never walk. Yet the mere suggestion that I could get back into leg braces filled me with optimism. I fantasized that I would miraculously confound the experts and progress from braces to crutches to . . . Well, if Diane Skorupski could walk with the help of braces, why couldn't I?

I knew the answer to this question all too well, but it didn't stop me from getting excited at the prospect of wearing braces again. After more than four years at Belchertown, leg braces had come to symbolize my struggle against not only the physical effects of my handicap but everything that was wrong with the institution.

My spirits continued to soar for the next month or so. Then, on April 14, 1967, all of that changed.

.FLOWER.RED.SPAGHETTI.

It was a Friday, and it started out routinely enough. I woke up as the morning shift was filtering in, and waited quietly while the attendants began their daily routine of changing soiled bedclothes and getting everybody ready for breakfast. An attendant changed my diapers, and a bit later Wessie gave me breakfast in bed, which isn't such a treat when that's how you get every meal. I never was big on breakfast, and it didn't take me long to have my juice and toast. After exchanging a minute's worth of conversation, Wessie went off to feed someone else.

Rosa had been dressing me lately, but she hadn't arrived yet. I watched what was going on with some of the other girls and contemplated yet one more day of lying around in my chairbed. Out of habit, I tried to guess the spot on the ward where I would pass the day.

Rosa showed up about a half-hour later, in a hurry as usual. I was her last chore on the breakfast/dressing detail. Once she got me into some clothes and squared away in my chairbed, she could take her morning coffee break.

I mentioned earlier that Rosa's rough ways had scared me at first. As time went on, her attitude softened and she took a more relaxed approach. But in the past few months she had returned to her old, harsh ways. Carol had overheard several attendants saying that Rosa was getting divorced, and she passed that news on to me. Rosa was treating everyone coldly, not just me. She wasn't even paying much attention to Carol, her favorite.

For that reason, it didn't bother me when Rosa rushed through my stuff without even talking to me. But on this particular morning, she was off in a cloud somewhere. After yanking my nightclothes off, she pushed and pulled me into a faded jersey and a pair of baggy pants. Then she picked me up and dumped me into my chairbed. In the process, my right leg clipped one of the big sidewheels and bent up under my rear end as she set me down. My leg was doubled up like that when I landed.

I cried out as I felt something snap just above my knee. I would have screamed, but the first wave of pain took my breath away. Rosa heard my cry, though, and seeing the problem, quickly untucked my leg. She muttered something like "Sorry, Ruthie" and wheeled me over to the other side of the ward.

My right leg immediately began to throb and ache, and my face must have been the picture of pained surprise. But Rosa didn't notice. She just wheeled me over to join some other girls and went off for her break.

I was very angry at Rosa because of her carelessness, but I knew it had been an accident. So I tried to ignore it, and hoped that the pain would go away.

It didn't. Over the next few hours, the dull aching developed into a sharp, steady throbbing. Whenever an attendant walked by, I made sounds to try to get her attention. But my cries were lost amid the random clatter of the ward.

By the time my friend Mary came by to say hello and feed me

lunch, I was really hurting. Mary took one look at my face and knew that something was terribly wrong. I looked up at her, moaned softly, and looked down at my right leg, a grimace on my face. Mary immediately asked if my leg hurt. Raising my eyes to the ceiling, I replied with a pained "Yes!" I arched my back and shoulders and lifted myself up on my elbows for added emphasis.

Starting around the ankle, Mary began to squeeze my leg lightly and asked me if that's where it hurt. When she reached my knee, I hollered. Mary understood, and asked me if I wanted her to take a look at my knee. I could have kissed her! I quickly responded with an emphatic yes, and Mary carefully rolled my pants down to my ankles.

"Oh my God!"

Mary spoke for both of us as we saw the swollen, discolored skin just above my right knee. Just looking at it made my leg hurt a lot more. Mary checked my face just to make sure it hurt as badly as it appeared it would, and then she ran off to fetch some help.

In a few minutes she returned with Wessie. After one look at my leg, Wessie told Mary to get some ice and a towel. Wessie asked me how this had happened, but Mary came back before she got much out of me. Wessie applied the ice to my leg, told Mary to hold it in place, and then hurried off to find one of the nurses.

A little while later, Wessie returned with Roseanne, who spoke to me in a reassuring but very concerned manner as she examined me. Roseanne said that my leg looked like it was broken. She and Wessie agreed that I needed immediate medical attention, and Roseanne said she was going to call the Infirmary doctor right away. Before she left, she put a pillow under my knee and gave me some pills with pineapple juice for the pain.

Three days later I was taken by ambulance to Wesson Memorial Hospital in Springfield to be treated for a broken leg. The delay wasn't Roseanne's or Wessie's fault. They did everything they could to get me to a real hospital right away. The problem was that I already was in a "hospital" at Belchertown, and the State School's procedures had to be followed before I could be taken off the grounds, even in an emergency.

In order to go to Springfield for medical treatment, I needed the approval of the Infirmary doctor. But on that Friday afternoon he was nowhere to be found. Roseanne tried to find the Infirmary x-ray technicians, but they too had taken off early for the weekend. Without the doctor's approval or an x-ray indicating that the leg was broken, I couldn't leave for treatment; without the doctor's approval, I couldn't go elsewhere for an x-ray.

Roseanne tried desperately on Friday night and Saturday to find the doctor. He finally came to see me on Sunday. Actually, two doctors saw me that day: Dr. Franz, the Infirmary doctor, and Dr. Virginia Kasparyan, the medical supervisor. They agreed that my leg appeared to be broken, but they wanted to be certain. That meant I had to wait still one more day until the x-ray technicians returned and took a picture to show what we had all known for three days.

Once Roseanne realized on Friday afternoon that I wasn't leaving the Infirmary so fast, she moved me into a small room down the hall from the ward. I developed a high fever on Friday night, so they put me on a strong dosage of antibiotics. Along with the painkillers, these kept me floating in and out of a daze until Monday. Roseanne and another nurse, Margaret Clark, tended to me round the clock, but there was little they could do other than apply ice to my leg, prop up the pillows, and feed me pills.

In my lucid moments that weekend, I wondered why I hadn't already been taken to a real hospital. Roseanne and Margaret explained the situation to me, but they really didn't answer my question. I thought the reason they had moved me off the ward into that little room was that I was dying. I couldn't ask any questions, and the people caring for me seemed to be in the dark.

Everything depended on what the doctors said, and they didn't show up until Sunday.

Besides the intense pain and the agonizing wait, one other thing stands clear in my memory of that weekend. At some point on Friday, Wessie asked me how this had happened. She knew that I couldn't have injured myself, that some attendant, maybe Rosa, must have messed up. When she asked me about this, my head was still clear but I acted woozy. For one of the few times in my life, I was glad I couldn't talk.

I didn't want to squeal on Rosa. She was my friend, and I didn't want her to lose her job. It had been an accident, and I was sure she hadn't realized initially how badly I had been hurt.

Why Rosa didn't come forward later and admit her responsibility—even if only to me—is another question altogether. Maybe she never realized it was her fault. Or maybe she sat back and let it slide because nobody confronted her about it. To my knowledge, Wessie was the only one who asked many questions about what had happened.

When the x-ray technicians came into work on Monday morning, they took the picture of my leg. Then I was "rushed" to the hospital in Springfield, where they took another x-ray and promptly put me in a plaster cast that enclosed my right leg, ran up my side, and wrapped around my chest. Once the leg was set in the cast, it felt much, much better.

A few days later I began to feel pain in my left hip. I tried to tell the doctors and nurses about it, but I couldn't communicate with them. Nobody had told them about my facial signals. The nurses didn't know if I was deaf, dumb, or what. The nicer ones spoke to me slowly and loudly, as if this would make it easier for me to understand them. I wanted to tell them that English was my native language and I understood them very well, but I couldn't get that message across. The nurses kept telling each other "I guess she doesn't understand us" while I was flashing my yes expression so hard that my face hurt. Sapped by the ordeal of the past few days and loaded down by the painkillers and other drugs, I couldn't summon the energy to change their minds.

As usual, the doctors couldn't be bothered to let me know what was going on, or even ask me how I was feeling. They just assumed that I was incapable of understanding anything. This has been the story of my life as far as doctors are concerned, and it has usually caused me a lot of grief. This time was no different. The x-rays told the doctors all they needed to know about my leg, but that didn't make it any easier to hear them talk about me as if I weren't even there. It also didn't tell them about my hip.

If the doctors or nurses had only asked me how I was feeling, I would have told them about my hip. A frown and a negative sound would have indicated that I didn't feel well. Then either my eyes or a few intelligent questions would have led them to my hip. But they never asked, and I couldn't tell them without some help.

I remained at Wesson Hospital for two weeks. During that time, Mother came to see me every day. I had little trouble telling her about my sore hip, and I'm sure she told the nurses about it. But as far as I could tell, they never told the doctors, and my hip was simply ignored.

Mother's visits cheered me up enormously. She usually came in the evening so she could feed me dinner. The nurses had given me baby food the first few meals because they didn't know what else to do. Mother informed them that I could eat normal food if they cut it up for me to swallow, and she told the nurses what to prepare for the next day. That turned out to be hit or miss, depending on which nurse worked which shift. Despite Mother's best efforts, I ate a lot of baby food at the hospital.

Mother also told the nurses that I understood everything I saw and heard. I guess they didn't believe her, because none of them made any attempts to talk to me. She told them to brush my teeth regularly, but they ignored her on that one too. Since I enjoy dragon-mouth as little as anyone else, I was glad that Mother remembered to brush my teeth when she visited me.

My parents knew from my 1966 Christmas visit that things had finally begun to improve for me at Belchertown. They had been told by the physical therapist that I might be getting back into leg braces soon, and they shared my excitement over this prospect. When they learned that I was in the hospital in Springfield with a broken leg, they were shocked.

Since I was extremely weak from the ordeal, their initial concern was for my survival. As my condition stabilized and then slowly began to improve, my parents became increasingly angry. Not only were they upset about the injury, but they were furious that no one at the State School could, or would, tell them how it had happened.

When Mother asked me about it, I told her that it had been an accident caused by a careless attendant and that no, I absolutely would not divulge her name. As with Wessie back at Belchertown, I saw no good coming from telling Mother about Rosa. Besides, it would have been an extremely difficult message to express, because Mother didn't know the attendants' names.

My parents never did find out about Rosa. The authorities at the State School told them even less than I did. Once Mother understood that I was covering up for someone because I liked her, not because I was afraid of her, she gave up trying to pry the name out of me.

Before I left the hospital in Springfield, the doctors decided to operate on my leg. They didn't think it would mend properly in the first cast, so they cut that one off. Then they took me into surgery, inserted three screws in the bone to fuse the break, and put me in a second cast that enveloped my body from chest to toe. This cast relieved the pain in my left hip, for which I was grateful. Otherwise, I hated that thing. I felt like I had been stuffed inside a plaster box. They cut out a hole around my rear end for toilet purposes, and they also inserted a catheter, which irritated me even more than the cast.

On May 1, 1967, one week after the operation, I returned to the Infirmary. The attendants moved my bed to the end of Ward 3, next to their station, so they could keep a close eye on me. This turned out to be a smart move, because within a few days I was running a fever of 104 degrees and was placed on the Infirmary's critical list. I stayed on that list for the next fifteen months.

The dangerous fever broke after several weeks, but I remained feverish and weak for the three months I was in the body cast. It was a nightmare. July was especially bad; the sticky summer heat and dead air of the ward were twice as unbearable in that plaster sweatsuit, and the catheter continued to bother me.

I was a physical and emotional wreck. My body was broken and weak, and my spirits were being roasted by the heat and the fever. My appetite, which had never been robust at Belchertown, virtually disappeared. After five years at the State School, which had ranged from dreadful to nearly tolerable, I concluded that the harder I tried to improve my lot, the worse it got. For the first time in my life, I was totally without hope.

If possible, I would have overdosed on pills or slashed my wrists to end the misery. But I couldn't even ask someone to do it for me! I was trapped in a body without a voice, wrapped up in a plaster box, confined to a ward behind brick walls and iron gates, and surrounded by wardmates whose mental infirmities compounded their physical impairments. There seemed to be only one way out for me, and that was off the deep end.

But I didn't take that route, and I know why. My father used to describe himself as "two hundred pounds of tough Polack." Although I was only a thirty-five pound chip off the old block, I had enough of that tough Polack in me to survive that perilous summer with my sanity intact.

I might not have made it, however, without the special attention I received from my friends. Wessie, Hazel, Rita, Mary, and others gave me extra encouragement, even though they were continually behind in caring for everyone else on the ward. When Wessie observed through the hole in my cast that my lower back was irritated, someone brought in lamb's wool and stuffed it up against the cast, so the lanolin would soothe my skin. And my friends showed their concern by frequently stopping by to make small talk, or to prop up my pillows.

Even so, my real lifesavers were the two nurses at the Infirmary, Roseanne Wroblicki and Margaret Clark. They gave me the large doses of tender care and pampering that no doctor ever prescribed for me but that were so essential for my survival. Roseanne and Margaret had pulled me through that dangerous weekend when I was stuck in the Infirmary waiting to be x-rayed, and when I returned from the hospital in Springfield, they picked up where they had left off. Since I was on the critical list, it was their job to monitor my physical condition and satisfy my medical needs, either by themselves or with whatever help they could get from the attendants. They performed this task quite well, but more important — most important — they treated me with respect, consideration, and gentleness, very rare commodities at the State School.

Roseanne and Margaret quickly became my closest friends. They recognized my desire to communicate with them and actually gave me the chance to do so. Roseanne read Mother's letters to me. They were warm, caring letters, and that's how Roseanne read them, whereas some of the attendants read the letters as if they were grocery lists. Recognizing my strong ties to my family, Roseanne asked me many questions about them. From Mother's letters and my answers, she developed a good understanding of my background and upbringing.

Both Roseanne and Margaret provided me with many opportunities to answer their questions. As a result, I did much more "talking" that summer than at any time before at Belchertown. For the first time at the State School, two staff people regularly engaged me in extended conversations that concerned more than whether my pillows needed adjusting or the soup was too hot. Although I did suffer from severe fits of depression, the damage was limited by the genuine concern of my two nurses. I dread to think what might have happened if Roseanne and Margaret hadn't been there.

One day, while I was still in the mummy cast, Margaret told me that Theresa Ladue said hi and wanted to know how I was doing.

I was stunned. I thought none of the staff had observed that Theresa and I had been friends. We had never hidden the fact, but there were lots of things the staff never noticed because they simply never looked. But Margaret was different. She had been talking about me to an attendant on Theresa's ward, and Theresa overheard the conversation and reacted to it. Margaret noticed her interest. By asking Theresa the right questions, Margaret discovered that we had lived side by side on Ward 4.

I was very impressed, and grateful. Although Theresa lived only a hundred feet down the hall, it might as well have been across the ocean for all we had seen or heard of each other in the four years since I had left Ward 4. By acting as a messenger between Theresa and me, Margaret helped to reestablish our friendship. She told the attendants on both wards about us, and pretty soon Theresa and I were chatting with each other again.

The key to my ongoing contact with Theresa was Hazel Ritter, who spent a great deal of time with me during the winter of 1967–1968. Hazel's sister, Chris Boswaite, worked on Theresa's ward. With some sisterly collusion, Theresa and I met in the corridor, looked into each other's eyes, talked with sounds, facial expressions, and body language, and shared our lives for a few minutes each week.

Oddly enough, I went outside more often when I was in the mummy cast than during any of my previous summers at Belchertown. Two or three times a month the attendants carted our ward, and sometimes another ward, out for an afternoon of fresh air. Nothing felt as good when I was in that cast as sitting under a shade tree in a cool late-afternoon breeze.

Since I couldn't take my summer week of vacation at home that year, my family came to visit me a few extra times. Each time I met them out in front of the Infirmary; parental inspection of the wards still was not encouraged. At this point that was fine with me, because it gave me more chances to get outside. My folks brought Marie, Shari, and Howard with them, and Mother turned the occasions into family picnics, bringing delicious home-made goodies to eat. Gramma Ruth even came to one of these gatherings.

.TALK.BOX.TALK.EAR.

While I was in the mummy cast, I was also treated to many visits from Wessie's teenage daughter, Mary Lou. I had met Mary Lou earlier that year, several months before my leg was broken. She and Gena Hildred, whose mother, Yvonne, also worked at the Infirmary, came by the ward one Saturday after-noon looking for Wessie. The girls, both about thirteen years old, wanted to tell Wessie they were going out for a walk. When they couldn't find her, they left the message with an attendant who was propping me up in my chairbed. The attendant introduced us, we chatted for a while, and then the girls left — but not before Mary Lou promised she would come back the next day to visit.

I was very impressed with both Gena and Mary Lou. They had been dropping by the State School for about a year, but this was the first time either one had walked onto a ward at the Infirmary. They weren't supposed to be there, because only staff and resi-dents were allowed on the wards. But the girls didn't gawk or stare at anyone; they didn't act afraid or hesitant; they didn't giggle nervously. When we were introduced, they said, "Hi, nice to meet you," and started right in talking to me like I was a class-mate. It was the first time I had felt like a "normal" person in five years.

After our introduction, Mary Lou kept her promise and re-turned to see me the next day. She visited me three or four more times before my leg was broken, but when I was in the mummy cast, she saw me every weekend and also came by on an occasional weekday after school.

Mary Lou was quiet at first, but after we got to know each other, she gradually opened up and became very outgoing. Mary Lou shared her fantasies with me. We dreamed out loud about romance, movie stars, and all of the wonderful and exciting things we would do when we grew up. By the way she confided in me and invited me to fantasize along with her, Mary Lou reminded me very much of Shari, who was the same age.

Mary Lou was my best friend at the State School in the years after my leg was broken. She was always interested in finding out what was on my mind. Gena, in contrast, was a delightful chatterbox. Listening to her talk was like watching a live soap opera. Gena also visited me during this time, although not as frequently as Mary Lou.

These two young women provided me with a sense of what "normal" teenage girls thought, said, and did together. I really missed out on being a teenager by living at Belchertown all those years, but my contact with Mary Lou and Gena at least helped me learn what I was missing.

On August 14, Dr. Virginia Kasparyan, whom we all called Dr. Virginia, visited me on the ward and told me that it was time to remove the cast. This made me very excited, but my excitement soon turned to terror when she plugged a little power saw into the wall outlet and proceeded to cut the cast off my body. I imagine that almost anyone would find the thought of another person running a power saw within a half-inch of her body scary. For me, it was positively terrifying.

My lifelong physical immobility has made me wary of things that most people ignore, such as a sudden movement in my direction by a fly, or an unexpected sound. If someone so much as snaps his fingers behind me, I jump up in my wheelchair. You can well imagine, then, how I felt watching Dr. Virginia slicing away at my cast with that little saw. She could have cut my toes off and I wouldn't have been able to move my foot away, although I would have felt the pain as intensely as anyone else. Luckily, she had me out of that cast in a few minutes without a scratch.

Even stranger than having the cast cut off was seeing my legs and stomach for the first time in over three months. After the cast was gone, my knees were propped up on some pillows. I examined my legs. The skin was dried out and flaky, and felt tingly and prickly in the open air. This worried me at first, but I was reassured that this would clear up in a few weeks, and that's exactly what happened.

It was quite a relief to be freed from that cast. My body was immediately cooler, and my constant bouts with the fever disappeared as soon as that damned catheter was removed. My right leg, the broken one, didn't feel too bad, but both of my knees hurt for the next few months. They didn't begin to feel right until the following spring.

Most of my discomfort, however, came from my left hip, which had continually throbbed in the cast. It started hurting a lot more after the cast was removed, but I didn't see any discoloration there. It really acted up on rainy days; otherwise, I tolerated it fairly well. As with the aching in my knees, I thought the hip problem was only a painful side effect of being in the cast for so long. I assumed from its on-again, off-again nature that one day the pain would go away for good.

Despite these physical problems, my spirits improved throughout the fall of 1967. One big reason was the cementing of my friendship with Diane Skorupski. Although she was still helping out on our ward, particularly with her blind friend, I hadn't seen much of her in the months before I broke my leg. She was busy filing and typing in the Infirmary office, and although we were still friends, we had drifted apart since the days of the Bob fan club.

My accident changed that, however. Diane typed up some of the reports about my broken leg for the Infirmary records, and she visited me right after I returned from the hospital in the mummy cast. She saw that I was in desperate straits, and immediately devoted most of her spare time to me. She continually tried to keep me out of the doldrums, feeding me lunch and good conversation several times a week and dropping by for an after-dinner chat nearly every evening. She kept to this routine faithfully for about a year, until the following spring.

During this period, Diane really came out of her shell. Like Margaret and some of my other shy friends, she used me as a sounding board. I couldn't have been happier. Diane had been at the top of my list ever since I had met her, and as a result of our revived friendship, we grew closer than ever. Once I was liberated from the cast and on the road to recovery, I no longer saw Roseanne or Margaret that often. Diane picked up the slack. She took over the job of reading my letters from home, and like Roseanne, she became acquainted with my family in the process.

.ON.FACE.EYE.POCKETBOOK.

Near the end of 1967, Diane and I began a routine that helped break up the monotony on the ward. Just about every day after she fed me lunch, she put makeup on my face. This treatment usually consisted of lipstick, eyeliner, and eye shadow. I loved it because it made me feel like a normal teenage girl. Occasionally we got silly and Diane painted my face with gaudy rouge and bright red lipstick.

Diane also told me about her frustrations in living at Belchertown. She was determined to leave the State School and develop a life for herself on the outside. I shared this dream, and Diane was the first person I talked to at Belchertown about living and working in the real world like a normal adult. For years I had set my sights on returning to live with my parents in Springfield. Now I began to think in terms of leaving the State School for a home of my own. Diane was much further along with this concept than I was, but hearing her talk about the independent life she would lead quickly convinced me that this should become my goal as well.

.C.H.A.R.

By November 1967 I was feeling much better, both physically and emotionally. The recurrent fever was gone, my appetite had improved, and I began to gain some weight. The old chairbeds were gone too, replaced by wooden-framed wheelchairs with metal wheels. The back of my new chair came up over my head in an arch. Since it basically was an unpadded wooden board, the first time I sat in it I felt like I was strapped to the wing of an old airplane.

The chair had foot rests, and with some pillows stuffed under and around my arms and knees, I could sit upright. Even though my knees and hip were still hurting, sitting in the wheelchair was better than lying on my back in bed. My endurance improved steadily, and by the end of the year I was spending several hours a day in the wheelchair. This made my hip hurt more, but since I wanted to get out of bed as much as possible, I did my best to ignore the pain.

Sitting in the wheelchair also enabled me to take better advantage of the new social program on the ward: television. Shortly after I returned from the hospital in May, a TV set was placed on a table at the end of the ward near my bed. It quickly became the focal point of most of the residents' lives.

The attendants laid four mattresses on the floor in front of the TV for the benefit of the girls who couldn't sit in wheelchairs. Up to a dozen residents occupied the mattresses for a morning or afternoon of viewing. They encountered the same problems I had experienced in the Box: the thrashers and rollers wreaked havoc on the more passive viewers, despite the staff's best efforts to separate people with pillow walls. An attendant had to keep a constant watch on the mattress audience and untangle the mess when one of the thrashers got going.

Since my bed was nearby, I missed very little of the action on, and in front of, the tube. I passed many evenings in the fall of 1967 this way, usually in the company of Diane Skorupski. It was easier to watch from my wheelchair, and I gradually joined nearly everyone on the ward in huddling around the television for most of our waking hours.

At first, watching TV was a huge improvement over the monotony of the ward. It opened a window to the outside world, letting in a variety of people, places, sounds, cars, game shows, music, soap operas, commercials, and news. It was a great diversion for a while, but as most people realize, watching television for many hours on end, day in and day out, tends to numb your brain, like taking large doses of tranquilizers on a regular basis. Still, it was impossible for me not to watch it for six, seven, even eight hours a day. There was nothing else to do. The State School used television very much like it used drugs.

My favorite shows were the soap operas. I had been hooked on soaps when I was ten years old, living at home in Springfield. Watching them again was like being reunited with a bunch of dear old friends after a five-year separation. For many years thereafter, the soap world made up a large part of my real world, much more so than my actual surroundings. At a time when I was starving for social stimulation and development, the soaps fed my needs. For both diversion and survival, I eagerly plunged into *The Edge of Night*, *As The World Turns*, and *The Days of Our Lives*, and although I knew they were melodramatic, I remained in the soap world long after the programs ended each day. I became a regular occupant of that landscape — walking, talking, kissing, conniving, laughing, and crying with the rest of the characters.

By early 1968 I was definitely one of the TV crowd, parked in my wheelchair in front of the set every day. It was painless enough until somebody got the bright idea of "socializing" me with the girls on the mattresses. I was laid on my back on the outside mattress, my head propped up on a pillow. A wall of pillows to my left was supposed to provide a barricade against unwanted visits from my neighbors. Nonetheless, I feared that someone was going to crash into me at any moment. I hated lying down there. It was cold and drafty, and once again I was being treated like a baby.

My fear, discomfort, and bruised ego lasted about three days, until Roseanne walked by and spotted me on the mattress. I caught her eye and shot her an exasperated look, accompanied by a high-pitched whine that pleaded for her assistance. She didn't say anything to me then, but she must have said something to someone, because I was watching TV from my wheelchair the next day. Roseanne stopped by a few days later and told me she was glad to see me back in my chair. From the wink she gave me, I knew that I wouldn't have to worry about going on the mattresses again. Roseanne had helped me out of a real pickle, because those mattresses remained on the ward until 1973, when the whole Infirmary was reorganized.

.LEG.SORE.

In the summer of 1968, I began using a conventional metal wheelchair. The attendants continued to stuff the chair with pillows, towels, and rolled-up blankets to pad it and to keep me upright. The new wheelchair was truly mobile, unlike the wooden chairs. For the first time at Belchertown, I was taken outside for walks several times a week, a brief but welcome relief from the television syndrome on the ward. In the evening I returned to my old wooden chair for sitting around and doing nothing.

Perhaps as a result of spending so much more time in the wheelchair, the pain in my left hip grew worse over the summer. I repeatedly tried to tell Wessie about this, but I couldn't get the message across. We kept having the same conversation. Wessie would come by and ask me how I was feeling, and I would give her a sour expression, usually accompanied by a pained sound.

She then would ask me if my leg was bothering me, and I would indicate yes and then no, because I knew she was referring to my right leg, the broken one, but I wanted to draw her attention to my hip. She took my mixed response to mean either that I was having only a little trouble with the broken leg or that it hurt more than usual. For some reason, her usually sharp ability to read my mind failed when it came to the problem with my hip. Unfortunately, I had no better success in communicating my plight to anyone else on the ward, and I spent an extremely frustrating summer of suffering in unwanted secrecy.

One rainy night in September, the pain in my hip kept me awake all night. My broken leg, which hadn't bothered me for some time, decided to act up too. I became very angry over the whole situation, and determined to redouble my efforts to communicate the problem to someone.

I tried and tried, but nothing changed. Every time I attempted to tell someone about my hip, she just assumed I wanted to tell her something about my leg. This inability to communicate was like a repeating nightmare, and it made the physical pain worse. I spent many nights crying myself to sleep, trying to forget my emotional and physical distress by dreaming of walking alone in a meadow full of spring flowers.

It wasn't until October 1969, when I resumed physical therapy, that my hip problem was finally discovered. The therapist was a young woman named Joan, who was in her early twenties and new to the State School. She started me with light stretching of my arms and legs, but in the very first session she observed that any motion of my legs caused severe pain. She knew that I had broken my right leg above the knee, but she also knew that it had healed well and that it shouldn't be so sensitive to very simple movement. By asking a few simple questions while she manipulated my legs — "Does it hurt when I do this? Does it hurt here?" — she was able to pinpoint the problem in short order.

I was elated. Wessie was informed immediately, and her first question to me was why I hadn't told her before. From my exasperated response, and a few follow-up questions, Wessie finally understood that I had been trying to tell her for nearly a year and a half.

Within a day or two, the Infirmary doctor examined my hip and pronounced with great authority that it was sore. He ordered no x-rays, and no changes were made in my routine, other than to cancel physical therapy and prop another pillow under my hip when I was in the wheelchair. The extra padding, along with gentler handling, relieved my discomfort a little, and I felt much better emotionally now that my unwanted secret was known. But I was very angry, although not surprised, that the Infirmary doctor didn't do a thing to help me. The pain didn't go away as a result of one more pillow and his neglect.

On May 5, 1970, I was again admitted to Wesson Memorial Hospital in Springfield, this time for the scheduled removal of the three screws from my leg. I was given a local anaesthetic in the operating room, so I was half-awake during the procedure. I remember feeling cold all over from the anaesthetic. It was very strange to watch the doctor remove the screws from my leg. It seemed like it took only a few seconds, but the operation actually lasted about thirty minutes. (I know this because I watched the clock in the operating room.)

Although no one paid attention to my hip at this time, the surgeon who removed the hardware discovered that my right leg had grown a bit longer than my left leg. He told me that this was because of the calcium pills I had been taking to help the bone heal. I concluded that this fact, along with sitting in uncomfortable, badly supported positions in different wheelchairs for three years, had caused my hip problem.

Another unwanted and extremely disappointing result of this uneven leg growth was that all ideas of refitting me with leg braces were permanently abandoned. While this too came as no surprise, it did dash my remaining slim hope of fully recovering from my broken leg and eventually improving my physical condition.

The book on my hip was pretty much closed in December 1971. A new doctor had begun working part-time at the Infirmary, moonlighting, I believe, from a regular medical practice on the outside. I think that because he worked in the real world, not just at Belchertown, this doctor actually knew something about medicine. After examining me in response to my continuing complaints, he suspected a dislocated hip. He ordered x-rays to see about a possible operation. I'm not sure what the x-rays showed — nobody ever told me — but the surgery was never recommended. The doctor did prescribe Darvon to alleviate the pain, which helped. At least I was able to sleep better, although I disliked the side effects of the drug. It made me feel spacy, and time seemed both to slow down and to speed up, all at once. I was happy when the dosage was reduced so that I could get some relief from the pain without becoming totally disoriented.

My hip improved with better padding and better care, so that by early 1973 I no longer needed the painkillers on a regular basis. Occasionally I took a pill to help me sleep, but mostly I just accepted the pain as another fact of my physical life.

In 1967–1968, there had been a small but significant increase in the staff at the Infirmary. This meant that there were almost enough attendants to tend to the basic physical needs of the residents. I think this was why they started phasing out diapers and began dressing us in clothes. There was a similar staff increase in 1970. Again, this translated into better direct care for the residents. I benefited at this time by getting out of diapers — at the age of twenty. But as with everything else at Belchertown, change came slowly, and they kept me in diapers at night until early 1972.

Another noticeable improvement in 1970 was the quality of the food. Almost overnight, the food changed from repulsive to tolerable. The standard menu stayed the same — chicken and rice, watered-down chicken soup, hot dogs, hamburgers, pork, and fish and potatoes every Friday. But all of a sudden I no longer had to force myself to eat for sustenance. I even started to look forward to some of the meals.

SCHOOL.HOWARD.

As important and welcome as these changes were, they were insignificant compared to one other development at this time: I started school.

Our teacher was Howard Shane, a recent college graduate who was new to the State School. Although some of the verbal residents at the Infirmary, like Carol Muse, had been receiving basic education for some time, Howard was the first person at Belchertown to teach nonverbal residents. Our class started in December 1969, in one of the small rooms off the hallway between the wards. There were six other girls in the class, most of them from Ward 3.

The first class was quite memorable. One of my classmates, a retarded girl who was about sixteen years old and confined to a wheelchair, caused a commotion by taking off her clothes. That was her last day in the class. The rest of us continued, meeting for one hour on four mornings a week.

Two of my other classmates, Carol Muse and Marie Dionne, could talk. Carol, of course, was one of my first friends at the Infirmary, and our friendship stayed pretty constant. She was bright and vigorous, and despite our surroundings, she remained perfectly normal from the waist up. In contrast, "normal" is not the word to describe Marie Dionne. She too was bright and fully verbal, but she suffered from spina bifida, and was handicapped by a severely hydrocephalic head and an accompanying inability to sit upright. She stayed in a chairbed most of the time, with the back raised for support.

Despite her extreme physical disability, Marie had a lively personality. She was about ten years old, and like everyone else I knew with spina bifida, she had pretty useless legs, but her hands and arms functioned perfectly. She had no trouble feeding herself, and was able to read and write by herself in our class.

A few months after school started, Marie's leg was broken on the ward in an accident similar to mine. She attended classes for a while with her leg in a cast. I certainly could identify with what she went through on that score, although luckily for her, she didn't experience as many problems from the break as I did. In that respect, she was better off for having no feeling in her legs.

Howard Shane was faced with an unusual group of students, but after that bizarre first day, we settled down to business. He worked with us on both a group and an individual basis. I started on the fundamentals—the alphabet, rudimentary spelling, and simple arithmetic. Although I had mastered these skills at Crotched Mountain, I had grown rusty during my eight years at Belchertown.

Fortunately, my mind hadn't atrophied from inactivity like my arms and legs. From the outset I was thrilled about being in a classroom again, especially with Howard. He never got hung up on our physical infirmities in relating to us and teaching us. Instead, he asked questions and actually listened to our answers, reading our faces and our eyes when necessary, or taking cues from the sounds we made. Howard very quickly came to understand the particular nonverbal language that each one of us nontalkers used. He was gentle and patient, and never patronized any of us.

Howard was also our zealous advocate. He regularly challenged the Infirmary and State School administrators—but not the direct-care staff—about our overall treatment as well as our educational needs. He sharply criticized the lack of activities and social interaction for the residents of the Infirmary.

I never doubted that I was capable of benefiting from a complete education, and Howard felt this way about me too. Moreover, he believed that with professional training and hard work, I could communicate my thoughts to others well beyond my yes-or-no facial expressions.

Although I wholeheartedly agreed with Howard's progressive ideas, much of the staff at the Infirmary and nearly all of the administrators at the State School did not. Our class met with Howard regularly until the summer of 1970, when he returned to college to work on an advanced degree in speech disorders. I'm sure that his constant battles with the administration had something to do with his return to school. I'm also sure that when he left that summer, many of the people in charge at Belchertown breathed a sigh of relief.

About a month after Howard left, I was moved to Ward 2, on the other side of the Infirmary. The reason for the move was never explained to me, but it didn't matter much. The staff was the same, and the residents on Ward 2 were all women, most of them physically handicapped and many of them mentally retarded as well, just as on Ward 3. I still watched television for many hours at the same location between the wards, and I saw my same group of friends just as frequently. All in all, the move was insignificant.

Fortunately, our school sessions continued after Howard's departure. Our new teacher was a young man named John, who picked up where Howard left off. Although he lacked Howard's sparkle, he applied the same dedication and progressive approach to his teaching. With his help, I continued to make progress in learning how to read and spell simple words.

Our group continued working with John until May 1971, when the class abruptly ended. As with so many other things at the State School, we were never told why. One day we went to class; the next day we didn't.

Interestingly enough, someone at the Infirmary decided to try occupational therapy for me several months later, in August. I don't know why the activity was called "occupational" therapy;

it consisted of trying to teach me to feed myself with an oversized spoon and fork. I hadn't been able to master this simple physical skill eleven years earlier at Crotched Mountain, when my hands and arms had been much stronger and more flexible. Not surprisingly, my occupational therapy was abandoned after four months of sporadic and futile attempts to learn the impossible.

7

In 1970 a man named Ed Hebert began the Speech, Hearing, and Learning Center at the State School. His goal was to help the residents develop their communication skills. He worked alone at first, with no staff, no funds, and no equipment. At this time the institution had about 1200 residents, almost all of whom suffered from some kind of speech, hearing, or learning impairment.

Within a year or so, a group called the Friends of Belchertown, consisting mainly of parents and relatives of residents, began to pressure the authorities to improve conditions at the State School. As a result of this and similar pressure from other groups in the early 1970s, Ed's program really took off. He was provided with funds to hire several professional speech therapists in the spring of 1971. That summer, four graduate students in speech pathology, including my former teacher, Howard Shane, joined the program. In the fall, three undergraduates started as student interns, and Ed became the director of the Communication Disorders Clinic. Although hundreds of people at Belchertown had serious hearing problems, the clinic had no money to outfit residents with hearing aids; it didn't receive funds for conducting hearing tests until 1972 and even then the first funding came from the Friends of Belchertown.

By the fall of 1974, the program was again renamed, becoming the Communication Resource Center. These name changes reflected the evolving sophistication in the new field of communication disorders. The clinic had grown to a full-time staff of ten speech pathologists, a similar number of graduate and undergraduate interns, plus two supervisors and a new director, Lissa Carroll, who had begun as a student intern with Ed in 1972.

Soon after it started, the clinic became the highlight of my existence at the State School. With its help, my communication skills took huge leaps forward, especially in the first several years.

I began in the summer of 1971, when Howard Shane returned to the State School as an intern. Almost immediately Howard began working with me at the clinic. Another graduate student, Kathy Elias, also worked with us on a regular basis.

It was great to see Howard again, and even better to concentrate on an individualized program aimed at developing my communication skills. I met with Howard or Kathy twice a week for sixty-to-ninety-minute sessions. Weather permitting, I was taken to the clinic building, which was very different from anywhere else at the institution. The atmosphere was dynamic, charged with the energy and optimism of young professionals who were at the forefront of a new field.

I wasn't treated like a State School resident at the clinic, nor was I considered a patient or even a client. Howard, Kathy, and I were participants in an ongoing experiment. We were partners in discovering what worked and what didn't in developing the most usable and unlimited communication techniques possible for the verbally disabled.

When I started going to the clinic, I could spell one-syllable words. For example, Kathy would ask me how to spell a word, and I would signal with my eyes or a sound to choose the letters as she ran her finger across an alphabet chart. At first Howard and Kathy taught me graphemes from the initial teaching alphabet (ITA). This system is made up of forty-four graphemes, one for each sound in the English language. They believed that mastering the ITA would make it easier for me to learn how to read and spell. Later, in the fall of 1972, they switched back to the regular alphabet, and we began to work intensively on my "sounding out" and spelling words.

Although I tried very hard, progress came slowly, and I became very frustrated at times. It's difficult to learn how to spell when you can't talk or write, when you can't feel the sound of the words coming out of your mouth, can't watch the letters take shape on paper at the point of your pen or pencil. I could only sound out the letters in my head and write them out longhand in my mind. As a result, I had a tough time spelling words that used different letters but sounded alike. Words such as "bin" and "been," or "pain" and "pane," or "seen" and "scene," or "cuff" and "cough," were very difficult for me to master. Likewise, I had trouble with the vowels *a, e,* and *i,* and the letter *y,* and all the different forms these sounds take on paper.

The concept of the ITA was great for someone with my physical limitations. The idea was to teach me the basic sound combinations that were the building blocks of words, without confusing me with the numerous variations these sounds take in different spellings. But I couldn't say the graphemes or the sounds out loud, and I later became confused between the graphemes and the actual spelling of particular words.

Unfortunately, I was never able to overcome this confusion and generate anywhere near the number of words that most people can write out accurately. If I could have stuck with the ITA, I might have been okay. But written English does not follow the regularity of the forty-four graphemes of the ITA. To this day, the only way I can read or produce words is the old-fashioned way — I memorize them!

.PIE.LIGHTS.HAND.WATCH.SMALL.WATER.

In the spring of 1971, I tried out my first communication board. Kathy and Howard developed it for me at Ed Hebert's urging. It consisted of the ITA graphemes and pictures of about ten items (food, drink, clothing, a happy face, a sad face). With Howard holding the board in front of me, I selected a particular picture by directing him with my eyes and my yes-or-no expressions. Once he recognized the item, he could ask me questions for further details. (I selected the graphemes by a similar process, but we used these only for spelling practice.)

Compared to the boards I use now, which have five sides with over 1800 words and phrases, that first board was quite primitive. But it was a radical breakthrough at the time, both for me and for the State School — and as far as I know, for severely communication-disabled people everywhere.

At the same time I also began experimenting with an automated communication device that Howard developed with help from several electrical engineers at the University of Massachusetts. He called it "the expressor." It was a wooden box, two feet high by two feet wide, with a circle of forty alternating red and green lights on the front. Howard made up circular templates out of cardboard to stick inside the ring of lights. The templates were divided into quadrants, within which there were anywhere from four to forty pie-shaped sections.

When the expressor was in operation, the lights flashed on and off in sequence around the ring. If I wanted to choose a particular section of the template, I raised my forearm, which triggered a mercury switch attached to a band on my wrist. By tripping the switch, I stopped the flashing sequence at a particular bulb, hopefully in the section I had chosen. My teacher could then see my selection, and we proceeded accordingly. When I raised my forearm and triggered the switch again, the expressor resumed flashing the lights around the circle.

The first template I used was composed of eight pictures showing basic messages — a smile, a frown, a TV, musical notes, a plate of food, a pitcher and glass, and a bathroom. (I know that's only seven; I've forgotten the other one.) We used it to learn how to operate the expressor on a fundamental level, and it worked quite well. It was exciting for me to produce messages, even such simple ones, without anyone's assistance.

Our work with the expressor became more challenging when we began using templates with some of the symbols of the ITA. We began with four sections, and soon worked up to sixteen of the total of forty-four symbols. At that point we had only four lights flashing within each section (there were forty lights on the expressor), and the timing of operating the switch became a definite problem, even when the machine was turned down to its slowest speed.

After several months Howard began operating the switch for me. He would sit behind the machine, facing me and unable to see the template, and take the cue from my eye signals to hit the switch. This solved the basic operational problem, but it also took away one of the best aspects of the expressor — my ability to operate it myself.

We stopped working with the expressor in the spring of 1972. Our work with it was more experimental than anything else. Fourteen years later I began operating a computerized communication device by using a headswitch to select words and phrases on the screen, which the computer stored and later "spoke" aloud at my command. In 1987 I began working with a new device that allowed me to construct phrases based on a limited number of symbols I patched into a computer with a headswitch; these phrases also are spoken aloud by the computer.

Although Howard's device was crude by the standards of such microcomputers, it was revolutionary for 1971. My electronic machines today are state-of-the-art, but their basic premise is the same as Howard's light-bulb-and-wood expressor. The common goal is communication, with technology that enables me to use my limited physical powers to overcome my handicaps.

Howard wrote his master's thesis at the U. Mass. Speech Department based on his work with me and Ron Benoit, another resident at the Infirmary with similar disabilities. Not surprisingly, he went on to a Ph.D. in speech pathology and has worked for years at the Children's Medical Center in Boston — and he helped develop the computer software I have been using in the late 1980s.

Howard left Belchertown for good in September 1972. I was very sorry to see him go. He taught me a lot during the years we worked together, and we became very good friends. But his most important contribution was to reawaken my pre-Belchertown belief that I could overcome my physical limitations by hard work and education.

In February 1973 the Infirmary was completely reorganized. All of the ambulators were moved to the four upstairs wards, and all of the people in wheelchairs came downstairs. On the first floor, Wards 3 and 4 were female, Ward 1 was male, and Ward 2 became coed, with kids and young adults. I stayed on Ward 2.

When the wards were reorganized, the staff finally got rid of the mattresses in front of the TV set. The younger kids had been wasting away on those things for years, and it was quite an improvement for them to be able to sit in wheelchairs throughout the day.

During June and July, my communication therapy lapsed. It resumed in August with a new speech therapist, Donna Einfurer, and two women named Chris — Chris Dendor and Chris Ramsey. Both Chrises had recently started working at the State School as Boltwood volunteers; this was a student-run program that placed college students as interns with the Communication Resource Center.

Donna was an innovative teacher, at times quite dynamic. She was quieter and more reserved than Howard, and sort of old-fashioned in her attitudes. She definitely was not a feminist, for example. Her approach to working with me was matter-of-fact, and she expected me to work hard during our sessions. We enjoyed a good relationship, because I usually did just that. But

Donna never took the time just to chat with me, and although she was very sensitive to my speech problems, she was slow to realize that my emotional outlook sometimes affected my ability to work. As a result, I wasn't as inspired by her as I was by Howard and some of the other therapists with whom I developed a friendship.

Probably because they were more outgoing and interested in me as a person, I grew closer to the two Chrises. Chris Ramsey had light brown hair, was short, and was very extroverted and opinionated. Chris Dendor also was short and opinionated. She was exactly my age, wore glasses, and kept her dark hair cropped. Chris D. had a great sense of humor, and her moods changed quickly and dramatically. She was a strong advocate of the women's movement, and in the course of our discussions I became increasingly enthusiastic about it too. Like many of my other attendants and teachers, before and since, Chris D. openly shared her thoughts and feelings with me. More unusually, though, she viewed communication with me as a two-way process, and she gave me plenty of opportunities to express myself.

I worked with both Chrises, and with Donna, on basic spelling and sight reading. About a month after we started working together, Donna showed up with a new word board for me to use on the ward. She had developed it under the supervision of Ed Hebert, with help from my two interns. Although I was excited about having a communication device for everyday purposes, I was annoyed that I hadn't been involved at all in its formulation. But that feeling passed quickly as I learned how to use it.

The board was very basic, consisting of about thirty words, including *mom, dad, sister, radio, TV, toilet, home, money, food, drink, foot, arm, eye, finger, fingernail, elbow, nose, lips, leg,* and *head.* We operated it just like the first communication board. My helper held it in front of me, and by giving directions with my eyes and facial expressions, I indicated what I wanted to communicate.

This second board, my first real word board, made a great impact on my life. In addition to using it in my training sessions, I used it on the ward with some of the staff—Wessie, several of the nurses, even Rosa. Although it was limited, it opened up a whole new breadth of communication for me. It was especially helpful for little things, like telling someone I was thirsty or that I needed to use the bathroom.

Most of the staff didn't like the word board—after all, it was a change—and they used it only on my insistence. True to form, however, Wessie understood right away what an important breakthrough it was for me. Although it was completely new for her too, she thought it was great, and she worked with me on it at every opportunity.

.BOSTON.LAW.
.I.FEEL.BAD.

About a month after I started using the new word board, I was having a session with Chris Ramsey in Wessie's office. Our work was interrupted when John, a male nurse from the Infirmary, poked his head in the door. He had fielded a phone call for me from home, with the message that my Gramma Ruth had died.

I had seen John every once in a while around the Infirmary during the past year. He always said hello to me, and I think he was working part-time at the State School while attending college. He was quite sensitive and considerate about telling me this very bad news. When he asked me if there was anything he could do, I was sure that he meant it. I deeply appreciated his thoughtfulness at the time and have never forgotten it. I was extremely pleased years later when this man, John Kerry, was elected the junior senator from Massachusetts.

After John left that morning, Chris R. and I talked about the news. Chris understood how close I was to Gramma Ruth, and she was very sympathetic and supportive. Our conversation helped to solidify our friendship. Although my emotions must have been obvious on my face, I used my new word board to give her the following message: .I.FEEL.BAD. It was especially gratifying, and of historic significance for me, to be able to state *in words* my feelings about such an important event.

At the end of 1973, mainly because of school schedules and vacations for the student interns, I was working on my word board only one hour a week, usually with Chris Ramsey. This picked up somewhat during the next few months, and I got a big lift in May 1974 when we began using a new, improved word board. Chris developed it, and this time she sought my input for the words and organization.

The new board was much more sophisticated than the earlier ones. It was divided into eight sections: people, places, objects, body parts, food, time, emotions, and clothes. Within a few days I mastered three of the sections: body, people, and clothes. It didn't take me long to become fluent with the other sections.

.MAD.TALK.YOU.

Wessie's daughter, Mary Lou, began working at the Infirmary in 1972 as part of the cleaning staff. She dropped by once in a while during breaks, and we frequently chatted after she finished work in the afternoon.

I loved Mary Lou as much as ever, but she had adopted a one-way approach to our conversations that was beginning to bother me. Even after I mastered my first word boards, she rarely sought, or listened to, my responses. By the summer of 1974 I was really irritated by this, and I decided to tell her how I felt. One afternoon I gave her the following message on my word board: .MAD.TALK.YOU.

After a few questions, Mary Lou caught my drift—partially. She realized that I was upset over something to do with our conversations, but she couldn't figure out exactly what was bothering me. Was it something she had said? Did she talk too much?

I answered yes, then no, then yes again. I wanted to tell her that it wasn't what she said or even that she talked too much, but that she didn't let me respond. Unfortunately, I was unable to explain this to her.

When Mary Lou left that day, she was confused and hurt. In the next two months she visited me only three times, and she was nowhere near her bubbly old self. This turn of events distressed me to the point that I literally stopped eating. I felt lost without Mary Lou's frequent, upbeat visits. I also believed that it was my fault for giving her the wrong idea from my message on the word board, which frustrated me no end.

Wessie noticed that something was wrong, both from my demeanor and from Mary Lou's absence. She asked if her daughter had said something that bothered me. When I gave her the same yes-no-yes response I had given Mary Lou, she understood that there wasn't a simple answer. By asking a few more questions and studying my facial and vocal responses, she figured out the problem.

Wessie told me she would talk to Mary Lou, and she probably gave her some advice about letting her friends get a word in edgewise, especially those of us who couldn't talk. Mary Lou visited me a few days later. She told me she had misunderstood what I had tried to tell her. Just as I had feared, she thought I didn't want to see her anymore because she talked too much. Thereafter, our friendship grew stronger. We remained close friends for another year, until Mary Lou got married and stopped working at the State School.

As with Mary Lou, I had developed a steady relationship with Gena Hildred from the day the two girls walked onto the ward years before. I began to see Gena much more frequently after she started working full-time at the Infirmary kitchen in 1973.

Gena understood that I had never had a chance to be a teenager. I had never dated, never chatted all night with my girlfriends about clothes and school and boys and TV shows and rock stars. She did her best to compensate for that by encouraging me to speak my mind in my own fashion, which Gena understood quite well. And she did more than sit around and shoot the breeze with me: she wrote letters and made telephone calls to my family, and scurried around the State School to deliver messages for me. More than anyone else I ever knew at Belchertown, Gena made me feel like a "normal" member of society.

BORED.SMART.YOUNG.DEPRESSED.

My spirits received another big boost in the fall of 1974 when I was moved to Ward 3 with the other adult women. Since the Infirmary reorganization in February 1973, I had been surrounded by younger girls — there were a few teenagers, but mostly children — on Ward 2. At first this hadn't made much of a difference, because I was wrapped up in my communication therapy. But as the novelty of working with the word boards wore off and my time with the speech therapists was reduced, I became increasingly bored and depressed on Ward 2. I was twenty-four years old, and once and for all I wanted to be treated like an intelligent adult.

I repeatedly expressed my frustration to Wessie, and to Chris Ramsey and Chris Dendor. They all understood my feelings and agreed with me, but it still took six or seven months of nonstop complaining before I was moved to an adult ward.

.SINK.HIGH.BENCH.
.BURN.HAND.

One morning in late September, just after I had moved, I was sitting in the "potty chair" in the "slab room." In the Infirmary lingo, this meant that I was sitting on the toilet in the bathroom.

"Potty chair" is a familiar term, since it usually refers to those little contraptions used to toilet-train toddlers. It was widely used at the State School to refer to the portable toilets used by the "kids" (the residents, regardless of their age), which gives you some idea about the attitudes of the staff, even in 1974. The term "slab room" was also widely used at Belchertown, as at other state institutions. It was derived from the two huge porcelain sinks, only a few inches deep and about waist high, in the bathroom. The residents were bathed right in these sinks, with a hose that had a showerhead attached to the end — a relatively efficient setup, I guess, but not one that does a lot for your dignity or self-respect. Besides, the water was always cold, and that porcelain was freezing against your back.

On the morning in question, I was strapped onto the "potty chair" by an attendant, as usual, and left for several minutes to take care of business. Another resident was tied onto the potty next to mine. When she tried to get up, she bumped into me. It was a very minor collision and my chair moved only a few inches, but that was enough to push my right hand up against the hot metal bedpan sterilizer, which was beside my chair. As a result, I received second-degree burns on my knuckles and fingers.

My hand was bandaged for a few days, and it really hurt for some time. Why I was set down so close to that sterilizer, unattended, is beyond me. Despite the accident, the sterilizer wasn't removed from the bathroom, and I was left alone many more times in those same circumstances.

.TAKE.ME.

Along with such never-ending bad things, good things continued to happen to me. One very good development occurred when I met Michelle Busquet. Michelle was eighteen years old and had just started working at the Infirmary as an attendant. We hit it off immediately, but our friendship was truly established one day in November 1974 when Michelle took me to do some Christmas shopping at the Eastfield Mall in Springfield.

As part of the slow process of breaking down the walls of the institution, a few of the "easier" residents recently had been allowed to go on day trips with friends or staff (on their own time). When I heard that someone on another ward had done this, I asked Michelle to take me away for a day. I also wanted her to meet my sister Shari, who was her age, so I asked Michelle to call Shari to set something up.

Suddenly, leaving the State School was easy. Michelle simply loaded me into the old car she was driving, threw my wheelchair into the trunk, and off we headed for my parents' house to pick up Shari. Once we got there, what was supposed to be a quick stop turned into a major delay because Michelle couldn't get her car started up again. My brother Howard, who was fifteen at the time, took a look and announced that he could fix it. After much good-natured and very funny harassment from Michelle and Shari, he got us under way again. We made it to the mall, where Michelle and Shari kept the jokes going full tilt.

Our activity for the rest of that day was to laugh our way around the mall. In the process, we caught a lot of sidelong stares from other people. But I just laughed harder and harder as Michelle and Shari cracked jokes about everybody who gawked at us.

Without a doubt, that was one of the best days of my life.

In early 1975, my best friend at the Infirmary, Theresa Ladue, moved onto Ward 3. It was very important to have Theresa living near me again after all those years. Wessie told the other attendants that we were friends, so Theresa and I spent a lot of time together, watching the days go by. This changed my life tremendously, because now I had someone with whom I could communicate spontaneously by a look, a sound, or a gesture, someone who understood what it felt like to be trapped in a nearly useless body in the Infirmary in the State School.

Theresa and I had seen enough of each other to stay current with our personal language of hand signals and facial expressions and sounds. Within a few days of our reunion, we were talking to each other more clearly than ever. But some things had changed, of course, in the thirteen years since Theresa and I had lived together on Ward 4.

I was now using my word board to communicate with some of the attendants, and Theresa was quite interested in this. She had never received any formal education, worked with speech therapists, or used a word board. Nevertheless, as she watched me "talk," she immediately appreciated what an important breakthrough the word board was for us. She keenly observed the dozens of words and phrases it added to my "active vocabulary" in 1975, and understood the virtually unlimited potential it offered for our ability to communicate in the future.

Right away Theresa told me that she wanted her own word board and that she wanted to work with the speech therapists too. I was happy to try to convey this message to Chris Ramsey and Chris Dendor, but I ran into difficulties. No matter how hard I tried, I couldn't get the message, simple as it was, across to either of the Chrises or to Wessie. Like me, Theresa was very persistent, and she kept at me to tell someone. I kept trying, and she tried too, but we struck out. Such an obstacle certainly was nothing new to either of us, but our long histories of frustration in communication heightened the pain.

.BIRD.MOVE.ARM.AIRPLANE.SIDE.

About the time Theresa joined me on Ward 3, rumors began circulating about the renovation of the Infirmary. From eavesdropping on staff conversations, I learned that as a result of a lawsuit brought by the Friends of Belchertown, the court had decided that the Infirmary was one of the worst buildings at the institution and had to be cleaned up right away.

Our whole ward was supposed to be moved into other buildings on the grounds in March 1975. When that didn't happen, I heard that we had been rescheduled to leave in a month. Still on Ward 3 in April, I learned that we were to move out in yet another month. I was confused, nervous, worried, and happy. Nobody on the Infirmary staff explained what was happening, and I didn't want to put too much faith in the rumors flying around. Still, with all of the other recent changes at Belchertown, improvements in our residential facilities were long overdue.

After nearly thirteen years of unwanted and unnecessary hospitalization, I finally left the Infirmary for good in May 1975 and moved to a building called Tadgell. Although it was only a few hundred yards away, Tadgell was drastically different. It was spacious, bright, well lit, and recently renovated. It was a one-story building, with a central kitchen, a TV area, and male and female sleeping quarters divided by common bathroom facilities. Some handicapped children were housed at the other end of the building, but we were pretty much separated from them.

Twenty people, ten men and ten women, moved to Tadgell from the Infirmary. All of these individuals were physically handicapped but either intellectually normal or at least high-functioning retarded. This setup gave me an opportunity to meet new people as well as spend more time with friends I had made at the Infirmary. Also, for the first time in my life at Belchertown, I was able to socialize somewhat normally with male residents. The mingling of men and women was a real improvement, part of a very new and different concept: to allow at least some of the residents to live in a less institutional environment.

After we moved in, I learned that Tadgell was supposed to be a temporary stopover. Within a few months our group was to move next door to Alpha House. Typical of the State School, however, we remained in our "temporary" quarters for a year and a half.

Even though the men's sleeping quarters adjoined the women's, we maintained a fair amount of privacy. I slept with four other women in an open area, with small privacy screens around our beds. With a brighter group of people, there were very few disruptions caused by roommates who were unable to control their behavior, so I had more actual privacy than at the Infirmary.

Although the kitchen at Tadgell was big enough to serve the whole group, our meals were still supplied from the central kitchen of the institution. But the attendants frequently prepared snacks in our kitchen, and they also bought beer and other alcoholic beverages for us. I usually kept a bottle of Kahlua on hand for an occasional sombrero, and it was common for the residents and attendants to drink beer at birthday parties. Not that this should have been a big deal — after all, I was twenty-five years old, and all of the other residents were adults as well — but it was an earthshaking innovation for the State School.

Tadgell fell far short of community living, but it definitely beat the Infirmary. At least I was halfway free. The attendants were helpful and considerate, and several used my word boards regularly. All of them gave me the time and the opportunity to communicate with them.

A woman named Marge Sibley took over my physical care in much the same way Wessie had done. Marge was an older woman, very easygoing and talkative. She was extremely gentle and respectful of my needs and wishes, and would have done anything for me. Of everyone at Tadgell, Marge spent the most time working with me on my word boards, and in short order our relationship grew almost as strong as my bond with Wessie.

I still missed Wessie dearly, though. I also missed Gena. Luckily, she was dating a man named Paul Lachut, who worked as an attendant at Tadgell. As a result, I saw Gena in between her mad dashes from the Infirmary to Tadgell, when she ran in to see Paul during a break. Occasionally she would drop by to talk to me after work.

A few months after I moved to Tadgell, Gena and Paul were married. They both continued to work at the State School, and a short time later Gena started taking me to their house for day trips, usually on weekends. This provided me with a much-appreciated break from the scene at the institution, and it also gave me a chance to catch up with Gena on all the gossip, to listen to our favorite songs on the radio, and just to spend time with her. Then, as always, Gena did everything she could for me. Being with her always made me feel like I was plugged in to the real world.

Of the nineteen other residents at Tadgell, five people stood far above the rest: Diane McCabe, Ron Benoit, Theresa Ladue, Rick Leaman, and Norman Mercer. Over the next three years at the State School, by our own choice, we spent nearly all of our waking hours together. Although we shared physical handicaps of varying degrees, the six of us also shared more or less "normal" mental abilities and an increasingly intense desire to leave the institution once and for all.

I had met Diane McCabe back in 1968, a year or so after my leg was broken. Diane was two years younger than I was, and she also had cerebral palsy, although she was not as physically incapacitated as I. She sat without problem in a wheelchair, used her hands to feed herself, and pushed her wheelchair along with her feet. Although her speech was garbled, I understood nearly everything she said, and I had little trouble figuring out her sounds and gestures. In turn, Diane read my eyes and sounds well, especially in regard to my emotions. For the most part, we only shared common space at the Infirmary, and didn't become friends until we moved into the less oppressive atmosphere of Tadgell.

I mentioned Ron Benoit earlier, when I described working with Howard Shane on the expressor; he was the other resident who used that device with Howard. Ron was about seven years younger than me and was similar to me physically. He was very sharp, and was something of a hell-raiser. Throughout the 1970s at Belchertown, Ron and I were in the forefront in trying out new communication techniques and devices.

I met Rick Leaman, who was about my age, at the Infirmary in 1969. Like Carol Muse, he had spina bifida, which rendered his body mostly useless from the waist down. But Rick spoke perfectly, had full use of his hands, and could be very witty, outgoing, and charming. He also possessed an exceptional memory, and could tell you what happened to whom at virtually any time or place. He was one of the most intelligent residents at the State School, and we became friends soon after we met.

Rick was also very spacy. He often would sit for half an hour and stare at nothing, rolling his head back and forth, mumbling nonsense to himself. He sometimes became extremely upset over small things, which was understandable, considering that he had been dumped at Belchertown, abandoned by his family, when he was four years old. For the next twenty years, he had been surrounded by mentally retarded residents and treated as though he were retarded too by mostly unsympathetic attendants. Despite his physical handicap, Rick was bright enough to have been a teacher or a lawyer or a businessman. But he wasn't strong enough emotionally to withstand the institution while he was growing up there.

Rick's best friend was Norman Mercer, who was forty-four years old when we moved into Tadgell. Like Diane, he had cerebral palsy but could move his hands and feet. He had a sharp mind and spoke a few words, but you had to develop an ear for his growly way of talking. Norman had lived at Belchertown since he was five years old, and had experienced some nightmarish situations during those years.

Norman's earliest memory of the State School was of A Building, where he was attended by a female resident who was about twenty years old and mildly retarded. This young woman helped the attendants by taking care of Norman, but she wouldn't let him talk to anyone else. If she saw him talking to another resident, she spanked him and made him cry.

Norman was very close to his mother, who used to take him home every Saturday. She taught him the alphabet, counting, and other simple skills. When he was nine, his mother told a supervisor that he was a bright boy and asked whether he could go to classes with some of the other children. The request was refused because the building where the classes were held was inaccessible to wheelchairs. Norman never did receive any educational instruction at the State School.

When Norman was twenty-five, his mother died at Christmastime. He never went home again. No one else in his family ever came to see him, and he wasn't even taken to his mother's funeral. Ever since, Christmas had been a melancholy time for him.

For many years, "discipline" was a big part of the care and treatment provided to the residents at Belchertown. Norman told me that the attendants used to make him wear a dress — a johnny, like we wore at the Infirmary — when they didn't like his behavior. For "disciplinary reasons," they used to lock up residents' eyeglasses. If a resident wandered away from where he was supposed to be, he was likely to have his head shaved. People who "misbehaved" were forced to wear a monkey suit (a combination of jumpsuit and straitjacket) for a day. Still others spent days in "the dog house" — solitary confinement — and the only time they saw another person was when their meals were brought to them in a metal bucket.

Amazingly, although Norman saw and experienced all of this and more for forty-four years, he somehow stayed immune to the craziness. He was outgoing, funny, fun-loving, friendly, and very perceptive. Of all the people I met at Belchertown, Norman was probably the least affected by the institutional syndrome that destroyed or damaged so many residents and soured so much of the staff.

Like me, Norman had enjoyed a very strong relationship with his mother, and she had maintained that relationship for as long as she lived. He too had been committed to Belchertown out of necessity, not by his mother's choice. According to Norm, if it hadn't been for his mother's continuing efforts to see him as much as possible, and for the few good people he met, he never would have survived "that goddamned place."

I had met Norman at the Infirmary, back when we used to live in front of the television set, but I didn't really get to know him until 1974. At first we had a great deal of trouble understanding each other. He didn't know anything about my communication methods, and I could only understand a few words of what he said. But we connected as friends nonetheless. As we sat together in the TV area, we gradually began to figure out ways to communicate.

One activity our group started just before moving out of the Infirmary, and continued with greater frequency at Tadgell, was bowling. Once a week, all or most of the six of us went out with a couple of attendants to a bowling alley in Holyoke that had candlepins and the little balls. We needed a modified system to roll the balls down the lane, so we used a wooden ramp set up right behind the throwing line. With our wheelchairs pulled up alongside, we could direct an attendant in aiming the ramp and then give the ball a push to get it going toward the pins.

Some of the others, especially Rick, could direct the ball down the ramp by themselves. My ability to move my hands and arms was so limited that it took a big effort just to nudge that little bowling ball down the ramp. Although I never became very enthusiastic about the game, I thoroughly enjoyed the opportunity to leave the State School for a few hours.

.TIC.

In the spring of 1975, right about the time I moved to Tadgell, I began using the Tufts Interactive Communicator, or TIC. This was a sort of electronic spelling device that was under development at Tufts University. The Communication Resource Center was able to get hold of one for me through Howard Shane and his contacts at his new job at the Children's Hospital in Boston.

The TIC had the letters of the alphabet arranged in rows and columns, with a tiny red light next to each one. The letters were arranged in order of frequency of use rather than alphabetically, and the lights flashed in sequence down the rows. By hitting a headswitch at the right moment, I could select a letter, which then would appear at the top of the grid. In that fashion I could spell out words and even form sentences for whoever was working with me.

Of course, that sounds a lot easier than it was. First, I had trouble with the speed of the flashing light pattern. Although I could operate the headswitch by moving my head sideways, I couldn't always time the movement to select the letter I wanted. I started off at about a five-second switching interval for each selection, which was very slow. This allowed me enough time to hit the switch, but at that speed it took forever to work through the TIC's sequences. I also tired quickly from both the repeated head motion and the mental effort of concentrating. And when I made a mistake, it was a real pain to start from the beginning again.

An even greater problem was my difficulty with spelling and reading. At the outset, Chris Dendor and Chris Ramsey decided that I should work on spelling with the TIC and continue to try to learn spelling and reading in the conventional building-block fashion. That is, rather than having me memorize the position of words on my word board or recognize words by sight, they kept trying to teach me how to spell by "sounding out" words on the TIC. They believed that once I mastered these fundamental skills, I would eventually be able to read books and newspapers independently.

.QUESTION.PARTY.

In May 1975 I had been working on the TIC with Chris D. or Chris R. every day for about six weeks. The routine was the same: we chatted for a few minutes and then set to work on spelling exercises and operating drills on the TIC, which was set up permanently on a table near my bed at Tadgell. The daily chats not only provided me with social contact with two good friends, but gave me a chance to improve my skills on my word board, which by now was constantly expanding with new words and expressions.

One afternoon when Chris Dendor picked up my word board for one of our pre-TIC conversations, I indicated the word "question."

"Do you want to ask me something, Ruth?"

I responded with a negative facial expression, and repeated the word "question" on my board.

"Do you want me to ask you something?"

I responded with another negative expression.

"Do you want me to ask someone else a question?"

I raised my eyes and gave Chris a big smile, telling her she had guessed correctly.

There were a few names on my word board, and after Chris went through them without success, she started asking me names of all of my friends at the State School. When she said Ray, I lit up.

Ray worked at the Infirmary as a physical therapist and recreational attendant, which was a new position at Belchertown. He was in his early twenties, a big, handsome guy with dark hair who looked like a baby-faced Robert Urich (the television actor who played Dan Tanna in *Vegas* and more recently Spenser in *Spenser for Hire*). I had met him the previous summer, when he and some of the other new people on the recreational staff took about six people from our ward over to the U. Mass. pool once a week. Ray was very strong, and very gentle with us, in and out of the pool. He seemed a bit shy, but he was dedicated and genuinely interested in improving the quality of our lives.

After Chris guessed that I wanted to ask Ray something, I still had to tell her what question I had in mind. I indicated "party" on my word board. Chris understood this clue immediately, and we both started laughing.

"You want to ask Ray to go to the prom with you?"

Bingo! My laughter turned into high-pitched howling, and I

stood myself up in my wheelchair in a gleeful burst of excitement—as much over the fact that Chris understood my message
as over the topic of our conversation.

After I calmed down, Chris asked if I wanted her to relay my
question to Ray. I looked over at the machine, and Chris immediately understood that I wanted to ask him myself on the TIC.

Believe it or not, there really was a prom at the State School. I
think that the first one was held in 1970, and they held one every
spring until 1977. Any resident who wouldn't disturb everybody
else could go. The proms, which were held in the auditorium,
were attended by about four hundred people. A real dance band
played, the men wore ties and jackets, the women wore long
dresses, and people sported a fair number of corsages and bou-
tonnieres. As the years went by and the resident population at
Belchertown decreased, the staff began to outnumber the residents at the prom, and assorted friends from the outside also
attended.

I had gone to a few of the proms before and had always enjoyed myself. I was really excited about my first one, but it turned
out to be somewhat disappointing: same people, same place,
trying to be something different but not quite making it. In 1974
I went with Norman Mercer, but that wasn't really a date; Norm
and I were just friends. As a matter of fact, my last date of
any kind had been with Jimmy Saywich, fifteen years earlier, at
Crotched Mountain. I was ten years old then!

Chris Dendor sensed that I was a little hesitant about asking
Ray to go to the prom with me. I had a mild crush on him, but I
didn't want him to go with me out of pity. I certainly wouldn't
have been heartbroken if he had said no. Chris and I talked about
this, and she encouraged me to ask him. We both agreed that it
was a great chance for me to use the TIC as a real communication
device.

With Chris's help, I learned how to spell out the message:
"Will you go to the prom with me?" It took a full week of practice, because I had to spell out every word letter by letter, and

trial and error on the TIC was a very slow process. But once I got it down pat, Chris arranged for Ray to come by Tadgell and I punched out the message for him.

Ray was at a loss for words. He had seen me operate the TIC on spelling drills, but this really surprised him. After an awkward silence, he told me that he would think about it and let me know.

A few days later, Rose Milano, who worked with Ray, told me that he would be happy to take me to the dance. She told me the color of his suit so I knew what kind of boutonniere to buy for him, and she also told him the color of my dress so he could get a corsage.

I wore a white and yellow gown, with puffy lace sleeves and a lace bodice with lace trim. (One of the attendants lent it to me.) Ray made the evening very special by giving me a half-dozen long-stemmed roses when he picked me up. This was the first time a man bought me flowers.

At first we were both a little nervous, but that faded as soon as we went to the dance and started talking to our mutual friends. I liked listening to the band, and it was especially fun when Ray held me in his arms for a few slow dances. As I said, he was a big, strong man, and because he had held me in the swimming pool many times, it wasn't at all strange for him to hold me in his arms on the dance floor. A few other couples were dancing this way, too. It was a little awkward and uncomfortable, but I really liked the sensation of my whole body moving to the music as if I really were dancing.

The highlight of the night came when a friend of Ray's walked over to say hello. His name was Hans Toegel. He was a psychologist at the State School, and he had come to the prom with a woman I knew from the Infirmary. Hans had sharp, piercing brown eyes, dark hair, a moustache, and a magnetic smile. As he talked to Ray, it struck me that he was the handsomest man I had ever seen.

Ray introduced us — maybe because I kept staring at Hans —

and I turned beet red from a combination of shyness and embarrassment over the strange excitement I was experiencing just from looking at this man. I was deathly afraid that Ray or Hans would figure out what I was thinking about Hans at that moment, but that never happened. Hans simply said hello, and then left to talk to other people at the dance.

We didn't speak again that evening, but I followed him with my eyes all over that room. I had never reacted that way to anyone before — or since, for that matter.

As always, though, Ray was a sweetheart. If he noticed anything about my instant infatuation with Hans, he kept it to himself. Despite his quiet personality, Ray managed to keep a pleasant conversation going, and he showed me a wonderful time.

.A.V.O.N.

A few months later, in the fall of 1975, I became very upset when my participation in the swimming program abruptly ended. It wasn't Ray's fault; I think a supervisor figured that since I would never be able to swim by myself, it couldn't be doing me any good. Typical of Belchertown, that supervisor never asked me whether I wanted to continue with the swimming program, which I did — floating in the water was very relaxing. I don't think Ray's opinion was solicited either.

Ray and I didn't see much of each other after that, except for once every month or so when he dropped by to say hello. About a year after I stopped the swimming program, Ray told me that he was leaving the area and moving to South Carolina. I became teary, but kept my composure and dealt with the bad news pretty well. I said goodbye to him at Christmas, when we were exchanging gifts with friends and staff. I gave him a bottle of cologne from Avon, as I had the year before, and he told me he would write and come back to visit.

Nothing has been as consistently painful in my life as the departure of friends who have worked with me. Despite the best intentions, and regardless of the physical distances involved, almost every time a friend has left for another job, we have lost contact for good. It didn't hit me until I returned from my Christmas vacation at home at the beginning of 1977 that I probably would never see Ray again. Even though we hadn't seen much of each other in the past year, we had remained good friends. His departure made me very depressed for a few weeks.

Ordinarily, Ray's leaving would have had a more devastating effect on me. After all, I didn't have many handsome, personable male friends at the time. But luckily, shortly after the prom in the summer of 1975, Hans Toegel started coming over to Tadgell a few times a week to counsel some of the other residents. Whenever he ran into me, he would chat for a few minutes. I always tried to act cool and nonchalant during our chance meetings, but I looked for Hans every day, and it took months before I could keep my face from turning red every time I saw him.

The summer of 1976 was an eventful time. There was an old-fashioned carousel at the State School, about a mile and a half from Tadgell, near A Building at the other end of the grounds. The carousel had been a fixture since several years before my arrival in 1962. It had originally been located at Forest Lake in nearby Ware, and was quite run-down from its years of service at Belchertown. But the Friends of Belchertown restored it, repairing the big wooden horses and benches and applying fresh paint to everything.

My memories of the carousel are less than fond. The few times I was taken outside during my early years at the Infirmary, it was usually to the carousel, which blared out the same old stale music of the fifties all the time — the attendants loved Elvis, and the carousel played nothing else. Usually I would be parked nearby, where I could enjoy the outdoors and watch the merry-go-round or the trees or the sky. Then an attendant who didn't know me very well would run up and say, "C'mon, Ruthie, let's take a ride on the merry-go-round, you'll love it."

I always responded with my sourest grimace and most negative sounds, my version of "No, anything but that." Without fail, the attendant would ignore my clearly stated wishes, lift me out of my wheelchair, plunk me down on a hard wooden bench on the carousel, scrunch me up in a terribly uncomfortable, sometimes painful position, and take me for a ride. Then he or she would tell me how much fun we were having. The carousel would turn round and round, Elvis would sing, and I would get sick to my stomach.

This lovely experience repeated itself several times a year throughout the sixties. As conditions at the State School improved in the 1970s, I was taken to the carousel more and more. By the summer of 1976 I was having a picnic lunch there, listening to Elvis and watching the wooden horses chase each other, at least once a week. The more we went there, the more I despised the thing. But I kept going anyway, because it was outside and it was the best place at the State School to watch and meet people.

One afternoon at the end of July, I was returning from a brief visit to the carousel when the front wheel of my wheelchair got caught in a rut along the edge of the paved sidewalk. The chair abruptly tilted forward and, terrified, I catapulted out. I landed on the pavement, face first. When the attendant picked me up, my mouth was bleeding profusely, my face, hands, and knees were badly scraped, and I had one less tooth in my mouth.

Back at Tadgell the attendants cleaned me up and closed a small cut on my chin with some butterfly bandages. I was sore all over, and my mouth hurt like hell where that tooth had been. It was a pure accident and I didn't blame anyone for it, but I was pretty depressed for a few weeks about the gaping hole in my smile.

To cheer me up a few weeks later, my friends Pat Borges and John Foley invited me to a party at John's house in Amherst. Pat and John were college students who had been doing volunteer work at the State School for about a year. They understood me very well and treated me like a normal person their age (although I was about five years older than they were). Both were easygoing and friendly, and very matter-of-fact about people's handicaps. I was in a wheelchair, they weren't; they could talk, I couldn't. But we all could see and hear and think and laugh. So they pushed my wheelchair, asked me lots of yes-or-no questions, and checked out my vocal responses and facial expressions for punctuation.

In June, John and Pat had taken me out to dinner at a Chinese restaurant (I love Chinese food). I had never gone out to dinner with anyone but my parents. I felt very self-conscious as the people in the restaurant stared at me, and I was afraid we were going to get kicked out when Pat started feeding me. I was nervous, she had never fed me before, and I'm not the world's quietest or most genteel diner. My trouble with swallowing causes me to make gurgling sounds while I eat, and I always cough or spit out some food during the course of a meal. At some point, though, John or Pat cracked a joke, the tension broke, and we all started laughing. I think the people in the restaurant got used to the sight of me, and we ended up having a good time. But I did experience the mixed feelings I have had ever since about dining in public.

Back to the party. It was on a Saturday night in late August, about the time when everyone was going back to college. Pat and John picked me up at Tadgell and loaded me and my wheelchair into Pat's old Pacer for the ride to Amherst. John's house was near the U. Mass. campus, and by the time we arrived the place was filled with their friends, and friends of friends, from the university and elsewhere. There was music and dancing and drinking and everything you would expect at a college party in 1976.

I was the only person there in a wheelchair. For a while I felt out of place. After all, this was my first "normal" party since the birthday parties in our old neighborhood in Springfield, back when I had never even heard of the State School. But Pat and John were great, and they made me feel like one of the crowd. They introduced me to everyone simply as their friend Ruth, as opposed to "Ruthie, one of our clients from Belchertown." Pat stayed nearby throughout the evening and included me in her conversations.

At around midnight, with the party still going full tilt, I said goodbye to many new friends, and Pat and John started to take me back to Tadgell. John was maneuvering my wheelchair down the front steps of his house, but he was a little tipsy; as he started to ease the chair off the top landing, one of the front wheels slid off the edge and the chair lurched forward. For the second time in about three weeks I was airborne, landing flat on my face on the pavement. Both times I had been wearing the safety belt attached to my chair, but I popped right out of it when the chair tipped over.

Again I came up minus a front tooth and with a bloody mouth that really hurt. Pat ran into the house to get some ice for me, then she and John rushed me back to Tadgell and alerted the night attendants to the accident. The attendants applied another ice pack to my face and gave me some Tylenol.

Within a few days the pain had subsided, but I was twice as depressed as before. In less than a month I had lost two front teeth!

In early September 1976, I became friends with another U. Mass. student, Debbie Loomer, who began working with me several times a week as part of her internship program in communication disorders. Very shortly after we started, Debbie's father died, and she missed a week of sessions with me. When she returned, she shared her grief and told me a lot about her family.

Debbie had a younger brother who was physically handi-capped. He could speak all right, but was confined to a wheelchair. Debbie told me about her brother's problems at home, about her feelings toward him, and about the way the rest of her family related to him and his handicap. It was clear that this experience had motivated her to work at the State School. Debbie instinctively understood me and my feelings and frustrations. We became close friends on the spot.

Most of the work I did with Debbie involved the TIC. Throughout 1976 I spent about an hour a day working on that device, which was set up right next to my bed so I had ready access to it. When I began working with Debbie, I was concentrating on increasing my speed on the TIC, building up my vocabulary, and practicing grammar so that I could construct sentences. I was also making some headway in spelling phonetically.

For one of our basic exercises, Debbie would say a word and I would spell it out phonetically on the TIC. Debbie would then correct my spelling. After studying the corrections, I would try to reproduce the word. Some of the words I mastered at this time were *dress, who, what, when, where, like, need, hair, chair, sister, brother, sheet, seed, butter, ring, necklace, like, soda, leg,* and *sun.* I also negated sentences by adding "no" at the end, both on the TIC and on my word boards.

Debbie and the other student interns in 1976–1977 were supervised by two young, talented, and dedicated speech pathologists from the Communication Resource Center, Steve Calculator and Dave Bickford. I worked a little bit with Steve on my word boards and on the TIC, but I worked more with Dave, who was terrific. He especially helped me that year in improving on my word boards.

Dave made an important contribution by developing what we called Ruth's Code. This was a typed list of words and phrases, organized by places to go, things to eat, my favorite shows on TV, people, basic needs, and other categories that I used regularly in everyday communication. Each category had about ten words or phrases in it. To use Ruth's Code, I first had to indicate to my listener that I wanted to say something with it. Once my helper discovered the right category by a process of elimination, he or she would run through the specific items. Again I indicated my choice with a yes expression.

Ruth's Code was a shorthand version of my word boards. I used it only for quick messages. As I became more adept with my word boards, they replaced the code even for those simple expressions. But the code served a useful purpose for a time: it helped me master the word/phrase communication technique that I have continued to develop ever since on my increasingly sophisticated word boards.

.BOOK.

In the fall of 1976 I decided to write a book about my life. I discussed the idea with Pat, who had been working at the Communication Resource Center, and with Debbie. They both thought it was a great idea. At the same time, and quite coincidentally, Norman Mercer suggested that I put my story into words. When I told him that I had already decided to do just that, Norman became (and remained) very enthusiastic about my project.

During the next few months, I spent a lot of time talking to Debbie and Pat about different ideas for my book. By the end of the year I was starting to outline the basic elements by punching out subjects on the TIC and responding to questions about them from my speech therapists.

8

.GO.AWAY.BSS.

Another, even more important project also began to develop in 1976. Two of Norman's friends, Carol and Paul Shelton, came over to Tadgell one evening and spoke to Norman, Rick, Ron, Diane, Theresa, and me about leaving the State School — for good!

I had met Carol Shelton in 1969 when she worked as an attendant at the Infirmary. She always respected the rights of the residents, and she was very responsive to my physical and emotional needs. She took as much time as possible to talk to me, which in those days was especially important. Norman met Carol at about that same time, and they became good friends. After she became a recreational therapist a few years later, Carol began taking Norman home for visits on weekends and holidays.

Carol, Paul, and their four children lived on a small farm in Belchertown. Although none of their children was handicapped, the Sheltons were dedicated advocates, and both belonged to the Friends of Belchertown. In 1973 they opened a group home for the mentally retarded, and they began talking to Norman about moving out of the State School.

Norm had been desperate to leave for many years, and he

wanted to move into the Sheltons' group home. But that program was not geared to someone with Norm's mental abilities and physical limitations. Very reluctantly, Carol and Paul had to say no. At the same time, they promised him that they would get him out of Belchertown as soon as possible.

This was no simple task, however. Norm caught flak at the State School just for visiting the Sheltons' farm on weekends. Maybe the staff resented him because he rolled in late on Sunday night, or because he drank Jack Daniel's there, or because he enjoyed himself, or because he hated to come back. Whatever it was, the more he left the institution, the more grief he got on his return.

Likewise, every administrator scoffed at the idea of Norman leaving the State School to live in the community on a permanent basis. Where would he go? What would he do? Who would take care of him? What if an attendant got sick? Who would manage his finances? How would he see his friends? How would his friends see him? And so on and so forth. Some of these questions made sense and some did not, but they all had their source in one prevailing attitude: handicapped people can live only at a huge institution like the Belchertown State School, surrounded by other handicapped people, separated and insulated from the rest of society.

Carol and Paul Shelton vehemently rejected this concept. By 1976 they were willing to extend the promise they had made to Norman to his friends who wanted to leave the institution with him. When we first met with them at Tadgell to discuss leaving, my mind already was made up. I wanted out!

True, I was scared and worried about those same questions — where would the money come from, who would take care of us, where would we live, could I take my mattress with me? I was also afraid that I would miss my friends from Belchertown very much. Yet I knew that before long, I would dry up and rot unless I left the institution and lived in a normal place, saw different people, ate normal food — lived my life. I was afraid, but I was also ecstatic over the possibilities.

I drew inspiration from my friend Diane Skorupski. In the fall of 1975, Diane had moved out of the State School. With the help of a new organization in Amherst called the Stavros Foundation, an advocacy and support organization for the physically handicapped, she had set herself up in an apartment and started a new life. From all I heard, she was doing just fine. Although Diane had skills that I didn't have — speech and the use of her hands — I figured that if she could make it on the outside, I could too.

I knew that I was lucky to have the help of two people like Carol and Paul Shelton, who were sincere, dedicated, and tireless. After several more meetings with our bunch at Tadgell, and dozens of meetings with officials at the State School, they developed a plan to place us in a group home by the end of the year.

Our biggest obstacles were funding and a location. We were all receiving small amounts of disability compensation from the government, but this was nowhere near enough to live on. Carol and Paul had to work out a detailed program, with a budget plan and funding request, and then push it through a very reluctant bureaucracy.

After much searching, the Sheltons found a house in Chicopee and tried to negotiate a down payment. But the deal fell through for lack of funds. After that, we changed our approach from sharing a group home to pairing up and renting several apartments in the same complex. Meanwhile, 1976 turned into 1977, and we still were living at the State School.

.OLD.MATTRESS.ROUGH.NIGHT.

We did leave Tadgell, however, in October 1976. Our group of eighteen "highly functioning" residents finally was moved next door to Alpha House, which was supposed to be a kind of halfway house on the institution's grounds. Although it wasn't that different from Tadgell, it represented a radical step for Belchertown, at least in theory. It was intended to be our last stop before moving into the community.

Alpha was the first place at the State School that was limited to such a small number of residents with relatively similar needs. It was divided into four living areas, two at each end, one small, one big. There were twelve men and six women. The men were split up evenly in the large areas, and the women were split up in the small areas. To provide some privacy, each section was divided into individual spaces by movable partitions. We each had a bed and a dresser, so it was like having my own small room.

My first night at Alpha was rough. I slept on an old mattress that was hard and lumpy, and I missed my comfortable bed at Tadgell. Also, I was anxious about the change, and my mind wouldn't stop racing. Alpha was supposed to prepare us for living in the community, with a different approach from anything I had experienced at Belchertown. I had no idea of what to expect.

As it turned out, there was nothing to fret about. Alpha was very similar to Tadgell, although the quality of life did improve slightly. One important aspect was the food. For a while we ate the usual tasteless meals from the institution's central kitchen. Fortunately, there were food warmers in the serving trays, so at least we could get our meals hot. Then, in the spring of 1977, the attendants began preparing our meals at Alpha, in a small kitchen off the central common area. This was terrific, because we now could choose from several alternatives for each meal. The food itself tasted much better too, probably because it was cooked right there. The cooks knew us, watched us eat their food, came to know our individual likes and dislikes, and wanted to please us.

I ate better at Alpha than at any other time at Belchertown. The food was better, but so was my frame of mind. The increased privacy made me feel more like a real person, and the overall atmosphere at Alpha was happier. It also helped me to know, or at least to believe firmly, that I wouldn't be living at the State School much longer.

.TALK.BABY.ALPHA.

As with everything else at Belchertown, the good was accompanied by the bad. Even at Alpha there were attendants whose attitudes toward me were kindly but prehistoric — more like those I encountered when I first arrived in 1962 than what I was accustomed to in 1976. The worst example of this was one attendant who talked to me exclusively in baby talk. She would talk nonsense to me in a high-pitched voice, then turn to another attendant and talk about me as if I couldn't understand a word she said. This was very annoying, but I ignored it as best I could.

The highlights of my life at Alpha were working on my TIC every day and seeing Pat Borges. I talked to Pat about my book several times a week. We went over ideas and organization, and she asked me questions about my life. She also gave me an ongoing tutorial in current events and the world outside the State School. We spent hours talking to each other about what goes on in high school and college, how you get a driver's license, how the president of the United States is elected, and anything else that came up.

During the summer of 1977, I saw Pat nearly every day. She worked intensively with me on both my word boards and my overall reading skills. She also came home with me a few times and met my family. When she returned to school in the fall and we saw each other only a few hours a week, I really missed her. Luckily, Gena Lachut had joined us early on at Alpha House as a full-time attendant, and her energetic presence invariably kept me in good spirits.

Although Alpha was supposed to be wheelchair accessible, the bathrooms were laid out so that the bathtubs were up against a wall and it was difficult to get to them in a wheelchair. I had to be lifted out of my chair and carried into the tub for a bath. The shower stalls, however, were accessible, and some of the residents took showers sitting in their wheelchairs.

One memorable feature of the bathtubs was their spray hoses, which could douse people who were out in the hallway. Some of the residents, especially Norman, loved to start water fights when they were taking a bath by getting an attendant to spray whoever happened to be going by in the hall. I was ambushed my share of times. Even though nobody likes to get soaked when they're fully dressed, the water fights did keep things lively.

One day in the fall of 1977 the new crop of college volunteers in the Boltwood program were touring Alpha for the first time. On a dare from Gena, Norman streaked them. By then Norm had been equipped — or maybe "armed" is a better word — with a motorized wheelchair. He operated it with his feet, by pressing buttons on a footplate. He was quite a sight for those curious, well-intentioned college kids, cruising up and down the hallway stark naked, howling like a lunatic.

.DREAM.HAPPY.

I continued to see Hans Toegel, the handsome psychologist, quite often after I moved to Alpha. As he had done at Tadgell, he came by Alpha several times a week to counsel some of the residents, and he usually stopped to chat with me. I had long since gotten over my self-consciousness with him, although I became even more infatuated with him as I got to know him better.

Several times at Tadgell I had spelled out .I.L.O.V.E.Y.O.U. on my word board during conversations with Hans. Each time he had laughed with embarrassment and quickly changed the subject. He reacted the same way when I repeated the message during a conversation after we had moved to Alpha House.

My friends Pat and Gena knew that I had a serious crush on Hans, and one afternoon in January 1977, when I was talking to him alone in a small room at Alpha, Gena locked the door on us. She left us locked in there for about ten minutes, and we all thought it was pretty funny.

But at that time, neither Gena nor Pat knew how deeply Hans had affected me. For the first time in my life, I was experiencing erotic dreams. In my fantasies, Hans and I would be at his apartment — which I had never actually seen — and we would make passionate love. Sometimes I would stay for breakfast. In some of these dreams I was handicapped; sometimes I wasn't. When I dreamed I wasn't handicapped, I looked a lot like Shari, and Hans picked me up at my parents' house in Springfield. When I was handicapped, he would pick me up at the State School and take me away.

Shortly after I began experiencing these dreams, I tried to tell Gena about them. Despite several attempts, the most I could communicate was that I still had a crush on Hans. Although I had been told the facts of life a few times before — by Wessie, Debbie Loomer, and Pat — these had been clinical, educational discussions. Nobody had ever talked to me about my sexual drives and frustrations, what my realistic expectations should be, and how I could best cope with them. Hans certainly never knew that he was my lover in my dreams, and nobody suspected that my sexual fantasies about him were so vivid that I was experiencing orgasms.

.TALL.TENNIS.SHOES.

In late spring in 1977, Gena helped me plan a date with Hans. Using my word board, I asked him out to see *The Sting* at a local theater. The movie had been around before, and I think Hans had already seen it, but I hadn't. The last movie I had seen in a theater had been *Mary Poppins*, which Mother took me to see before I came to Belchertown.

They did show some movies at the State School, but these were usually Elvis Presley films or old stuff like *The Wizard of Oz* or *Around the World in Eighty Days*. The institutional "theater" was in the basement canteen of the school building, which doubled as a nondenominational church on Sundays. I wasn't interested in the church services and never attended, but I would have gone to the movies — even if the films were old or corny — just for something different. For some reason, I was never allowed, or asked, to go.

Anyway, Gena helped me plan everything for my big date. She took me to J. C. Penney's at the mall in Hadley to buy a new outfit. I wanted to look very sexy, so I selected a yellow pantsuit with a halter-top blouse. Unfortunately, we couldn't find any matching shoes that fit my feet, so I ended up wearing white high-cut sneakers! (My toes curl over, and I've always had a lot of trouble finding shoes that fit and don't look like boxes attached to my legs. Since then I've discovered soft, elasticized slipper-type shoes that are comfortable and look halfway decent.)

Excited though I was about it, the date turned out to be pretty boring. Pat Borges came along to help me out, and even though I enjoyed the movie, it wasn't like a real date. It was more like three friends going out to see a movie, which was okay too, I guess.

I didn't know it, but Pat was dating Hans at the time. Her relationship with him, and her friendship with me, must have prompted Hans finally to talk to me a few weeks later about our future as a couple.

.SORRY.BODY.

Shortly after our date, I asked Hans to the prom, and he readily accepted. During one of our conversations about it, he started telling me that he thought I was a beautiful woman with a good mind locked up inside an unfortunate body. He said that he liked me very much as a friend, but he didn't think we would make a very good match romantically.

I understood what he was saying, and I was heartbroken. For the first time in my life, I realized that I would never be able to enjoy a romantic relationship with a "normal" man. It finally dawned on me that no nonhandicapped man would ever be sexually attracted to me — certainly no nonhandicapped man to whom I was attracted, anyway. Since I had never been physically attracted to men with disabilities like mine, I concluded that I would never enjoy a sexual relationship with anyone.

This was a bitter pill to swallow. It certainly took the excitement out of going to the prom with Hans. Not that it changed my feelings about him — or my erotic dreams about him, for that matter — but it definitely affected my general outlook. I realized that my romantic fantasies about Hans were just that — fantasies.

I matured quite a bit in those few weeks.

.UPSET.ANGRY.

I maintained a close, friendly relationship with Hans for the rest of the year. We continued to see each other frequently, and I continued to carry a torch for him, although a bit more soberly.

One day in December, a few days before Christmas, Hans dropped by Alpha and told me that he had to speak to me alone. He looked very serious, and he stayed that way as he told me that he was taking a job in Boston and would be leaving the State School in January.

I was stunned. Even if he was unattainable, he was still *there* every day, talking to me, clowning around, with a twinkle in his eye. Very soon my shock turned into anger as I realized that once again I was locked up inside Belchertown, unable to maintain any kind of relationship with my friends who left for bigger and better things. I too wanted to leave and do bigger and better things, and I was getting very, very tired of waiting for my day to come.

Fortunately, Gena was there to console me. She let me cry on her shoulder about Hans's departure, and in talking out the whole situation, I finally succeeded in getting the message across that Hans had been my imaginary lover. I felt much better once Gena understood the true extent of what he meant to me. As usual, she was extremely sensitive to my feelings.

Just by his presence in my life, even without any return of my romantic feelings, Hans provided me with the closest thing to a love affair I had ever had. At the age of twenty-eight, I was long overdue. For many years after he left, I continued to dream about him. No one since has had that kind of effect on me.

.HOME.NOVEMBER.DISAPPOINTED.

In November 1977, about a week before Thanksgiving, I was told that I could go home for the holiday. For the first time in fifteen years, Mother's request that the State School authorities allow me to go home for turkey and cranberry sauce was granted. I was very excited. Not being able to go home for Thanksgiving had come to represent nearly everything that was wrong with living at Belchertown.

As it turned out, however, the holiday was a big disappointment. I felt awkward and in everybody's way at home. With the exception of Mother, who was great as usual, nobody seemed relaxed or comfortable around me. Even though I had been coming home for a week in the summer and at Christmas every year, I felt distant and out of touch, like a long-lost cousin who suddenly shows up on the doorstep and doesn't quite fit in despite everyone's best efforts to make her welcome.

I think that I had been drifting away from the rest of the family for a long time; it probably began as far back as 1965. Somehow, I didn't fully realize how apart we had grown until the normal Thanksgiving routine — me at Belchertown, the family at home — was upset. I returned to the State School a few days later feeling more isolated and alone than I had for many years.

.DREAM.TEACHER.

One night a few months after we moved into Alpha House, I dreamed that I was a speech therapist at the State School. I was still in a wheelchair, but I could talk normally and had the full use of my hands. In my dream, I was teaching the people who in reality were my co-residents at Alpha House.

Another dream that I often had involved a total reversal of roles and situations. The handicapped people in my dream, the people I was teaching, were Wessie, Rosa, Dave Bickford, Howard Shane, and Lissa Carroll. None of them could walk or talk. My fellow staff members, all of whom could walk and talk normally, were Norman Mercer, Rick Leaman, Diane McCabe, and Theresa Ladue.

Both of these dreams recurred dozens of times for several years. When I walked normally in my dreams, I always talked and looked a lot like my sister Marie — tall and a bit chubby, with a strong resemblance to my mother, except for my brown eyes and blond hair. I used to wish that I looked more like Shari in these dreams, because Shari was thinner and prettier than Marie. But I think that I usually resembled Marie because our personalities are so similar — both of us are strong-willed, ambitious, and aggressive. Shari is physically more attractive, and a much gentler soul.

.LIKE.A.WOMAN.

Early in 1977 I met a young woman, Susan Downie, who became a role model for me. Sue was a U. Mass. student who was physically handicapped and confined to a wheelchair. Under the auspices of the Stavros Foundation, she and another handicapped student, Laura Rauscher, conducted weekly peer counseling sessions for some of the residents at Alpha House. These sessions were invaluable in helping me come to grips with the obstacles I would face when I left the State School and entered society as an independent adult.

Sue met with me once a week through 1977 and the spring of 1978. She freely recounted her experiences of being handicapped and trying to live a normal life on a college campus that wasn't particularly concerned about physically disabled students. In October I visited her room at U. Mass., which was on the second floor of one of the newer tower buildings. At the time only one dorm, Patterson, was designated as fully wheelchair accessible.

Sue didn't want to live there because it was like a ghetto for handicapped students, so she lived at Southwest, the cluster of high-rise dorms, with most of the "normal" undergraduates.

Sue was studying to be a speech therapist. The classes for this field of study were held at Arnold Hall, which was not accessible for wheelchairs. Since there was no elevator, Sue's classes were moved down to the ground floor.

A year and a half after I met her, in her last semester at college, Sue was driving around town—unassisted—in her own customized van, complete with a lift ramp and special brake and accelerator controls that she operated by hand. I respected her for many reasons, but first and foremost for the fact that she treated me like a woman. She inspired me to strive for an education, and I began to dream of attending college myself one day.

.SIZE.HEAD.

There were several other women in my life whom I greatly respected because they too treated me like a woman: Mother, Pat Borges, Gena Lachut, Diane Skorupski, and Jean (Rosie) Rosenberg.

I first met Rosie in 1976 when she was working at Belchertown as an occupational therapist. She later switched over to the new Adaptive Design Workshop at the State School, where she remained for five years, doing great work. In addition to becoming a close friend, Rosie improved my life greatly by helping to develop and upgrade customized wheelchairs for me.

Then, as now, I spent nearly all of my waking hours in a wheelchair. In many ways, being comfortable in my chair is like being comfortable in my skin. With my leg and hip problems and the lack of strength and flexibility in my muscles, correct padding and support in my chair is critical.

To some degree this is common for every person with cerebral palsy, and I suppose for every person confined to a wheelchair for any reason. Yet I spent fifteen years at the State School before I was fitted with a wheelchair that even began to address these basic needs. And my needs were not unusual at Belchertown, where there were hundreds of residents in wheelchairs.

The first attempt to customize a chair for me was undertaken in 1975 by a woman named Joan Newbanks, a physical therapist. Joan worked with Ray, and was one of the therapists who used to take us swimming. Before I met her, the attendants used to prop me up in a conventional wheelchair by stuffing pillows around me. This met with varying success, depending on who did the stuffing. Joan was the first one to fit my chair with a semipermanent padded headrest that wrapped around my head and gave me the kind of support I required to sit upright. She also placed vinyl-covered foam padding in various spots to make me more comfortable and, again, to help me sit upright. But she did not have the tools, material, or budget to create a wheelchair that was truly adapted for me. This job fell to the Adaptive Design Workshop, which was just getting off the ground.

In the summer of 1977, my friend Rosie and her co-worker, Tim Casey, began designing a customized, padded-in-all-the-right-places, fully supportive wheelchair. I think this was the first original, completely adapted wheelchair the workshop did. Rather than take a conventional metal wheelchair and pad it, as people had done in the past, Rosie and Tim built a wooden chair frame to my specific requirements and mounted it on wheels. Then I tested mockups of different padding arrangements and we reviewed the chair's performance. Adjustments were made in the padding—it was just foam and duct tape at that point— and we tried it out again.

It took several months to perfect the design. I finally received a custom upholstered, form-fitting, fully supportive wheelchair at the end of 1977. What a difference it made!

.$?*!

Late in the summer of 1977, Paul Shelton started up a day program of sorts for the five of us at Alpha House who were planning to leave together—Norman, Rick, Ron, Diane, and myself. Theresa Ladue had decided to stay at the State School. I think she was afraid to leave after all those years, and she probably wanted to see how we did out on our own before she made the big leap.

A fellow named Arthur ran this program for Paul. Arthur had attended U. Mass. and had become friends with Ron Benoit through the Boltwood volunteer program. Hans Toegel introduced Arthur to Paul as someone who could help put together a support organization for us when we left Belchertown.

Paul wanted to set up the day program before we moved out of the State School and into a community residence. He envisioned an individualized educational program that would prepare us for living successfully in a deinstitutionalized setting. Unfortunately, the program got off to a shaky start. It didn't focus on much of anything. It was run on a skimpy budget, about $12.50 per day per client. Hans and Paul tried to find volunteers for the staff, but they didn't meet with much success.

Occasionally Hans or Joan Newbanks took us out for the day; those were always our best days. More often, Arthur took us off the State School grounds a few times a week, usually in groups of two or three. We drove over to U. Mass. by car to spend the day at the Campus Center. Arthur had contacts that enabled us to use a conference room there if we reserved it ahead of time. When we had a room, we sometimes worked on reading, communication, or other educational activities. When Arthur hadn't reserved one, we just hung out in the coffee shop all day long.

For a long time, going to the U. Mass. campus was very intimidating. There were hundreds of people constantly milling around, and although a handful of students were in wheelchairs, I didn't feel like I belonged there. The students were very friendly; they rarely gawked at us or made comments when they passed by. But we didn't know many people, and little was done to fill us in on what was happening on campus. It took a long time, and some basic changes in our program, before I really felt comfortable about spending time there.

The main problems with the part-time day program were disorganization and our lack of input. Occasionally we wandered around a shopping mall or went to a movie. Sometimes we went to the Sheltons' farm in Belchertown and visited Carol or Paul. But Arthur didn't ask us what we wanted to do. He would simply announce that we were going somewhere on a particular day, and that was it.

As the months wore on, Norman, Rick, Diane, and I began to dislike Arthur intensely. We didn't complain, though, because Paul was having enough trouble keeping the program afloat. He was still fighting nearly everyone at the State School about springing us into the community.

.APARTMENT.SPRINGFIELD.

By 1978, Paul's efforts finally were nearing success. A new apartment complex named Linden Towers, a modern building with fifteen floors, opened in Springfield. Having been specially designed to accommodate elderly and handicapped residents, Linden Towers was fully accessible for wheelchairs.

As soon as he heard about it, Paul made inquiries to see if any apartments could become available for us. Although it seemed like the best place in the area to suit our particular needs, he met with a lot of resistance from the people who ran the building. Nearly all of the residents at Linden Towers were retirees, and they were very wary of having handicapped people from Belchertown as their new neighbors. Paul kept hearing a lot from the management about "medical concerns" and whether enough attendants would be working with us to provide adequate care.

With some help from the mayor's office, Paul managed to convince the Linden Towers people at least to let us see the place and talk to us about living there. One morning in February, Norman and I drove down to Springfield with Paul and met with one of the building managers and a nurse who worked there.

The meeting went really well. Norm and I particularly hit it off with the nurse. We managed to show her that despite our handicaps, we possessed fully developed personalities and were capable of living productive lives in the community. The message we got across, with Paul's help, was that we did not belong in a hospital or an institution like Belchertown.

I was quite impressed with Linden Towers. It seemed very big and looked great, partly because it was brand new. I really liked the open layout of the apartments, especially the kitchens and bathrooms, which left plenty of room for wheelchair traffic. There was also a sliding glass door that led out to a little patio overlooking the highway. Although it was much noisier than what we were used to out in the sticks, it was very exciting. I liked the idea that I would be able to sit out on the patio on a warm night and watch the cars go by. It made me feel like I would become part of the action going on in the city.

By that time, February 1978, our plan called for me to share an apartment with Diane McCabe. At first I wasn't crazy about the idea of sharing a place with anyone. I had spent the last sixteen years sharing my whole life with all sorts of people at the State School. Although Diane and I were friends, I wanted to have my own place. But once I visited Linden Towers and saw how the apartments were laid out, I realized that Diane and I would each have our own bedroom and that there was plenty of room for both of us. This made me feel much better, and the idea of having a roommate didn't bother me anymore.

With all the negative stuff that the staff at Belchertown was whispering in our ears and behind our backs about moving out, it was a wonder that any of us stuck with our plans. The administrators, and many staff members, were criticizing Paul for "getting our hopes up only to let us down." Paul's response was that if all that came of his efforts was to give us some hope, then that alone was worth it.

The same old nagging questions kept being repeated: What if there was a fire in our apartment? What if an attendant didn't show up for work? What if there was an emergency? Meanwhile, the mother hens were working on us too: "If you move to Spring-field, Ruthie dear, how will I be able to visit you?" My unspoken response to such questions was something like "That's the basic idea, lady!"

All of us agreed with Paul's belief, which he stated loudly and clearly again and again, that the State School was an embarrass-ment to our whole society, and that everyone should be working together to move all of the residents out and shut the place down for good.

.GREAT.

On March 10, 1978, I made my first public appearance as an advocate for the rights of the physically handicapped. With the help of my friend and peer counselor, Sue Downie, I gave a pre-sentation to an audience of about fifty women at the Interna-tional Women's Week Conference at the U. Mass. Campus Cen-ter.

Sue, Rosie, and I had worked for weeks on my remarks, which Sue read for me at the conference. Our talk lasted about ten minutes, and it summarized the ups and downs of my life and my treatment by society — from home to Lakeville to Crotched Mountain, back home, and then to Belchertown.

One of the themes I stressed was my lifelong dependency on other people and the fact that I was rarely respected as a woman and an individual. Through Sue's voice, I told the audience how I had expanded my communication techniques, with hard work and lots of help, from simple facial expressions to the use of sev-eral word boards and the TIC. We ended our talk by explaining that I, like many other people with a disability, constantly strove to become a useful and productive member of society.

I was extremely anxious about our presentation and how it would be received. My nervousness remained unchecked until Sue finished and the audience gave us warm, sustaining ap-plause. A few people asked questions, and I enjoyed being able to answer with both my yes and no facial expressions and my word board.

After our session ended, we attended other workshops on women's issues. Nobody paid too much or too little attention to me. I was just there, involved and interacting with dozens of women from all walks of life, contributing to the conference. It was great!

.GO.

We were scheduled to leave the State School once and for all on June 30. The preceding months were hectic and full of uncertainty. We had seen other moving dates come and go in the past year and we were beginning to wonder if we would ever get out of Belchertown.

Although it wasn't as good as a house, Linden Towers looked promising, and our apartments seemed to be set. In those last few weeks, the people at the State School finally accepted the fact that we were leaving. We even began to hear complaints about how we were taking our wheelchairs and beds with us.

The situation loosened up a little with some help from a friend named Kay Gillespie. Kay was a member of the Friends of Belchertown and worked as a volunteer at the State School. She wrote to Dr. Jones, the superintendent, and asked him to help us out with some of these problems. I believe that Dr. Jones passed the word down to the staff to cooperate. Nevertheless, the social workers managed to screw up some important details, like providing the wrong forwarding addresses for our mail and submitting incorrect paperwork to the federal government for our disability (SSI) benefits.

We had reviewed our program very carefully with Paul Shelton. He had secured funding from the state and had set up an administrative staff and hired attendants to provide us with around-the-clock personal care at our apartments. Although we weren't happy with the part-time day program, we believed that once we left the State School and started up full-time, it would improve. We particularly wanted more input into how it was run. I looked forward to benefiting from a program of individualized teaching and developing my communication skills.

As I waited to leave Alpha House, I felt comfortable and optimistic about the future. The move itself, however, was quite disorganized. I was annoyed that my clothes and personal articles were crammed into boxes and scattered all over the place. I was certain that at least half my things would end up getting left behind. I didn't have much money, and I worried that with the tight budget we were going to be on, I wouldn't have enough for clothes, furniture, or other essentials for setting up our apartment. My last night at Belchertown, I was a nervous wreck.

The next morning we left the State School in the new, customized yellow van (complete with motorized wheelchair lift) that Shelton's Inc., our "providing agency," had purchased for our program. As we drove through the country roads and headed for Springfield and Linden Towers, I knew in my bones that the worst chapter of my life had just ended.

.LINDEN TOWERS.

I had never had a place of my own. As a result, I had never worried about buying groceries and planning meals, paying the rent and the phone bill, balancing a checkbook, making appointments, figuring out how to keep the appointments I made — all of the things adults just do. But starting out in society at the age of twenty-eight, after living at a state institution for the mentally retarded for sixteen years, I found these everyday tasks confusing and wonderful and frightening.

A lot of it was fun, especially at first. Simply making a grocery list and going shopping at the supermarket was exciting. I quickly learned, however, that food was expensive for someone on a fixed income of about $250 a month. This was all I received in benefits. It had to pay for food and rent (which was subsidized; I paid $51), as well as my general expenses. I didn't have any money in the bank, and my parents didn't have much money either. Since Shelton's budget was very tight, with all of the funds allocated for our personal care and staff needs, there was no extra money available to me from anywhere else.

I quickly found out how expensive it was to set up an apartment from scratch. According to plan, Diane McCabe and I shared a two-bedroom apartment on the fifteenth floor of Linden Towers. Paul Shelton scraped up a few dollars for us to buy furniture with, but we soon discovered that we couldn't afford anything even halfway decent. We managed to find a passable kitchen table and a new loveseat for under $200. I took my waterbed from the State School, but I had to buy a cheap bedroom set and put the water mattress on the frame that came with it. Mother brought over my grandmother's old TV set, and some of our friends and relatives donated miscellaneous plates, silverware, pots and pans, sheets, towels, and other basics. We didn't have anything extra, and it certainly wasn't fancy, but we made do.

Our situation was made worse by the fact that we didn't receive our monthly SSI checks for a couple of months because of the bungling back at the State School. While that was being straightened out, I was flat broke.

A key part of our program involved becoming as self-sufficient as possible, so we took a crash course in money matters — budgeting, personal finances, and other issues we never had to face at the institution. Of course, this meant starting, and controlling, a checking account.

The people at the local bank didn't exactly jump for joy when I rolled through the doors as a new customer. Like most people, they didn't know what to make of me. I couldn't write, so I couldn't sign my name on checks or other papers. I couldn't really make "my mark" either, but since they needed something, I scratched out a squiggle while somebody held a pen in my hand. I couldn't talk, so somebody had to explain the situation every time we went into the bank to do any business. (For obvious reasons, I love today's automated banking machines. I just tell my attendant what to do, give her my card, and the machine does the rest.)

As with so many other obstacles that seemed insurmountable at first, the banking situation cleared up once we figured out how to handle it. The people at the bank got to know me as a regular customer, and I got used to making my mark. I later bought a rubber stamp with my name on it, which enabled my assistants to "sign" my name as necessary.

I was hoping that the same process would work for our group in making friends with the other tenants at Linden Towers. Initially, we met with one of two reactions from most of the residents, nearly all of whom were retired people: they openly resented us for living there, or they patronized us. I can't tell you how many of these people pinched my cheeks and called me "cutie," "sweetie," or "poor little thing" in our first month. Even so, most of the old people thought that having handicapped neighbors placed a stigma on Linden Towers. A lot of them also were very nosy and tried to meddle in our business, questioning our attendants and telling them how to care for us ("Do you really think it's safe to leave her alone in her apartment while you're downstairs doing the laundry?").

These reactions were understandable at first, and we all figured that given time and the opportunity to get to know us, our neighbors' resentment and lack of understanding would fade away. Unfortunately, it didn't work out that way. We never were accepted there, except by a handful of people.

Linden Towers was a very active place, sort of like a retirement community. There were frequent social activities in the community room off the lobby — parties, movies, and of course everybody's Monday night favorite (no, not football), bingo.

The building was equipped with a sophisticated central intercom system. Every apartment had a buzzer and a speaking device hooked up to the front door. There was a camera downstairs, and we could watch the front entrance on our television set. The intercom system could also be used as a public address system for every apartment, which lent an institutional feel to the place that I did not like.

Every Monday evening around six o'clock, I would be sitting quietly in front of the TV, watching the evening news or *Hollywood Squares*, when a scratchy voice suddenly would blurt out over the intercom, *"Bingo in the lobby, bingo in the lobby."* For months we cracked up whenever we heard that announcement. The refrain "bingo in the lobby" became a standing joke for everyone connected with our program.

For some time the staffing of our residential program was a problem. Paul had trouble finding a good supervisor, and we had mixed luck with our personal care attendants, or PCAs. Fortunately, we always had at least a few devoted, capable people on the staff, and we managed to avoid any major catastrophes. One male and one female attendant worked at all times to cover three apartments — Diane's and mine on the fifteenth floor, Norman's and Rick's on the fourteenth floor, and Ron's on the twelfth floor. The PCAs worked eight-hour shifts, starting at eight A.M., and they helped us cope with all of our everyday physical needs and chores.

Several of our stalwart PCAs deserve particular mention. One of the first attendants we hired was a Jamaican man named Winston Thompson. Winston spoke English like most other native Jamaicans — very quickly and musically. It took a while to get used to his style of talking, but we all hit it off with him right away. He was extremely devoted and hard-working, always came to work on time, and frequently worked extra shifts to cover for PCAs who didn't show up. Winston understood our different personalities and needs, and related to us as individuals in a caring and often humorous fashion. He became particularly close to Norman and Rick, and was their most reliable attendant for many years.

Another Jamaican, a woman named Queenie, became a mainstay of our residential staff two years after we arrived at Linden Towers. Like Winston, Queenie was extremely hard-working and dependable, and had a fabulous sense of humor. Most important for me, she was sensitive to my wants and considerate of my preferences. She took excellent care of me physically, and at the same time let me control my life. I told her my schedule, chose my clothes, selected my meals, and she helped me get it all done, always with a smile.

From early 1979 on, Dee Dee Motyka also was crucial to our program. She was a big, strong, gentle woman who was able to lift Rick, Norman, and Ron in and out of their wheelchairs for various caretaking needs. Like Winston and Queenie, Dee Dee was hard-working and reliable, and since she had a nursing background she was very matter-of-fact about our physical handicaps. She also had a keen sense of humor, and genuinely enjoyed all of us. Rick and Norman loved it when she flirted with them and jokingly gave them a hard time about nearly everything.

I liked Dee Dee very much, but somehow we couldn't avoid frequent hassles and minor disagreements. I resented it when she didn't take the time to find out through my word boards what my thoughts were or what I had planned. Sometimes she just forgot what I had told her the day before about where I had to be at a certain time, and I missed appointments entirely. I don't want to sell her short, however. She worked with us for three years, and provided all of us with super care and unswerving loyalty the whole time.

Other PCAs did a good job but had little quirks that we had to accept. One woman, Susan, worked with Diane and me for about two years. She was extremely soft-spoken and sensitive. We nicknamed her "Mrs. Clean" because she wore rubber gloves whenever she handled us for baths, dressing, or bathroom functions. Another woman, G., did a pretty good job despite the fact that she usually was high on pot. G. and I understood each other quite well, and she was very perceptive and intuitive about me. But she made me nervous because she didn't pay attention to what she was doing. This was particularly bothersome when she was handling me, or when she messed up my appointments.

We always had turnover problems at Linden Towers, but our worst problem was when people didn't show up for their shift. If this happened, the PCA on duty had to work a double shift or at least stay until someone else came in to cover. When this created difficulties, the residential supervisor was called in. If the supervisor was unavailable, then the buck stopped with Paul Shelton. In our first few months at Linden Towers, Paul worked more than his share of shifts.

After a month or two of hitting and missing with our PCAs, we told Paul that we wanted to become more involved in the hiring process. He understood our concern — he knew how things were going by the number of shifts he was working — and we soon were interviewing prospective PCAs and making the hiring decisions along with the residential supervisor. This didn't guarantee that we never had problems with PCAs, but at least we had nobody to blame but ourselves if somebody turned out to be unsuitable.

The residential program had to be well organized in order to comply with the requirements of the Massachusetts Department of Mental Health (DMH), which provided most of our funding. There were regular staff meetings, and we also participated in individual program conferences every few months with people from DMH, to review what was going on and to formulate plans for our educational and residential programs.

All of these meetings and conferences took time. They seemed like an awful lot of red tape, but they gave us a chance to begin to assert ourselves. At first we were so used to the way things had been run at Belchertown that we didn't even try to direct our own program. But as the months passed and we began to get a feel for how things were going and how we wanted them to go, we started expressing our opinions much more freely.

.$?*!

The turning point in our program came at the end of the summer of 1978. Arthur was still running what was supposed to be our educational program, but everything was disorganized and our concerns were not being recognized. Norman, Rick, and I complained to Paul and asked him to fire Arthur. Paul urged us to be patient, but things just got worse. Our PCAs were upset over problems the educational program was causing for their work at Linden Towers, particularly our late departures for and arrivals from U. Mass.

Our patience came to an end after we returned home two hours late one evening because of an unscheduled ride in the country. To emphasize our displeasure with the situation to Paul, we went on strike the next day. When Arthur came to pick us up to go to the university, we refused to leave our apartments. Diane, Norman, Rick, and I told our attendants not to let him take us out. This drastic action finally convinced Paul to fire Arthur.

.F.R.E.E.

We worked closely with Paul to find a replacement to run the educational program. In September we hired a woman named Laura Lee Jones, and the Fundamental Right to an Equal Education (FREE) program began to take real shape.

Laura Lee had a special-education degree from U. Mass. and lived in Amherst near the campus. She had worked at Belchertown and understood where we had been and where we needed to go in order to live successfully in the community. She was a good teacher and an excellent organizer, and she did great things for us.

First Laura Lee developed individualized teaching programs for everyone. She included us in the interviewing and hiring of the other staff for the day program, and by November we had three more excellent people working with us. We continued to meet at the U. Mass. Campus Center, but we now had a conference room every day (Laura Lee saw to that), and we had a real program. I worked on basic math, such as the skills necessary to balance a checkbook and budget my monthly expenses. I also concentrated on my communication skills, which included improving my reading and expanding my word boards.

Once our program was straightened out, I began to feel comfortable about being at U. Mass. Although we were not part of the university, I finally was receiving an education during the time we spent on campus. It also helped that we were no longer living at the State School, so we didn't feel like prisoners out on leave every time we visited the University. Whenever we ran into someone we had known at Belchertown, such as the many students who had worked as Boltwood volunteers, we felt more at home — and more liberated in being able to tell them that we no longer lived at the State School.

In November 1978 I received a new communication device called the Handi-Voice. Ed Hebert, the speech pathologist from the Communication Resource Center at Belchertown, and my old friend Howard Shane arranged for me to get it. This machine was about the size of a telephone answering machine and had an electronic display of numbers from 0 to 999, with each number representing a different word. By using the headswitch on my chair, I could punch in a three-digit number to cue up the corresponding word, and the Handi-Voice would actually "speak" the word. I also could store the words in sequence and construct phrases that the Handi-Voice would speak for me when given the proper command.

It was a terrific concept, and I worked long and hard on that machine for over a year. To help me with it, Laura Lee wrote in all of the correct numbers for the matching words on my word boards. Unfortunately, it was tough to memorize which word corresponded to which number. It also took a long time to punch in the three-digit numbers and cue up each word. I could string together a simple message like "Hello, how are you?" in about fifteen minutes, but I never got much further than that. As with the TIC, I found it very draining to work the headswitch and concentrate on punching up the numbers for any length of time. This put a real limit on what I could do with the Handi-Voice.

Still, it was exciting to generate even simple speech, and the Handi-Voice whetted my appetite for further advances in communication devices.

.LÍKE.TALK.

In January 1979 I began working with Steve Kaplan on writing my autobiography. I had been frustrated since leaving the State School over the total lack of progress on this project. Soon after Steve and I started working together at the FREE program, however, I began to hear parts of my story being read back to me. For the first time in my life, I was hearing myself "talk" in complete sentences and paragraphs.

.THINK.DAD.FEEL.

The only real difficulty I ever encountered in telling my story to Steve occurred the following March, when we began discussing my parents' decision to send me to the State School. I initially explained that my parents hadn't fully understood how bad the institution was in 1962. This lack of understanding, along with my mother's poor health, the three little kids growing up behind me, and our lack of money to hire help all contributed to my parents' decision.

This sounded true enough, and I almost sold Steve, and myself, on this explanation. But when we started talking about those first terrible years at Belchertown, about how I lost all that weight and was so unhappy, and about how I cried when I went home for Christmas and summer visits, Steve wanted to know whether I had ever asked my parents to take me back home for good (yes, several times), whether they had understood the request (undoubtedly), and why they hadn't agreed (no reply).

Mother met with Steve and me at Linden Towers in late March, and she told him what I had been like before the State School. She offered the same explanation for the decision to send me there as I had. She recalled how terrible those years had been for her, which was something I emphasized later to Steve. Mother's sincerity about this was unmistakable.

But in the weeks before and after that visit, I was holding back from Steve. He suspected as much and kept asking me, gently but persistently, if I was telling him the whole story, especially in regard to how I had felt about being sent off to live at Belchertown. At the time, Mother and Father had read some of the early parts of the book; they were very enthusiastic about and pleased with our work. I didn't want to hurt Father's feelings when he read my comments about being sent away. But after thinking the whole thing through, I decided not to pull any more punches.

.DAD.$?*!(*Asshole*)

It was my father's decision to send me to Belchertown, as well as to keep me there. He made that decision against Mother's wishes. He stuck with that decision throughout those awful early years, despite my obvious desire to return home, which I tried to make clear to him every time I saw him. As I have said, Father believed that he had to sacrifice me for the well-being of the rest of the family. Given the combination of our family circumstances and the lack of social programs and support services for families with disabled children, he felt that he had no choice.

I disagreed, then and now. We could have gotten help from relatives. Father could have taken a different job, one that didn't keep him away from home so much. If I couldn't stay home, my parents could have kept trying to get me into a different place, one more like Crotched Mountain.

My parents had a pretty fair idea of what Belchertown was all about when they put me there. And after they saw what the place was doing to me, any illusions they had must have been shattered. I kept trying so hard to talk to them about returning home, and they always avoided it. It couldn't have been easy for Father; I know it was hell for Mother.

I had been angry at Father for seventeen years — not so much for sending me to the State School in the first place as for not bringing me home when he saw what it was doing to me. Although I came to understand that decision as I grew older, I never accepted it or agreed with it.

After several sleepless nights, I told all of this to Steve. I realized that it was important to be honest about this issue. Father was a strong person, physically and emotionally, and I was certain he could handle the truth without being hurt or getting mad at me. Once I expressed my real viewpoint on these events in the book, I felt a lot better.

.JULY 4.

Father and Mother came over to our apartment on the night of July 4, 1979. The city was shooting off fireworks downtown by the Connecticut River, less than a mile from Linden Towers. We had one of the best views in town from our balcony on the fifteenth floor.

When the fireworks started booming and exploding, I started wincing, cringing, and laughing, even though they were far away and weren't terribly loud. Then Father picked me up out of my wheelchair and took me onto the balcony. He held me in his arms, and for the next half hour or so we watched the fireworks together. He cradled me gently but firmly, and kept cracking corny jokes and making me giggle just like he did when I was a little girl.

At the time Father hadn't read my account of being sent off to Belchertown. That part of the book wasn't to be drafted for another month or two. But by then it didn't matter, just as it didn't matter several months later when Father told Steve, "Put away the whitewash brush and tell the world that Ruth's old man was an s.o.b. who loved his family and made a tough choice." It didn't matter because Father and I buried the hatchet that Fourth of July in 1979, out there on that little balcony at Linden Towers, watching the fireworks light up downtown Springfield. I knew then that I was back in Father's life—perhaps I had never left it, really. And that meant so much to both of us.

.AFRAID.IN.BED.

One night in the summer of 1979, right around midnight when my PCAs changed shift, I was awakened by vicious yelling from the living room of our apartment. It was L and F, two of my attendants, and they sounded like they were about to kill each other.

L had been working with us since the beginning of the year. She was reliable, but she was not one of my favorites. She usually worked the night shift, so she was often the one who dressed me in the morning. I hated the way she threw me into any old clothes that she grabbed from my closet, without giving me a say in the matter. I also hated the way she loaded up my face with makeup. L was insensitive, and never really connected with my communication techniques or personality.

L's husband, M, worked part-time with Norman, Rick, and Ron, and they all liked him very much. M was very handsome and outgoing, and wore a black eyepatch over his right eye, which accentuated his good looks. He had a regular job as a hair-dresser, and he seemed to be quite the ladies' man.

F had started working with us in the spring, and she quickly became my favorite attendant and one of my closest friends. She was very pretty and observant, and had a terrific sense of humor. She also had a crush on M, whom she got to know when they both worked the evening shift at Linden Towers.

Evidently, while L was sleeping at our place at Linden Towers from midnight to eight in the morning, M and F were sleeping with each other somewhere else. At least that's how L presented it to F that night in my living room, although she phrased it a little more colorfully. L must have just found out, because she really was worked up.

F was nobody's doormat, and right or wrong, she wasn't about to back down one inch. So there I was, lying helpless in my bed, listening to my two PCAs screaming and swearing at each other. I was afraid that they were going to get into a fistfight right there in the apartment and break the whole place up. Either that or they would both take off and leave me alone for the night. Luckily, neither happened. After trading more threats and insults, F left, L stayed, and I eventually fell back to sleep. Needless to say, L wasn't very cheerful the next morning, but she didn't say anything about the fight. She worked with us for another two months or so, and then I never saw her again.

L's husband, M, left our scene right after that. F stayed on for another year and a half, and she continued to see M, who divorced L. Eventually F and M were married, and they later moved out west.

DIANE.JOHN.

In August, not too long after the argument, my roommate, Diane, dropped a bombshell on us: she was getting married in October.

For several months Diane had been dating a man named John Boomsma. John lived in an apartment on the tenth floor, and he too was handicapped. He was confined to a wheelchair, but he spoke pretty clearly and had the full use of his hands. He was thirty-five, about twelve years older than Diane. He had been raised at home with his parents, and had never lived in an institution.

At that time John was working at the Goodwill Industries in Springfield, doing piecework at a sheltered workshop for about eighty-five cents an hour. Although the program was supposed to foster independence and self-improvement for handicapped adults, John complained that it was more like slave labor. He hated it, but preferred working at some kind of job to doing nothing at all. Since he didn't know how to read, nothing else was available.

When Diane first told us of her wedding plans, we thought she was getting carried away in some romantic fantasy. But it soon became apparent that she and John loved each other and were set in their plans. Given that, we all jumped in and did what we could to help out.

.RAIN.

A week before the wedding, John's mother held a shower for Diane. About thirty women attended, mostly friends of Mrs. Boomsma's, although a few people came with Mrs. McCabe and Diane. I went with Diane and our PCA and good friend Bobbi Cohen.

Mrs. Boomsma's friends were like so many other phony people I had run across. They came up to me and rubbed my arm, stuck their faces close to mine, and remarked to nobody in particular, "Isn't she sweet, the poor dear." They went on talking about me for another minute or two as if I had disappeared, and then they ignored me for the rest of the party.

After Diane received all sorts of lovely gifts, we had lunch. Bobbi put one of my big blue paper bibs over my blouse (like what you might wear at the hairdresser's) and began to feed me. Right away one of Mrs. Boomsma's ladies announced quite loudly that she was getting sick from watching me eat. John's mother thereupon instructed Bobbi to take me into another room to eat. Bobbi said no, and we stayed put. Mrs. Boomsma then explained that it wasn't for her sake, but out of consideration for one of her guests. Bobbi replied, "Too bad." I was insulted and angered by both Mrs. Boomsma's and her guest's attitude, but Bobbi handled it perfectly and expressed my sentiments exactly.

We ran into the same brand of hospitality at the wedding. Norman, Rick, Ron, and I attended. The guys were stuck in the back of the room at the reception, off where nobody would see them. I was part of the wedding party, but Mrs. Boomsma asked that I eat in another room. As an alternative, it was suggested that I be fed after everyone else had finished. After consulting with me, our program supervisor (who was my companion at the wedding), Debbie Shepherd, ignored both requests. I ate dinner along with everybody else at the head table. Bobbi Cohen was there too. Mrs. Boomsma had asked her to feed the bride. For a long time Diane had been feeding herself. Although she didn't look pretty doing it — she awkwardly clutched the fork or spoon and brought it up to her mouth in jerky movements — she got the job done. Understandably, she didn't want to be fed at her wedding, and Bobbi had no desire to feed her, so that was that.

After their honeymoon, the newlyweds moved into our apartment and I moved into a one-bedroom apartment at Linden Towers. I enjoyed having my own place for the first time in my life.

COMMUNICATE.MEET.

Steve Kaplan stopped working full-time with the FREE program in August 1979, but we continued to see each other and work on the book. One Saturday morning in January 1980, he took Norman and me to the Nonvocal Communication Conference at American International College (AIC) in Springfield. The conference presented a number of workshops about educating vocally disabled children and was sponsored by an organization called the Northeast Communication Enhancement Group.

Besides my natural affinity for the subject, I had good reason for attending: my old friend and teacher Dr. Howard Shane was conducting a session on "augmentative communication" for nonspeaking people who possessed some communication abilities. Howard was now the chairman of the American Speech and Hearing Committee on Nonspeaking Communication, and had become a leading authority on this subject. We hadn't been in touch in years, and I was excited about seeing him again. Of course I was quite proud of him. After all, I had been one of his first students, and in some ways Howard had been one of my first students too.

There were about twenty people at the workshop, most of them public school teachers or administrators. Howard did a very good job in explaining the distinction between receptive language ability and expressive language handicaps, which is the key to helping anybody who is incapable of communicating verbally.

The most memorable part of the workshop was the participation of an eighteen-year-old boy named Ricky Hoyt. Physically, Ricky was much like me — he had little or no hand or foot movement and was unable to speak. Yet he demonstrated to a roomful of teachers how he maneuvered his brand new motorized wheelchair with a headswitch. A box near his right hand had six small lights on it, each one indicating a different command: forward, back, right, left, high speed, and off. Ricky hit the headswitch when the light flashed at the command he wanted; he hit the switch again to stop the chair's movement. This was the first self-directed mobility he had experienced in his life, and although he hadn't mastered it yet, he was ecstatic about his new chair. (Later that year I began to inquire about getting one of those chairs. Owing to delays in approving the funding through Medicare, and then to the time it took to have the chair designed and fabricated at the Adaptive Design Workshop at Belchertown, I didn't actually get one until March 1983.)

Ricky's mother, Judy Hoyt, told the audience how she had been fighting for years with the school officials in her town to mainstream Ricky — to put him in an ordinary school classroom with "normal" kids his age. Her main point was that even though mainstreaming wasn't perfect, it was essential in order to prevent a handicapped child's life from being wasted. I couldn't have agreed more.

Ricky never would have received a real education if it had not been for Chapter 766, the Massachusetts law requiring equal education for all handicapped people up to the age of twenty-one. As a result of the law and Judy Hoyt's tireless advocacy, Ricky attended public school, where he more than held his own. Judy told the workshop how he planned to attend college, and that she hoped he would live in his own place someday.

For a few days after the workshop, I was increasingly upset as I thought about Judy and Rick Hoyt. I couldn't help but think about how when I was Ricky's age, I was stuck in diapers, lying in bed all day at the Infirmary at the State School, watching my wardmates bang their heads against the walls and mutter nonsense to themselves.

NORMAN.MAYBE.

One morning in early May 1980, Rick, Norman, and I, along with two PCAs, were driving in the van up Route 91 on the way to Amherst. We were going to meet Laura Lee for breakfast at a little place called Rooster's. After that we would head over to U. Mass.

I was gazing out the window, watching the familiar highway scenery rush by, when Norman leaned over behind me and whispered in his raspy, hesitating voice, "I want to ask you an important question."

I started to stand up in my chair, and held back a shriek in anticipation of what I knew he was going to say. It took Norman a few seconds to wind up, and some stuttering in the delivery, but he finally blurted it out: "Will you marry me?"

A pure mixture of yes and no covered my face — eyes looking up, mouth frowning. I was still half-standing in my wheelchair, making excited noises as my teeth chattered and I gave my answer: "Maybe."

Norman was sitting behind me and couldn't see my response. Based on my standing up and making excited noises, he thought I had said yes. He couldn't see the doubt and confusion in my face.

I had known that sooner or later he was going to ask me that question. We had been friends since the early seventies at the Infirmary. Norman had always flirted with me, but there was no question that in recent months he had become more serious in

his tone. For years he had been saying—jokingly, I thought—
that I was the prettiest girl he knew. Lately he had been saying
it more and more, and now he sounded like he believed it.

Earlier that spring my parents had been visiting my apartment
when Norm was there. They had met a few years before, back
when we were living at Alpha House, and they knew that Norman and I were long-time pals. That day in my apartment, right
out of the blue, my father (blunt as always) remarked, "You
know, you two should get married. Hell, you're together all the
time anyway." I turned red with embarrassment, but I managed
to catch a glimpse of Norman's reaction. He was scrunched up
in his wheelchair, his head slumped over slightly, his right hand
slowly nudging up against his face. A trace of a grin formed on
his mouth as he said quietly and clearly, more to himself than to
any of us, "Yep."

So I had known for months that Norm would ask me, as soon
as he had thought it all the way through and worked up his
nerve. It was only a matter of time. But I still wasn't sure how I
would answer. Norman was twenty years older than I. We had
been friends for a long time, but never in a romantic way. We
had been through just about everything together, and I couldn't
think of anybody who understood me better, or with whom I felt
more comfortable.

But getting married? Despite months of concentrated thought,
the answer still wasn't clear. I knew that I loved Norman, but I
wasn't certain that I loved him like a wife should love her husband. Ever since my disappointment with Hans Toegel, I had
resigned myself to a life without physical love. Now here was
Norman, asking me to be his wife, not just his handicapped roommate—and I didn't know what to say.

.I.WILL.

A few days later Norman was visiting me in my apartment and
he asked me, "What kind of diamond do you want?"

Debbie Ramsey, one of my PCAs and a close friend, was with

us, and she saw from my beaming face that I had finally made up my mind. Although she didn't have to tell Norman what I was saying — we could read each other's faces, and minds, most of the time — she announced my decision: "Yes, I will."

Norman started kicking his knees up and waving his hand around his cheek. He was so excited that he nearly wriggled himself right out of his wheelchair.

I was excited too. The decision simply clicked in my head when Norman asked about the ring, and I knew it was the right choice.

Despite Father's earlier suggestion, my parents were somewhat stunned by the news, especially Mother. But they were thrilled nonetheless. They had always liked Norman very much. True to form, it wasn't long before Father was taking full credit for the whole idea.

I was a bundle of nerves all summer, but planning everything was a good distraction. Debbie and I had fun shopping for a wedding gown, but it wasn't easy. None of them fit! I've weighed about seventy pounds ever since I was in my mid-twenties, and not too many wedding gowns are made for someone my size. After much looking, we finally found something that I liked and that fit. Plus I got a great deal on it — the clerk at the store sold it to me for half price because it was last year's design.

Norman and I also spent a lot of time working out our invitation list. There were many people we wanted to invite, but we didn't have addresses for all of them, especially our old friends from the State School. We had a great deal of trouble tracking some of them down.

Initially, we didn't know what to do about a honeymoon. Neither of us had traveled any further than we could go on day trips. We were at a loss about how to deal with hotel reservations and travel arrangements, and it would be difficult to set up the necessary support staff to help us get away. Even worse, we didn't have enough money to do much more than go out to dinner, let alone go on a honeymoon. This problem was solved by our friends from Shelton's and FREE, who planned, paid for, and accompanied Norman and me on a three-day honeymoon trip to the White Mountains.

Part of my nervousness about planning the honeymoon involved our wedding night and sharing a bed with Norman. I had spoken with several of my friends about sexual relations, and I had a good idea of what to expect in general. But as to what I could anticipate from Norman, and even from myself, I had no idea whatsoever.

Although it took some time to figure out what works for us, I am happy to report that Norman and I have enjoyed an active and fulfilling sexual relationship since our marriage. Although our physical handicaps limit the scope of that relationship, we both have normal sexual drives and we are able to satisfy each other. I realized before we were married that Norman wasn't Hans Toegel, and Norman never expected me to be anyone else either. Quite simply, we love each other very deeply, and we also find each other physically attractive.

After our honeymoon, we planned to move into Norman and Rick's apartment on the fourteenth floor of Linden Towers. Rick was going to swap with me and take my single-bedroom apartment. Aside from the hassle of moving our stuff and buying a queen-sized waterbed, that part of our marriage plans looked relatively easy.

My family helped out with most of the wedding preparations. Mother and Marie gave a shower for me with lots of our relatives and friends, and it was really a blast. Mother and Father also took care of the church arrangements, and my brother, Howard, took photographs of the wedding. Mother enlisted some of our relatives to set up the refreshments for a reception in the church social hall after the service. Steve Kaplan's wife, Carol, was a professional floral designer, and she took care of the flowers for us.

SEPTEMBER 20, 1980.

Our wedding day got off to a shaky start when our PCA got lost driving us across town to the church. But the service couldn't start without us, and we weren't terribly late. In fact, we had to hold up the ceremony to wait for Debbie Ramsey, my maid of honor, who arrived even later than we did.

The crowd at the church included nearly everyone we knew and cared about. Pat Borges came from Providence and sang the Peaches and Herb song "I Pledge My Love" as our processional. Theresa Ladue, Donna Highland, and Carol Muse came from the State School, where, unfortunately, they were still living. Most of the people who worked with us at Shelton's and in the FREE program were at the wedding, as were old friends such as Dave Bickford. All in all, about 125 people attended.

Father walked me down the aisle and gave me away, and Paul Shelton was the best man. Steve Kaplan read a poem he had written especially for the occasion, and I cried.

When it came time for us to exchange our vows, Norman said "I do" nervously, but in an enthusiastic, willing, and intelligible voice.

I raised my eyes to say yes.

Afterword

After Ruth and Norman married in September 1980, they lived in their apartment on the fourteenth floor of Linden Towers. In October 1984, our good friend and Ruth and Norman's comrade from Belchertown, Rick Leaman, died of kidney problems related to his spina bifida.

In 1985 Ruth and Norman moved to an apartment in Northampton, Massachusetts, where they currently reside. Their basic care is still provided by Shelton's, Inc., of which Paul Shelton is executive director, and they still attend sessions at U. Mass. several times a week in a less structured version of the original FREE program. Diane McCabe and Ron Benoit left the program by their own choice before Ruth and Norman's wedding, but another good friend, Roma Roukey, was in the program with them for several years.

The biggest problems Ruth and Norman currently face are boredom and a tight budget. The federal and state funds they receive (about $700 per month) enable them to live at only a subsistence level. This severely affects their ability to enjoy any but the simplest social activities, and it renders impossible any travel beyond a simple day trip.

During the past three years, Norman has given several dozen presentations to grammar schools and junior high schools in the Springfield/Northampton area, on the topic of what it's like to be physically handicapped. Ruth occasionally joins him in these presentations, which have become the focal point of Norman's life.

.I.HOPE.TEACH.DOCTORS.

Ruth wants very much to address, and educate, professionals in all disciplines that deal with the physically handicapped. We hope that the publication of this book will provide her with the opportunity to engage teachers, speech therapists, doctors and nurses, social services providers, even politicians, and to raise their consciousness about the lives, needs, and aspirations of the Ruths and Normans of this world.

If anyone, after reading this book, still doubts Ruth's ability to present her point of view effectively, consider the following.

On November 20, 1983, a rally was held on the Belchertown Common by advocates of deinstitutionalization and community living for the physically and mentally handicapped. About five hundred people attended. Ruth was one of the featured speakers.

Here are the remarks she dictated to me several days before the rally:

.I.FEEL.(CLUE).TRASH.BELCHERTOWN.
.OLD.HOUSE.STINKS.
.(CLUE).HOT.BELCHERTOWN.
.I.GETTING.LEARN.
.I.GETTING.FOOD.MYSELF.
.PCA.ASK.ME.WHAT.WHEN.
.PATIENTS.MOVE.OUT.
.MONEY.PEOPLE.OUT.
.BROKEN.THEY.BUILDING.

At the rally, I provided a brief description of Ruth's background and experiences at Belchertown. Then I told the crowd, "I asked Ruth what she wanted to say to this gathering, and she had these comments: 'I was treated like garbage at Belchertown. The Infirmary stunk and the whole place was like hell. Now I am getting an education. I go grocery shopping for myself, and my personal care attendants ask me what I want to do and when I want to do it.

" 'All of the people still living at the State School should be moved out, and all of the money now being spent at the institution should be directed to handicapped people living in the community. The State School should be torn down, brick by brick.' "

On March 10, 1989, the Commonwealth of Massachusetts announced that the Belchertown State School would be closed by 1993. The remaining 266 residents of the seventy-year-old institution are to be placed either in community-based programs or in a comparable state institution, at the option of the individual residents and their families.

It is the unequivocal goal of Ruth, Norman, and other advocates of community living that the five remaining state institutions in Massachusetts soon follow the fate of the Belchertown State School.

West Hartford, Connecticut
March 1989

Afterwards
May 1996:

.I.DID.MEET.MARIA.YESTERDAY.TODAY.
.I.DID.MEET.JOAN.CAN.TALK.

In the months immediately following the publication of the book in June 1989, Steve and I appeared on a number of local and national television shows. Most of the Springfield and Hartford stations ran interviews with us, as did one of the Boston stations. But two nationally televised shows, Maria Shriver's "Yesterday, Today and Tomorrow" and "The Joan Rivers Show," stand out as the most exciting.

For "Yesterday, Today and Tomorrow," an NBC film crew recorded a day in my life with Norman. They also received permission to "recreate" some of my best and worst experiences at Belchertown State School, reenacting scenes from the book on the actual wards where they had occurred ten to twenty years earlier. My friend and attendant from Belchertown, Wessie, watched the filming with me, and we both advised the crew as to the proper set-up for the scenes on the wards. The staging was quite authentic, down to the old cribs, beds, and wheelchairs that were pulled out of storage for the filming.

The finished segment ran about fifteen minutes on the national news magazine, with narration provided by Maria Shriver. Despite some melodramatic acting in the reenactment scenes, I think the show packed a pretty strong punch in showing that the State School was a terrible place.

My trip to Manhattan to tape an interview with Joan Rivers was very different. The show put me up overnight at the Plaza Hotel, along with my personal services coordinator and longtime friend Debbie Shepard. Steve, and his wife Carol and son Spencer, joined us for lunch at the Palm Court before the show. Although it was one of the fanciest restaurants in the world, nobody seemed to give me or the way I ate a second thought. Perhaps that's because nothing is really new or unusual in New York City, or maybe it's because I had become something of a celebrity by then. A few people even stopped us in the lobby to say they had seen us on Maria Shriver's show.

At the television studio, we waited in the room with the other guests— several pretty young women who were wives of major league baseball players, and an elderly black woman who had been Elvis Presley's cook at Graceland. Joan Rivers came in for a minute before the show to say hello, and told me she had stayed up all night reading my book. She was much shorter than I'd thought, and her personality was incredibly energetic and strong.

For most of the interview, Steve explained how we had written the book, and Joan asked him some very good questions. She was very familiar with my treatment at Belchertown, and very vocal in her outrage over it. I came on for the last part, and she asked me a few simple questions that I answered on my word boards. I would have preferred more of an opportunity to speak for myself, but I guess there were time limitations for that on her show. Also, I think Joan was little nervous about how to talk with me.

.I.DID.AWARD.BOOK.GOD.

On February 22, 1990, Steve, I, and I Raise My Eyes To Say Yes were honored by receiving a Christopher Award. These awards are given annually by the Catholic Order in recognition of books, films, and television movies on the basis of their "affirmation of the highest values of the human spirit" and "artistic and technical proficiency." The presentation ceremony was hosted by Mary Alice Williams at the Time-Life building in New York City, and other recipients included Among Schoolchildren by Tracy Kidder (also edited by Dick Todd), the films Driving Miss Daisy, Field of Dreams, and My Left Foot, and the television specials "My Name is Bill W." and "A Mother's Courage: The Mary Thomas Story."

.AWARD.FROM.COMMUNICATION.WASHINGTON, D.C.

In the spring of 1990, I received another very exciting award. This was an Individual Achievement Award from the National Council on Communicative Disorders in Washington, D.C. This group arranged for Norman and me, along with Debbie and one of our attendants, Aimee, to drive to Washington and stay overnight at the Watergate Hotel. The awards ceremony was held at the Kennedy Center, and the Council also brought Steve to Washington to make the presentation to me.

The evening was hosted by the actress, Stephanie Beacham, who has a hearing impediment. She was very gracious in her remarks about me and the book. The event was even more poignant because the Americans With Disabilities Act had just been passed in Congress the week before, and Senator Tom Harkin, one of the Act's sponsors, also received an award. Another famous senator, John Glenn, was a presenter, and his wife, Annie, who has overcome a speech impediment herself, presented an award that was named after her.

It was another presenter I met that night, the comedienne Katherine Buckley, who provided me with my most enduring memory of the evening. Kathy Buckley is about six feet tall and is deaf. Her very funny routines are a combination of poking fun at herself and at others. Evidently, I made an impression on her, too, because a few months later I saw her performing on television and she had worked in some jokes involving Norman and me— again, at her expense. She said that when she first saw me at the awards ceremony, looking little and helpless in my wheelchair, she felt sorry for me. Then she found out that I had written a book, appeared on a bunch of television shows, and was happily married. Her point: that you never can tell about a person just by looking at her.

.I.DID.SICK.HOSPITAL.
.X.PHOTO.I.AM.POOR.
.I.FEEL.ANGRY.ABOUT.I.DID.SICK.STOMACH.I.

In the spring of 1993, I underwent surgery to have my right kidney removed. This culminated about six months of recurring health problems and several hospital admissions. During this period, I once again encountered my lifelong frustration of encountering doctors and medical personnel who discounted my ability to deal intelligently with my own body and medical condition.

During one examination, a doctor was reviewing one of my x-rays a few feet away and I heard him utter that I was a "poor little thing." I took this to be a polite way of calling me a "stupid moron." Prior to my kidney operation, a six-inch feeding tube was put into my body— without any explanation to me. I believe this was done as a "convenience" to the hospital, because no one there made the effort to talk to me and figure out how to feed me. I grew especially angry at my treating physician, a woman, who did not listen to Norman or me about anything.

.I.WANT.TEACH.PEOPLE.

In the nearly seven years since the book was published, I have given dozens of speeches and presentations to all sorts of groups, in many different cities. With the help of either an attendant reading my remarks, or in the last few years my computerized artificial voice, I have delivered my observations and comments to conventions and conferences of health care professionals, teachers, and providers of personal care for the disabled.

Much as I love to travel, however, and much as I love to share my experiences with anyone who is involved in working with the disabled, my favorite audiences have been the smaller groups and workshops in which I have participated with college students. There are two distinct groups that I want to reach in the future— teachers of the disabled, and the teachers of the people who provide care to the disabled. This last group is my most important audience, the people who are training and educating those who will teach doctors, teachers, and direct care personnel.

I hope that by keeping the book in print, and continuing to make it available to all of these groups, I can continue to teach as many people as possible about the lessons to be learned from my life.

> Ruth Sienkiewicz-Mercer
> Northampton, Massachusetts

SBK NOTES:

At first, Ruth and I would have been happy to print five hundred copies of this book and circulate it among our friends and families. Notwithstanding our optimism after Dick Todd and Houghton Mifflin agreed to publish the book, none of us anticipated the widespread attention and publicity which the book, and Ruth, received immediately following its publication.

Front page stories in The Boston Globe and The Hartford Courant, feature stories in People and PARADE, chapters excerpted in The Boston Globe Sunday Magazine and

Glamour Magazine, even an article in The Globe, one of those supermarket check-out tabloids! Very warm and appreciative reviews appeared in a number of major newspapers— Newsday, The Washington Post, The New York Times and The New York Times Book Review, The Boston Herald, The Cleveland Plain-Dealer, and The San Francisco Chronicle— and even better stories and reviews in smaller newspapers, like The Daily Hampshire Gazette (Northampton, MA), The West Hartford (CT) News, The Entertainment News (Hartford), The Patriot Ledger (Quincy, MA), The Desert Sun (Palm Springs, CA), The Sun-Sentinel (Ft. Lauderdale), The Grand Rapids (MI) Press, The North Georgia News, The Salisbury (N.C.) Post, The Times & World News (Roanoke, VA), and The Courier-Journal (Louisville, KY).

Then the television coverage— feature interviews on "Good Day!" in Boston, "Gayle King Live at Five" in Hartford, and "The Joan Rivers Show" in New York. Joan Rivers' on-air plug for the book stands out as my favorite review: "Anyone who doesn't buy this book is a fool!"

Our wildest t.v. experience was the lengthy segment on NBC's experimental news magazine, "Yesterday, Today and Tomorrow." Maria Shriver, whose family created and continues to expand The Special Olympics, convinced the authorities at the Belchertown State School to permit the network to "reenact" scenes from the book on the actual wards where they had occurred. I'll never forget discussing the program with her by phone and Maria asking me whether I had any connections that would permit NBC to film at the State School. I answered "No." Maria paused, then observed matter-of-factly, "Well, if they give us a hard time, I'll just call my uncle." No further contingency planning was necessary.

The NBC filming at the State School was eerie. I was standing next to Ruth as we watched them film the scene where the nurse puts Ruth into a wheelchair, doubles up her leg on the wheel, and breaks her leg at the thigh. We both winced, thinking we'd actually heard the young actress's leg snap, although she really wasn't hurt in the least.

It was even stranger to watch the show air a few weeks later. Ruth Sienkiewicz-Mercer was being lionized on prime time national television by the most highly achieving Kennedy of her generation. Eleven years earlier, and for the sixteen years before that, per the Commonwealth of Massachusetts, Ruth had been certified as just another "imbecile" committed to the Belchertown State School for the retarded.

A few months after Maria's show, photographers were taking Ruth's picture with Maria's co-anchor, Mary Alice Williams, and her brother, Mark Shriver, at the Christopher Awards Ceremony in New York. Ruth received her award alongside television and film people like David Brown and Lilli and Richard Zanuck. The next day, Ruth and Norman were back in their apartment in Northampton, watching game shows and back into the battle against boredom and stultification. Two months later, Brown and the Zanucks won the Oscar for best picture (Driving Miss Daisy).

Ruth's story struck a chord in a lot of people, and for a lot of different reasons. Understandably, advocacy groups for the disabled lavished high praise on her, and we both were the recipients of many kind words from a number of local and national organizations that invited us to address their meetings and conferences. Houghton Mifflin, our publisher, did a good job on the initial publicity and in pushing the book internationally. They arranged for its publication throughout the British Commonwealth, as well as in French, Dutch, and German translations. But given all of the attention and exposure, the actual circulation of the book has proven disappointing.

Thus, this new paperback edition. Although an American mass market paperback edition was published by Avon Books, it only stayed in print for about a year. With vanishing sales, the paperback never reached the educational audiences that we had urged the publishers to pursue. There is an irony here that I found intolerable. After struggling for thirty-six years to make herself heard, and then finally doing so with a sonic boom, Ruth was again being silenced— this time by marketing departments that were incapable of delivering her book to the audiences that were ready, willing, and eager to embrace it.

The Avon paperback edition never reached the mainstream educational market— the middle schools and high schools— where the account of Ruth's experiences would have such a profound and beneficial impact on adolescents who are being overwhelmed by their own self-doubt and alienation. I have spoken to middle school kids with and about Ruth, and their response is always the same: profoundly insightful and empathetic. Even younger, grammar school kids identify strongly with Ruth's struggle to express herself, to make adults hear and listen to her. Once they get past her wheelchair and her immobility, kids always warm to Ruth's energy and humor, and admire her combativeness and her ultimate success against the longest of odds.

Most kids, and most adults, too, relate more genuinely to Ruth than to Michael Jordan or Madonna. Many more kids have suffered their own versions of the frustrations that have permeated Ruth's life than have scored game-winning baskets. Of course they dream of becoming the next Ken Griffey, Jr. or Deion Sanders, or Mariah Carey or Kristy Yamaguchi, but they all have been Ruth many more times— stymied by an inability to communicate, or grappling with the same isolation and loneliness that we all experience in our own ways.

So a world of thanks to Dr. Bobbi Byrd and Dr. Ella Wallack, and also to the gently dogged Jim Hughes, for helping to get Ruth's book back into print. As Ruth likes to say, let's hope this edition enables her to keep on teaching the teachers, and their students, too.

Steven B. Kaplan
West Hartford, Connecticut

DATE DUE

APR 0 9 2000			
DE 13 '02			
MY 1 05			
TLL			
30 280282			
6/7/07			

GAYLORD   PRINTED IN U.S.A